Entanglements

University Press of Florida · State University System

Florida A&M University, Tallahassee
Florida Atlantic University, Boca Raton
Florida Gulf Coast University, Ft. Myers
Florida International University, Miami
Florida State University, Tallahassee
University of Central Florida, Orlando
University of Florida, Gainesville
University of North Florida, Jacksonville
University of South Florida, Tampa
University of West Florida, Pensacola

University Press

of Florida

Gainesville

Tallahassee

Tampa

Boca Raton

Pensacola

Orlando

Miami

Jacksonville

Ft. Myers

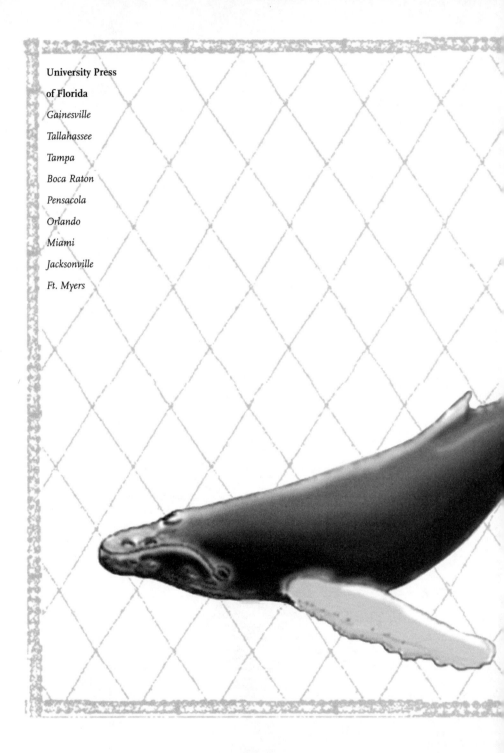

Tora Johnson

Entanglements

The Intertwined Fates of Whales and Fishermen

10 09 08 07 06 05   6 5 4 3 2 1

A record of cataloging-in-publication data is available from
the Library of Congress.
ISBN 0-8130-2797-7

Grateful acknowledgment is made for the excerpt in chapter 5 from the
January 13, 1997, *Boston Globe* feature article "Devil Doing the Angels'
Work?" by Scott Allen. Copyright 1997 by Globe Newspaper Co.
Reproduced with permission of Globe Newspaper Co.

The University Press of Florida is the scholarly publishing agency
for the State University System of Florida, comprising Florida A&M
University, Florida Atlantic University, Florida Gulf Coast University,
Florida International University, Florida State University, University
of Central Florida, University of Florida, University of North Florida,
University of South Florida, and University of West Florida.

University Press of Florida
15 Northwest 15th Street
Gainesville, FL 32611-2079
http://www.upf.com

In memory of . . .

Emily Argo
Jackie Ciano
Tom Hinds
Michael Newcomer

Contents

Illustrations

Maps

Figures

Acknowledgments

Mapping the political minefields of fisheries management and whale protection was made infinitely easier by the many people who offered patient instruction, practical help, indispensable advice, and boundless courage. I have been both buoyed and humbled by their trust. Bob Bowman, Stormy Mayo, David Mattila, Scott Landry, Jooke Robbins, and the rest of the staff at the Center for Coastal Studies in Provincetown, Massachusetts, granted me hours of interviews and access to a vast amount of information and candid advice. Jon and Judy Lien offered both hospitality and inspiration. Wayne Ledwell and Julie Huntington contributed a great deal to both the content and the heart of this book. Dozens of fishermen have given me their time and attention, often going out of their way to take me aboard their boats to observe them in their work. In Newfoundland, Lloyd Sullivan, Robin Butler, and Chris Butler offered me insights into Canadian fisheries. I am also grateful to the New England fishermen who trusted me to listen to and communicate their concerns, including Gary Ostrom, John Our, Ron Hemeon, Bill Adler, Leroy Bridges, and Bill Look. Ted Ames's and Robin Alden's tireless work on behalf of fisheries and fishing communities has been particularly inspiring. The staff at the U.S. National Marine Fisheries Service's Protected Resources Division, especially Mary Colligan and Diane Borggaard, were generous with their time and their thoughtful attention to my questions. Dan McKiernan with the Massachusetts Department of Marine Fisheries provided an incisive view of the take reduction process, and Laura Ludwig with the Maine Department of Marine Fisheries offered time and insights as well. Bob Kenney of the University of Rhode Island and Scott Kraus and Amy Knowlton of the New England Aquarium provided me with reams of technical information, as well as their observations from whale research and the take reduction process. Sharon Young, Richard Ellis, and Rosemary Seton offered a wealth of insight and information that lent a great deal to the story. Several anonymous sources were critical to filling in the story and are greatly appreciated, as well.

In many ways, College of the Atlantic was the ideal place to undertake a project like *Entanglements*. First and foremost, I wish to thank my advisors. Dr. Karen Waldron is a gifted teacher of writing and a supportive friend who always had just the right thing to say when my confidence flagged. Dr. Sean Todd's support and contacts among the top whale scientists allowed me to obtain interviews and opportunities that would otherwise have been impossible. Others at College of the Atlantic played pivotal roles in this project, including Steve Katona, Bill Carpenter, Ken Cline, and the dean of graduate studies, John Anderson. My students Santiago Salinas and Diana Choksey made invaluable contributions to my efforts to evaluate the Take Reduction Plan using geographic information systems. Sean Murphy, Ken Hill, and Kate Frank were immensely helpful in my survey research.

My editor, John Byram, and my agent, Stephany Evans, had the insight to know the value of this project and have worked hard to bring it to fruition.

Finally, I wish to thank my family. Cate and Bob Bowman's years of logistical support and many hours of kidsitting made this book possible. My husband, Chris Mullen, and my son, Wolf Mullen, showed seemingly infinite patience throughout this process. Chris has believed in this project from the beginning, and his continued faith and encouragement have helped me more than he knows.

About the Dedication

On January 26, 2003, a small plane conducting a routine survey of the right whale calving grounds off Florida and Georgia crashed into the Atlantic. The lives of three whale scientists, Emily Argo, Jackie Ciano, and

Tom Hinds, and their pilot, Michael Newcomer, were lost. This book is dedicated to their memories. It is my earnest hope that their efforts on behalf of Atlantic whales—and by extension, Atlantic fisheries—will not have been in vain. The nonprofit Wildlife Trust has established a memorial fund to honor the lives of these committed professionals by supporting marine conservation projects in keeping with their work and aspirations. If you wish to contribute to the fund, checks should be made out to Wildlife Trust and sent to:

Heroes of the Sea Fund
Wildlife Trust
1200 Lincoln Park Avenue, Suite 2
Prospect Park, Pennsylvania 19076

Abbreviations

CCS   Center for Coastal Studies

CHA   Critical Habitat Area (established under the U.S. Endangered Species Act)

CLF   Conservation Law Foundation

COSEWIC Committee on the Status of Endangered Wildlife in Canada

DAM   Dynamic Area Management Rule (under U.S. Atlantic Large Whale Take Reduction Plan)

DFO   Department of Fisheries and Oceans, Canada

ESA   U.S. Endangered Species Act

HSUS   Humane Society of the United States

MMPA   U.S. Marine Mammal Protection Act

NAO   North Atlantic Oscillation

NMFS   National Marine Fisheries Service (U.S. Department of Commerce)

NOAA   National Oceanic and Atmospheric Administration (U.S. Department of Commerce)

PBR   Potential Biological Removal

SAM   Seasonal Area Management Rule (under U.S. Atlantic
             Large Whale Take Reduction Plan)

TRP   Take Reduction Plan (Atlantic Large Whale Take Reduction
             Plan, implemented under the U.S. Marine Mammal
             Protection Act)

TRT   Take Reduction Team (Atlantic Large Whale Take Reduction
             Team, convened under the U.S. Marine Mammal Protection
             Act)

URI   University of Rhode Island

Introduction

During the summer of 2001, millions of people all over the world followed the story of Churchill, a North Atlantic right whale who had become tangled in fishing gear. With only three hundred right whales left in the North Atlantic, experts warned that even one reproductive female killed by fishing gear could doom the species to extinction. Beginning in June of that year, whale rescue teams made several desperate attempts to remove the rope that had become embedded in Churchill's upper jaw, causing an infection that sickened the mammoth creature. The rescuers approached the whale in inflatable outboard boats many miles from shore to attach a satellite telemetry buoy and inject the animal with experimental drugs designed to sedate the whale to allow the crew to remove the embedded rope safely.

Among those who followed Churchill's case most closely were tens of thousands of fishermen who set traps and gill nets in the right whale's habitat along the east coast from Florida to Labrador. Under U.S. law, one right whale killed by fishing gear could prompt a federal judge to halt lobster and gill-net fisheries, a move that would impact coastal communities already staggering after the crash of Atlantic groundfish populations in the 1990s.

Churchill's case was no isolated incident. In fact, recent studies show that more than 15 percent of all endangered right whales and threatened humpback whales in the western Atlantic become entangled in fishing gear *every year.* Eighty-eight percent of all humpback whales bear scars from encounters with fishing gear. Most entangled whales escape with minor injuries, but some do not. Those that aren't killed outright may carry rope or net with them for months or even years before dying of infection or starvation. Tensions between fishermen and whale advocates are nearing the boiling point as the stakes rise for whales, fish, and fishermen.

A handful of scientists, fishermen, conservationists, and government regulators have devoted much of their lives to solving the problem of whale entanglement in the United States and Canada, but in spite of their efforts, ineffective regulations and a clash of personalities could spell the end of both the right whale and many small-scale fisheries in the Northwest Atlantic. *Entanglements* is the story of the people at the center of the controversy over whale entanglement in the United States and Canada.

Stormy Mayo on Cape Cod and Jon Lien in Newfoundland began the first whale rescue teams in the 1970s and 1980s. These two men took on the work of wrestling with the leviathan in small inflatable boats with homemade tools, using the techniques of the whalers to release whales from fishing gear. The work begun by Mayo and Lien is continued today by a new generation, including David Mattila, who led Churchill's rescue operation, and Wayne Ledwell, who almost single-handedly runs the Newfoundland entrapment assistance program.

Scientists like Scott Kraus and Amy Knowlton at the New England Aquarium and Bob Kenney at the University of Rhode Island study the right whale in the field to track the health of the population and devise ways to see it through its current crisis. Others assess the Atlantic's humpback whale population, photographing them in the wild and spending tedious hours matching photos to determine the impacts of entanglement on America's favorite whale species.

While scientists and whale rescue teams go about their work, fishermen and conservationists trade volleys in the courts, in the press, and in the halls of Congress. In the late 1990s, Richard "Max" Strahan, a belligerent environmental activist with a two-page criminal record and no permanent address, filed a barrage of lawsuits, driving the U.S. government and the New England states to act on behalf of the right whale. In spite of his unorthodox methods and his vagabond appearance, Strahan is a shrewd operator who can work the system using money he raises by panhandling on the streets of Boston. No one can deny that he has forced action on the right whale problem, but many ask at what cost.

Even as Churchill was migrating north with a piece of rope embedded in his upper jaw, environmental groups took the U.S. government to court over the right whale. In 2001, a lawsuit filed by the Humane Society of the United States angered fishermen so much that many responded by vowing never to comply with new whale regulations. Rhetoric between the two sides has been reduced to what one observer calls "pissing on trees," staking out and defending territory rather than pursuing consensus. But fishermen, scientists, and environmentalists all agree on one thing: The complex set of federal rules now in place to prevent whale entanglement in the United States will disrupt already strapped fisheries without saving whales.

North of the border in Canada, whales and fisheries are faring no better. Wayne Ledwell's entrapment assistance program in Newfoundland covers the island's 15,000-mile coastline and disentangles dozens of whales each year, but he has a single inflatable outboard boat and an annual budget of $47,000 Canadian (approximately $35,000 U.S.). Meanwhile, Canadian fisheries managers are ignoring the growing problem of whales colliding with fishing gear on the Grand Banks, far beyond the range of Wayne Ledwell's outboard. The whales' life and death drama plays out against the backdrop of a province forever changed by the crash of the cod population, a calamity that devastated the Newfoundland economy and way of life during the 1990s.

Why has whale entanglement been such an intractable problem in the United States and Canada in spite of the best efforts of hundreds of people? The answers to this question, I have found, are complex and cut to the heart of our troubled and multifaceted relationship with the world's oceans. The sea and its inhabitants provide us not only with food but also with the stuff of culture, courage, myth, and beauty; the losses we would suffer in stripping the sea of its gifts are unfathomable. Different people seek different gifts from the sea, and many see the literal and figurative collision between whales and fisheries as a conflict between mutually exclusive interests.

Can whales and fishermen coexist? In my journey through the issue, I have come to believe that they must either coexist or both will perish. The fates of both are inextricably wedded to the fate of the sea. If human-caused blights like overfishing, pollution, and climate change strip the ocean of its ability to sustain the whales, what will be left to sustain us?

Moreover, the nations ringing the North Atlantic have embraced the notion that extinction is not acceptable. So if any of the great whale species fades and dies out because of collisions with fishing gear, the bitter struggle to save them will inevitably consume and destroy those fisheries. Where then will the displaced fishermen turn? Many will turn to other fisheries, using practices that may not conflict with whales but will likely impact some other species, just the next domino to fall in a centuries-long cascade of imbalance.

I was compelled to probe these questions because my own relationship with the sea is similarly conflicted. I am a former commercial fisherman, my husband is a commercial fisherman, and nearly all the men in both our families are or have been either commercial or charter fishermen. Over the past several years, I have written extensively on fisheries issues and have attempted, in some small way, to preserve the stories of a few old men whose way of living is disappearing in the space of a generation.

At the same time, my training is in marine biology, and I have spent much of my career advocating for and educating and writing about the natural world. I consider myself a conservationist, and though I have studied whales very little, I understand their importance both as a part of the marine ecosystem and as a symbol of past excess and newfound respect for the earth. Fishing, science, and conservation have been my calling cards throughout this project, gaining me entrée and trust among fishermen, scientists, and environmentalists and giving me a uniquely broad perspective.

In 2001, I returned to graduate school to study human ecology, a discipline that encompasses all aspects of human endeavor. I learned that literature, history, art, sociology, law, geography, and psychology could all shed light on some angle of the issue at hand. As a human ecologist, I hoped to attain and communicate a broader and deeper understanding of humankind's relationship with the sea.

To understand the nuances of the whale entanglement problem, I accompanied fishermen and whale rescue teams in their work in order to understand the details of their operations at sea. In addition to my studies in the field, I conducted many hours of interviews with the key players on all sides of the entanglement story—fishermen, environmentalists, scientists, historians, lawyers, fisheries officials, and fisheries advocates—hoping to pick apart the subtleties of the issue and understand the rancor and frustration that keeps the process at an impasse. My investigations also included sociological research in which I sought to understand perceptions about whales, fishermen, scientists, and environmentalists and how these perceptions play out in the decisions we all make. I have compiled and combed a library of resources and reams of scientific papers concerning many aspects of fisheries and whales and how they interact.

Finally, throughout the project I have sought to understand my own feelings, values, prejudices, and misconceptions about whales and fishermen. In some chapters, I have chosen to take you with me on this journey; in others, this self-examination serves as an underpinning, giving the story weight and boundaries without rising to the surface. In so doing I hope I will inspire, at least in some small way, the same reflective process in you.

In the end, my multifaceted approach to this book has led me to some very difficult, sometimes frightening, questions. There are many questions I cannot answer. The catastrophic collapse of the North Atlantic groundfish in the early 1990s and the perilous condition of the North Atlantic right whale are clear indications that we humans have been doing something very wrong. But getting it right will not be as easy as passing a slew of well-meaning laws that protect an animal here and a few trees there. Getting it right will probably involve a radical change in the way we look at the environment and each other. The fishermen and whales in this story have far more in common than just the rich North Atlantic waters they share. I hope we can come to understand those commonalities in time to head off two avoidable tragedies: the extinction of the North Atlantic right whale and the end of small-scale fisheries in the Northwest Atlantic.

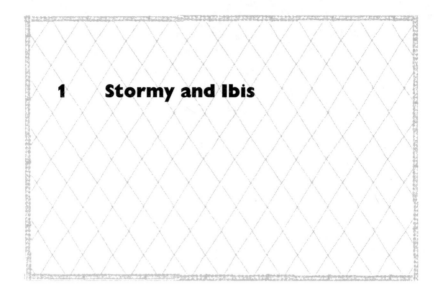

1   Stormy and Ibis

Reclaiming the Tools of the Whaler

This is clearly the direct collision between two endangered species,
and I have a transcendent involvement with both.
Stormy Mayo, February 2002

Stormy Mayo says he started rescuing entangled whales by serendipity
in October 1984. One afternoon he got a call at the Center for Coastal
Studies in Provincetown. A whale-watch boat had spotted a humpback
tangled in fishing gear that had snagged on debris near the mouth of
Gloucester Harbor, anchoring the animal and threatening to drown her.
Stormy and his assistant, Carole Carlson, gathered buoys, rope, snap
hooks, and knives and set out for Gloucester—about fifty miles across
Cape Cod Bay—aboard the Center for Coastal Studies' new thirty-four-
foot research vessel, *Halos*. An inflatable outboard boat, the Zodiac,
trailed astern. *Halos* had been donated to the center less than a year before. They had named the vessel *Halos* for Salt, the first humpback calf in
their study of the Cape Cod Bay population.

Stormy wasn't completely surprised to get the call. In August, Carole had told him that the female named Ibis had fishing gear on her. Carole worked with Stormy photographing whales to identify them by the markings on their flukes, so she knew all of the individual whales in the study. A blurry photo of Ibis out on Stellwagen Bank showed a gill net tangled in her mouth and around her tail.

"Ibis was a whale that I named. Her mother was Pegasus," Stormy says, looking back. He had expected her to return to Cape Cod Bay in 1984 with a calf. "We thought Ibis would come back with the first members of our second generation. Ibis was 'scheduled.' She was the first whale that we knew as a calf who was a female, who we thought . . . instead she came back with net around her. And it was clearly severe. She was starving."

Ibis had meandered into shallow water near Gloucester and caught the net on debris on the bottom. As Carole and Stormy motored *Halos* across Cape Cod Bay on that calm fall night, they wondered what they could do to help the thirty-foot creature out of her predicament. Both had worked with whales for years, but neither had ever tried to disentangle a whale. The task would be something akin to performing surgery blindfolded on a wild elephant with no anesthetic.

It was no secret that whales often became entangled in fishing gear. Stormy's father and grandfather, both fishermen, had talked about whales wrecking their nets. In fact, just weeks before, while working on a whale-watch boat near Plymouth, Stormy had seen a right whale struggling to free itself from lobster pots that were anchoring the immense animal to the bottom. That whale had eventually worked itself free, but Ibis was not so lucky.

When they arrived in Gloucester Harbor that evening, Carole and Stormy tied *Halos* to a pier and went ashore to spend the night with friends. Around ten the following morning, they motored out of the harbor in *Halos* towing the inflatable. When they arrived on the scene, they were accompanied by a flotilla of boats. A couple of fishing vessels, some folks from local whale groups, and a Coast Guard boat were on hand. The morning paper in the town had a brief report about the entangled whale, drawing a few tourists in their yachts.

"Carole and I found Ibis in the same place she had been reported the day before. That was odd," Stormy remembers. "She was anchored. The

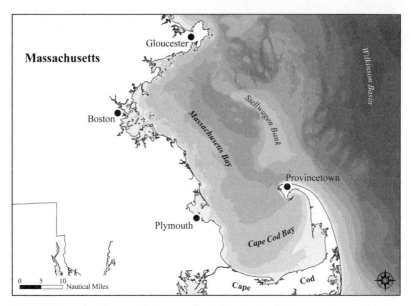

Map 1.1. Cape Cod Bay and Stellwagen Bank. Drawing by T. Johnson; data provided by Commonwealth of Massachusetts and GIS Data Depot.

net had tangled around a place where they had thrown a lot of trash and junk and engines and stuff outside the harbor. And she was tangled by the tail. The line through her mouth had wrapped around her tail. She was barely able at high tide to make her nostrils come to the surface. She was having a hell of a time, really threatened with imminent drowning."

Ibis had to struggle for each breath. To swim to the surface she frantically waved her tail, which was tightly wrapped with rope, dragging net and debris behind her. After getting her paired blowholes above water for a breath or two, she fell back exhausted and allowed the weight of the debris to carry her toward the bottom again.

Normally by October humpbacks are plump, having feasted on small fish and crustaceans for six months in the region's famously productive waters. Instead, Ibis was emaciated; the rope in her mouth had been interfering with her feeding. She had scant strength to struggle for each breath and had already been in this mess for more than fifteen hours. People on a dozen boats looked on as she labored. And the misfortune was not limited to Ibis.

*　　*　　*

Months earlier, somewhere along the rich coastal waters between Florida and Newfoundland, a fisherman, most likely a man, had driven his pickup to the dock and stepped aboard his boat just before dawn. The man—I'll call him Mike—checked the oil and water in his boat's engine, then turned the key to warm it up. Perhaps while Mike was listening to the weather on the VHF radio, his mate—let's call him Jimmy—stumbled aboard, bleary-eyed and cradling a paper cup of coffee. They pulled on orange foul-weather overalls and cast off from the dock to visit the fish pier where they took on fuel and ice in anticipation of the day's catch. Then they made their way out of the harbor—it could be almost any harbor—accompanied by the drone of the engine in the gathering light.

Mike stood at the wheel in the cluttered wheelhouse and turned on the loran, the fish-finder, and the local FM station. Jimmy gulped the last sips of his coffee and started getting ready to haul the net aboard, stowing fenders and docklines and rain gear, making sure the knives were sharp, maybe checking the fluid in the hydraulic system that ran the winch. He bent his knees as he stepped around the deck, swaying with the roll of a ground swell.

When they were past the moored boats in the harbor, Mike may have pressed the throttle forward, hoping to pick up his first string of gill-net gear before the wind picked up. If they were fishing for cod or haddock or hake, Mike may have pushed a worried thought aside: lately his catch had been dropping off. The fish were smaller and harder to find than they had been when he had fished with his father decades ago. Should he get one of those low-interest loans from the feds to buy a bigger boat? Maybe a dragger with radar and one of those expensive new electronic fish-finders? He would name the boat for his new baby daughter, or maybe his wife.

A day or two before, Mike had given Jimmy the word to toss one end of the gill net overboard. Jimmy had thrown the orange buoy first and maybe a high-flier, a small float with a flag attached used to mark the ends of nets. Keeping an eye on the depth sounder, Mike had motored away from the buoy as Jimmy paid out the line. When he reached the end of the float line, Jimmy had hefted the anchor over and stepped clear of the net that now snaked over the stern, tugged by the weight of the anchor toward the bottom. If he caught a boot in the net now, he could be dragged overboard, and it would be many minutes before Mike could haul him back like a gilled codfish. When the last section of net was whizzing over the stern, Jimmy picked up the other anchor and, timing his throw to avoid tangling it in the net, heaved it over, then tossed the buoy that marked the other end of the net.

"It's away," he might have called to Mike.

The gill-net string, or fleet, made of one or more rectangles of monofilament net a fathom high and as many as fifty fathoms long, now lay on the bottom. The top rope was buoyed with floats and the bottom was weighted, so the net formed a nearly invisible wall that caught groundfish by the gills and held them until Mike and Jimmy returned to haul the net. Each end of the net was marked by a float and held in place by a steel anchor if the current was strong or a strong plastic bag of sand if it was weak. To mark the spot where he had set the net, Mike had pushed a button on his loran, the electronic instrument that detected radio signals from shore-based stations to calculate the vessel's position, a precursor to the contemporary satellite positioning system.

The morning they returned to haul the net back, maybe Mike remembered that this set was on that sixty-foot spot where the cod often chased the capelin into a narrow bay. Or maybe it was on that sloping shelf where the schools of sandlance gather, attracting hungry groundfish. Or maybe it was that spot where he remembered longlining for cod with his father this time of year from an open wooden boat, filling the dory to the gunwales with brown and white fish they gaffed over the side. He could probably find the spot as easily as he could find his way from his house to the fish pier, so he may not have glanced at the screen on the loran. As they approached the area where they had set the net, Mike and Jimmy scanned the horizon for buoys or high-fliers. Perhaps Mike spotted a white puff of spray in the distance, then a humping black form with a curved fin, then a wide black tail lifted dripping into the air—a humpback chasing capelin or sandlance or mackerel or herring, just like the cod, the haddock, and several other species of fish targeted by fishermen.

But that morning when Mike arrived at the place they had set the net, he saw no orange buoys, no high-fliers. Nothing.

"Do you see it?" Mike might have asked Jimmy from the wheelhouse. It's always hard to see through wheelhouse windows crusted with salt from the ocean spray. "Keep your eyes peeled."

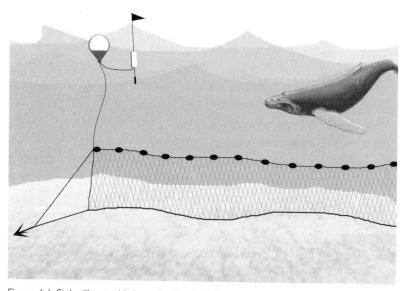

Figure 1.1. Sink gill net with humpback whale. Drawing by T. Johnson.

Knowing that the net could have drifted in the current while it was settling to the bottom, Mike steered the boat around the area, possibly using a search pattern. Still nothing. Then perhaps he spied the orange flag of a high-flier in the distance. He gunned the motor to investigate, but with a glance at the loran, he knew that net was probably not his.

After searching for a couple of hours, maybe more, Mike might have tried towing a grappling hook along the bottom to see if it might snag the missing net. He may have suspected that a whale had collided with the gill net and carried it off, but a careless trawler could also have run over it, or the gear might have been twisted when he and Jimmy had set it, dragging the buoy under. Finally, after hours of effort, he was forced to admit that the net was gone and set off to find his other fleet of gear—if he had another fleet of gear.

Losing a net or a string of traps is a risk you live with as a commercial fisherman, but losing thousands of dollars worth of gear is always hard to take. Thoughts of boat payments and mortgage payments and insurance premiums and doctor bills for the kids might have gone through Mike's mind. And the fishing just wasn't what it used to be.

While Mike looked for his net, Ibis, tangled and terrified, was probably many miles away. She had most likely been feeding, scooping up whole schools of tiny silvery fish in her maw, the pleats on her throat distended with barrelfuls of water. Ordinarily, she would have squeezed the water out between the fuzzy plates of baleen that hung from the roof of her mouth, then swallowed the wriggling mass of fish.

But this time Ibis swam into Mike's net, catching a line in her mouth. The more she rolled and writhed, the more the rope worked its way up between the plates of baleen. Eventually the trailing net and rope wrapped around her tail and tightened as she swam. She would carry it with her for months on the summer feeding grounds in Cape Cod Bay.

Stormy had been trying since August to devise a plan to disentangle Ibis if he saw her again before she migrated south for the winter in the Caribbean. One night over dinner Stormy sought his father's advice. Charles Mayo was a successful Provincetown fisherman in a long line of Provincetown fishermen. Well-known for his ingenuity, the elder Mayo had pioneered the tuna industry on Cape Cod, a fishery now worth tens of millions of dollars a year. After Stormy had founded the Center for Coastal Studies with his late wife, Barbara, and friend Graham Giese in the mid-1970s, the elder Mayo often served as the captain of *Halos*. So Stormy asked him to apply his ingenuity to the problem of disentangling whales.

"We had a picture of Ibis towing gear," Stormy relates. "I said to him, 'This is what we've got.' He listened to that and said, 'Why don't you keg it? Just put something on the gear.'"

In the 1930s, when Charles Mayo had hunted pilot whales using harpoons, he tied wooden kegs to the harpoon line and let the animal tow them around. Mayo would chase the whale, keeping his eye on the kegs floating at the surface. When the whale tired and could no longer fight or swim, he would approach the spent creature and finish it off. Kegging, in one form or another, had been used for centuries in man's effort to bring down the leviathan; the bigger the whale, the bigger the keg. Some northern indigenous cultures used air-filled seal skins; the Europeans and early Yankee whalers, like Charles Mayo, used wooden kegs. At the height of Yankee whaling, when the prize was the sperm whale, or cachalot—the strongest and most dangerous of the hunted species—the Yankees allowed the whale to tow a whaleboat full of men for many miles

Figure 1.2. Stormy Mayo. Photo courtesy of Center for Coastal Studies.

and often for hours, a rollercoaster sprint they called the Nantucket sleigh ride.

Once when Stormy was twelve years old, he and a friend took a little rowboat out into the bay, planning to catch a tuna on a baited hook. Stormy's father supplied them with a small keg and suggested that if they did hook a tuna, they should keg it to avoid swamping the boat while fighting the big fish. As it turned out, the boys hooked a 150-pound tuna, so they tied on the keg and heaved it over the side, then followed it around while the fish wore itself out trying to dive against the buoyancy of the keg. Finally, the fish was theirs. In an ironic turn of events, Stormy would now try to use kegging to save a whale.

So in October 1984, when Stormy and Carole went to Gloucester to try to help Ibis, they brought a few Norwegian floats, big orange balls to attach to the whale. They also had plenty of rope and snap hooks to fasten the floats to the gear. While a bevy of boaters looked on, they loaded all this equipment into the Zodiac, left a friend at the helm of *Halos*, climbed into the inflatable, and started the motor. They approached Ibis under the watchful eye of the bystanders on a flat, calm sea.

In retrospect, Stormy thinks they were perhaps more timid than they should have been, but they had no idea how the animal would react to their efforts.

Figure 1.3. Ibis blows at the surface in the mouth of Gloucester Harbor on October 23, 1984, during the first attempt to remove rope from her mouth and tail. Carole Carlson (center) rides in the Zodiac with Mike Williamson (left) and Perin Ross. Photo courtesy of Center for Coastal Studies.

"I remember feeling very puny with Ibis," he relates. Ibis could not hit them with her tail since it was wrapped in fishing gear and tethered to the bottom, but the mammoth creature, even in her haggard state, could easily have overturned their boat with her head or swiped them with six-foot flippers.

But Ibis was apparently too weak to worry about the humans that pestered her. Sometimes panicked humpbacks will trumpet when they surface for air, but Ibis was quiet when her knobby black head humped up at the surface. She made no noise, other than the "puh-huh" when her nostrils opened for a breath. At one point, Stormy and Carole lowered a hydrophone into the water to see if Ibis was making subsurface vocalizations. She was mostly quiet; there were no other whales around to speak with, anyway.

"The situation was desperate, so we kind of scrambled," Stormy says. "Ibis was charging up to the surface to get air. We waited until she rose to the surface and attached the buoys with snap hooks taped to a pole."

In this way, Carole and Stormy got two floats on her, but they were hooked on weak monofilament netting, not rope, so when the whale sank again to the bottom, the buoys pulled free of the gear. Again Carole and Stormy, with the help of friends from Gloucester, hooked the floats on Ibis, and again the buoys pulled free. For hours they performed this dance at the interface of air and sea, two or four minutes of waiting punctuated by frantic activity when the whale surfaced. The buoys kept popping off with little pieces of monofilament net attached to the snap hook. Finally, around two in the afternoon, Ibis stopped surfacing.

"There was a period when the whale was still struggling, then nothing," Stormy remembers.

They waited. Still nothing.

Finally, they returned to *Halos* and motored over the area, using the depth sounder to peer into the depths. They could see a mound on the bottom and could only assume it was Ibis, drowned. The return trip to Provincetown was a somber one. Stormy and Carole expected that the next time they saw Ibis she would be a bloated rotting carcass, floating at the mouth of Gloucester Harbor, tethered to the scrap on the bottom by a tangled fishing net. But Ibis never surfaced over the scrap heap. After a few weeks, they began to wonder if she had really drowned that day.

*   *   *

On a winter afternoon years later, I meet Stormy Mayo for lunch at Napi's Restaurant in quaint and cluttered downtown Provincetown. We sit at a tiny wooden table for two in the middle of a room that is loud with the bustle of locals visiting at each other's tables.

"I'm a native of Provincetown and the first of ten generations from the Cape that has not commercially fished," Stormy says.

Stormy looks more like a Cape Cod fisherman than a scientist. Crow's feet crinkle the skin around his eyes, telling of fifty-six years squinting at the sun on the water. He often wears a khaki canvas cap with a long black brim like the ones Cape harpooners wear when they chase swordfish or tuna passing by the sandy peninsula. In fact, in the eighteen years since his adventure with Ibis, Stormy has been in the bow of whale-rescue boats hundreds of times. And instead of throwing harpoons, he's been throwing specially designed grappling hooks to keg and slow entangled animals, applying the technology of whale hunters to rescue whales.

Stormy may be the first in ten generations of Mayos to work outside the fishing industry, but from my perspective he's not too far outside the fishing industry. Almost everyone I talk to about whale entanglement tells me that Stormy is one of very few who understand the problems of both fishermen and whales. As a member of the federal Atlantic Large Whale Take Reduction Team (TRT), he is trusted by fishermen and conservationists—no small feat in that divided group. Meeting Stormy now, I realize that his way of making those around him feel valued also earns him trust.

Stormy is quick to credit people for new ideas and listens thoughtfully to what others have to say. When he describes a scientific epiphany regarding the nutrition of right whales and their reproductive success, he tells me the idea actually came from his "brilliant assistant."

Over our Napi's soup and sandwiches, I learn that Stormy is a philosopher by nature, and on this overcast February afternoon, he seems to be in an especially reflective mood. He has recently hurt his shoulder playing soccer, and the injury will force him to retire, at least temporarily, from his customary position at the bow when the whale rescue crew takes to the water this year. Perhaps he sees this change as the end of an era.

Stormy's two almost-grown sons have been telling him it's time to step back from the physical work of disentangling monsters.

"It's time you didn't take any more chances," they say.

"And I've kind of tried to get out of the bow, although I haven't completely," says Stormy. "And it's cool." In spite of himself, he still enjoys the challenge of disentangling whales.

He says he has three main passions in life: marine environments, wooden boats, and dahlias.

"You know, it's all serendipity," Stormy says of the turns his life has taken. "Everything is serendipity." When Ibis got hung up in Gloucester, someone had just recently donated *Halos* to the Center for Coastal Studies so they happened to have a vessel that could cross Cape Cod Bay on short notice.

*   *   *

Like most people who pioneered whale research, Stormy began his career in a very different field of science. After growing up on the waterfront in Provincetown and working on his father's fishing boat in the 1960s, Stormy went to college to learn about fish. He got his doctorate in ichthyology from the University of Miami's School of Marine and Atmospheric Sciences, where he found he had a knack for growing tropical saltwater fish—a wet thumb, you might say.

After a stint working for the federal government, Stormy and his wife, Barbara, who also had a marine science degree from the University of Miami, settled in Provincetown for good in 1974.

"My wife and I had the charming idea that we could make a living back here," Stormy says. He planned to drop out of science. "I said, 'screw that, I've done that.' I'm not too much into the professional side of it, to tell you the truth. So I said, 'I'm going to build a schooner.'

"When I was sixteen, just after my birthday, my father took me down to a dock . . ." He pauses, trying to recall. "B Dock in Bahia Mar in Fort Lauderdale. He was running sailboats out of there. And he took me down after dinner with my mother out on B Dock and he said to me, 'This is the most beautiful, classic design of any American small sailing craft.' And in the darkness, there was a forty-three-foot Murray Peterson. That boat was called *Oceanus,* a schooner. I kind of always carried that with me."

With money Stormy and Barbara had saved working for the federal government on a major environmental assessment project in Puerto Rico, he bought a big stack of lumber and began to build a wooden boat at his house on the waterfront in Provincetown. And he soon became embroiled in local environmental politics.

"It happened that there was a big environmental issue in Provincetown related to a plan by a local guy to fill three acres of the harbor to make a pier complex. In the 1970s, that kind of approach was accepted," Stormy remembers. "In fact, it was this project among a few others that put the dagger in the heart of that concept that you could just pump up stuff and make land. The environmental battle engulfed Provincetown. Everybody chose sides. It was brutal."

Opponents to the proposed project eventually prevailed, but not before bad blood and death threats had flown around town.

While in the throes of this environmental battle, Stormy and Barbara hooked up with a physical oceanographer, Graham Giese from neighboring Truro. The trio founded the Provincetown Center for Coastal Studies in 1975, "just as a lark."

"We gave it an audacious name," says Stormy. "The center was founded just for the fun of those of us who had some academic background and loved the ocean. We had no physical plant. People would pay us fifteen bucks for a three-part course just to hear Ph.D.s talk about marine science. And amazingly, people did it. So we had these amateur courses, and a few of the people were damn bright and are still involved with the center. And then we grew from there."

Al Avellar, a fisherman who later came to own a fleet of Provincetown whale-watch boats, was running one of the first whale-watch cruises on the east coast. Avellar had known Stormy as a kid, and now that kid was a Ph.D. He hired Stormy to come on the cruises to talk to the passengers about whales and other natural curiosities, thus establishing a long-term cooperation between the center and Avellar's Dolphin whale-watch fleet.

Stormy says at first he was working for Avellar to make the twenty-five bucks a trip, but eventually he began to take an interest in the whales. He kept track of when and where he saw which species, how they behaved, and so on. He collected scientific data at a time when very little was known about the whales that commonly inhabited the waters just off Race Point at the outer tip of the cape.

As the Center for Coastal Studies grew and matured into a research institute, Graham Giese moved on to Woods Hole Oceanographic Institution and Barbara passed away, leaving Stormy at the center with an increasing interest in whales, largely because of whale watches.

"In those days, whale watches were not thought to be the way you collect scientific data. People in the field thought, 'not very pure,'" Stormy remembers. "And I was collecting scientific data. And it turned out to be the best database in the world, bar absolutely none. And now everybody is collecting data from whale watches. Maybe it's not pure, but I'll tell you, it's cheap."

The center acquired a couple of inflatable outboard boats, and Stormy began publishing papers on the whales of Cape Cod Bay. He took on assistants to help with his research. When a generous donor gave the center a research vessel in 1983, Stormy and his crew could begin collecting more systematic data on Cape Cod Bay's whales. The new boat also allowed them to begin rescuing entangled whales. Serendipity.

*   *   *

Thanksgiving Day 1984 dawned bright and calm in Provincetown. The Center for Coastal Studies crew all planned to spend the day together, cooking and devouring a turkey. That morning, Stormy was at his home on the water, gathering things to bring to the festivities when the phone rang. One of his assistants had arrived early to the party and had news that several humpback whales were milling around just outside the harbor.

"I went down to my beach, and I could see that there were several whales just at the mouth of the harbor," Stormy says. "So we thought 'yeah, what the hell, let's go out.' So we went out in *Halos* to get photographs of who was there, do a little sound recording."

Stormy's father took the wheel of *Halos,* and a couple of center staff members came along, including David Mattila, who would later serve as the director of the center's disentanglement program. As usual, they towed a Zodiac astern.

Stormy was below decks when they rounded the point and came upon two humpbacks.

"It's Ibis!" he heard someone yell. "There's net on that whale!"

"The first whale that we saw right at the entrance of the harbor was Ibis, tangled in gear, and another whale, Blizzard," says Stormy. "It turned out Ibis had apparently torn free in Gloucester; we had yanked her free of the bottom with the floats. And she had snuck away, with all the boats looking, in flat, calm conditions. She had snuck away from us. She was still alive—tangled, looking skinnier and bad. We knew she was going to start heading south on the migration and she obviously hadn't eaten."

The rope around Ibis's tail stock had tightened so much it had cut deep into her flesh, and a depression in the area behind her blowholes indicated that she had not laid on the thick blubber that was supposed to sustain her in the less productive wintering grounds. She would certainly die if the net and rope remained cinched around her body. This was the last chance to help Ibis. Everyone's holiday plans changed.

Stormy and David Mattila climbed into the Zodiac and circled Ibis, assessing the situation. Ibis kept her distance from the buzzing boats, punctuating what was already on David and Stormy's mind: A free-swimming whale is far more difficult to handle than one that's conveniently anchored, as Ibis had been in Gloucester a month before.

They all knew of the work of Jon Lien, a biologist at Memorial University in Newfoundland, Canada. For the past few years, with the help of his graduate students and local fishermen, he had freed literally hundreds of whales and the odd turtle or basking shark caught in cod traps or long gill nets. But most of the Newfoundland animals were anchored, stuck where they were. Even if it was anchored, working with a panicked behemoth was no picnic, but at least you could count on finding the animal when you looked, and when it dove, you had a limited expanse of sea in which the whale was likely to appear again.

Not only was Ibis free-swimming, it seemed she was not going to be a willing patient. Blizzard, her companion, appeared to be protective of Ibis, swimming between her and the boats.

In the Zodiac, David and Stormy discussed their options. They had the Norwegian floats and the hook-on-a-pole apparatus that Stormy and Carole had improvised in Gloucester, but they couldn't get close enough to Ibis to hook her. Each time they approached, she disappeared beneath the waves, leaving them guessing where to look next.

Finally, David said, "Look, we're not going to get a hook on this animal. Why don't we grapple her?"

They kept a grapple anchor in the Zodiac, so Stormy and David tied the grapple onto one end of a line and a few big Norwegian floats on the other. Then, while David maneuvered the Zodiac, Stormy took the first of many such throws from the bow of the Zodiac. On the second try, the grapple caught the rope that twined around Ibis.

"Jeez, we'd hung her by about ten or eleven," he says.

While *Halos* stood by, David and Stormy allowed Ibis to tire herself out like Stormy's kegged tuna. Blizzard milled nearby.

"We soon caught on to the fact that you can put the floats closer and closer on the line," Stormy remembers. "We moved them up every time we got the chance."

Ibis tried to pull the buoys under water and at first could drag them down for a short time, but she had very little fight left in her. As the day wore on and the tether got shorter, Ibis finally gave up, exhausted. By two in the afternoon, she was lolling at the surface, bobbing in the gentle swell with her big orange floats.

Word had gotten ashore of the attempt to rescue Ibis, and more people had joined the effort with another Zodiac. After some shuffling, Stormy stood in the bow of one inflatable, while David was in the bow of the other. They moved in to begin cutting the net and rope away. David took the head, and Stormy took the tail.

Blizzard was apparently distressed by their approach and began trumpeting, exhaling sharply through his blowhole to make a chilling sound of alarm.

"And it was just one of those remarkable things," Stormy recalls. "Here it was Thanksgiving, the weather happened to break perfectly, conditions were excellent. And by about three o'clock, we had two inflatables sitting on top of her. I literally had her tail in my lap at one point; she had lifted her tail.

"You know, there are seminal moments in all lives. A seminal moment in mine—it still gives me goose bumps—was this moment when this huge creature was lying there, literally immobilized by us. Blizzard, her associate, running around her, trumpeting and upset. And us in the middle of this swirl. I reached over the bow and her tail was there with this deep gash across, sawed into her tail stock. We'd been working on it, and I reached into that wound, which must have been six inches deep, ostensibly to feel how deep her blubber was. It was an open wound. And the seminal moment was when I reached in, and she started bleeding. You know, it was almost a bonding experience. Suddenly, just the blood said, 'I'm a feeling, sensitive creature.' I will never forget that moment when that blood came out. I'd obviously, probably hurt her."

Remembering this, Stormy shakes his head and looks in the distance, reliving the scene. "Wow."

While Stormy was holding Ibis's tail over the bow of his inflatable, David was in an epic struggle to get the line out of her mouth. He had cut the rope off short on one side and was pulling mightily where it emerged from the other side to draw the rope through the plates of baleen where it had been lodged for months. After many minutes of hauling, the line finally came loose. Stormy cut the rope and net that twined around her tail. Ibis was finally free. The small flotilla left her with Blizzard as the sun settled over the mainland to the west.

*   *   *

In the spring of the following year, Stormy was aboard a whale-watch vessel when Ibis was spotted for the first time since they had left her in the gathering dusk on Thanksgiving Day. In 1986, she returned with a calf, who was named Dowser in the humpback whale catalog compiled by the center.

Then, in 1990, Connecticut children's author John Himmelman published a picture book with a fictionalized account of Ibis's ordeal. The watercolor paintings illustrating *Ibis: A True Whale Story* portray Ibis and her friend Blizzard with big, expressive blue eyes (humpbacks have brown eyes). In the story, friendly Ibis loves to visit with whale-watch boats when they come to see her in the bay, and the red sea stars she sees on the rocks at the bottom of the bay give her a good feeling. Himmelman's depiction of the rescue effort in Provincetown on Thanksgiving shows the two Zodiacs with Stormy in his harpooner's cap and David with his bushy blond beard. Though Ibis is frightened when people begin to attach floats to her, she is eventually comforted by their hands, which resemble sea stars reaching into the water. After Ibis is freed, she thanks the team with a big blow. She and Blizzard poke their heads out of the water for one last look at the rescuers before they leave to frolic with their herd.

Of course, if my account were a storybook, the tale would end here. Ibis and her calf would live happily ever after; the fishing would pick up so Mike could buy a new net and make that mortgage payment after all; and the heroes who saved Ibis's life would ride their Zodiacs off into the sunset after doing their part to save the gentle giants of the sea. But this is not a storybook. In truth, the last two decades have been unlucky for whales, rescuers, fishermen, and fish.

What we don't learn in the storybooks is that Ibis, #0215 in the College of the Atlantic humpback whale catalog, was never seen again after 1986, the year she and her calf were photographed. She is presumed dead. Blizzard, #0291, was last seen in 1985. Both whales may have fallen victim to a biotoxin that accumulated in Cape Cod Bay mackerel in 1987; some scientists, Stormy included, believe this naturally occurring toxin caused seventeen known humpback deaths that year and is likely to have caused many others. Or perhaps Ibis was no longer able to sustain a calf after her ordeal. No one will ever know.

Ibis's mother, Pegasus—#0235, fared a bit better. She had three calves after Ibis and was found dead in December 1990.

Salt, the female for whom *Halos* was named, has led a relatively long life. Jooke Robbins, who studies humpbacks with the Center for Coastal Studies, told me in a recent email, "Salt has been seen regularly since, most recently in 2003 (with her ninth known calf)."

The fate of Dowser, Ibis's calf, is not clear. The calf was seen and identified by fluke markings only three times in the company of Ibis in 1986. Mason Weinrich, a biologist at the Whale Center of New England in Gloucester, tells me that often the markings on juveniles change over time, making it difficult to identify them after they wean. But Dowser, he says, had a distinctive fluke marking that would be unlikely to change enough to be unrecognizable, so the calf would have been a good candidate for identification. Dowser might still be out there swimming in a treacherous sea, but most likely Dowser is not.

Mike probably missed a mortgage payment or two, maybe more, when the Atlantic groundfish stocks crashed and fisheries in both the United States and Canada were shut down. If he's stubborn, he's still fishing (and many are that stubborn), but he's probably moved on to other fisheries. Maybe he's back on his feet now, depending on the lobster or the crab fishery for the largest portion of his income. If he's not that stubborn, he's probably building houses or finishing a retraining program at a local college.

Stormy has made hundreds of throws from the bow of a Zodiac, and Dave Mattila has earned veteran status in the business of rescuing whales. Both men are now talking about getting out of the Zodiac, though there seems to be no shortage of whales that need to be kegged and freed.

And as I write, at least two North Atlantic right whales—two of just three hundred remaining in the world—are swimming off the coast of New England with rope jammed between the plates of their baleen and wrapped tight around their upper jaws. It was precisely this kind of entanglement that killed Churchill in 2001 after an expensive high-profile effort failed to save him. Officials at the National Marine Fisheries Service have told Stormy that they can't let another right whale die, but the experts are hard pressed to think of a way to help the mammoth creatures out of their predicament without risking grave injuries to the rescue team—humpbacks are pussycats compared to right whales. If one or more of these right whales die, the courts could choose to start closing down trap and gill-net fisheries on the eastern seaboard, a move that could put Mike and tens of thousands of his colleagues out of work.

Whales and fishermen need a solution to the entanglement problem now, but the bureaucratic process that was supposed to produce a solution has ground nearly to a halt.

Meanwhile, a parallel story is unfolding on the craggy coasts of Newfoundland.

2 Jon Lien

The Whale Man of Newfoundland

Regardless of the politics, economics, and biological truths that swirl around the business of extracting food from the sea, the people out there are just doing what people do. They are ambitious, brave, frightened, rich, poor, confused, and amused, but fishing somehow differentiates them from other streaks of life.

Brad Matsen, *Fishing Up North*

On a summer day in 1978, Gilbert King, a fisherman in Trinity Bay, Newfoundland, made his way out onto the bay to check his gill net, only to find a humpback whale wrapped in the net, milling and snorting. Gilbert had a big problem.

Over the next few months, Gilbert and his neighbors did everything they could think of to get the gear off the whale, but nobody wanted to get too close, so they only succeeded in making the animal nervous and wary of boats. Gilbert's whale swam in circles, anchored to the spot, day after day after day.

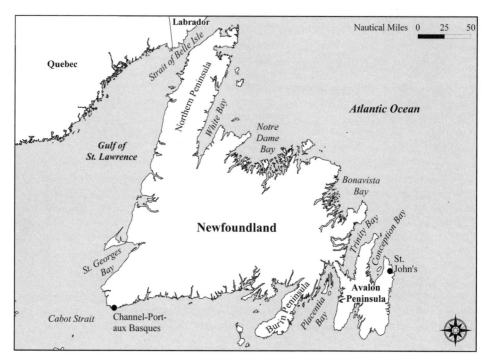

Map 2.1. Newfoundland. Drawing by T. Johnson; data provided by GIS Data Depot.

Gilbert called the Canadian Department of Fisheries and Oceans (DFO) and the Wildlife Division looking for assistance getting the whale out of his gear, but nobody would help.

"It's a fisherman's problem," they said.

Finally, Gilbert called someone in the administration at Memorial University in St. John's. That administrator called Jon Lien, a biopsychology professor at Memorial, to ask if he would try to help Gilbert out of his jam.

At the time, there were no whale biologists at Memorial and very few anywhere else in the world. But the administrator knew Jon had an interest in whale communication and that he was both generous and game for just about any challenge. Jon agreed to help Gilbert and brought a group of students from a biopsychology class up to Trinity Bay, a long stretch of sea between the Bonavista Peninsula and the northern arm of the Avalon Peninsula.

"Gilbert was a really poor fisherman and all his gear was on the one whale," Jon Lien remembers. "And the whale had been caught in it for three months."

Jon loaded his students into a Zodiac and made a few passes around the whale, sizing up the situation. But the wind was picking up, and a chop bothered the surface of the bay, so the group returned to the university. The whale wasn't going anywhere, and Jon needed to prepare, so he assembled an arsenal of tools for grabbing and cutting.

The following week, Jon and his class returned to Gilbert's whale in the Zodiac, caught the wary beast, and wrestled Gilbert's net off. The whale swam away, free of gear.

Then another fisherman motored up and said, "I got a whale, too."

"When did yours get caught?" Jon asked.

"Well, about three months ago," the fisherman answered.

Jon recalls, "And this guy had been shooting the whale all that time."

A scant few years earlier whales had been hunted along the shores of Newfoundland, just as they had been on Cape Cod. The Basques in the early 1500s were the first commercial whalers to ply the waters of the northwestern Atlantic—after they had winnowed the eastern Atlantic stocks of large whales. Yankee and European whalers soon followed, setting up seasonal tryworks for rendering blubber in nooks along the rocky coasts of Newfoundland, hunting for whales near shore, then towing the lumbering carcasses in to be processed. Once ashore, the whales were flensed—peeled of their blubber—and then the blubber was cut into pieces to be heated in the tryworks to extract the abundant oil. The men pierced great hunks of blubber with stout iron hooks, then labored with blocks and winches to lift them from the bulkhead and into the cauldron. They used long iron sticks to fish out the chunks of fried whale flesh that remained in the cauldron after the oil was extracted. They tossed this fried flesh on the fire, where it fueled the flames for further rendering of the same animal's fat, an irony that has been fodder for many a literary chronicler of the whale trade. While the blubber boiled in the cauldron, the men hacked out the plates of baleen from the whale's mouth. When all the useful parts had been extracted, they towed the carcass away where it joined the other rotting hulks that peppered the remote shores of the island.

Each year ships returned to cart away bundles of baleen and oil in wooden casks before the ice settled in for the winter. This was the cycle for a century or so until the intense whaling had largely exhausted the supply of whales that could be reached in small craft. Then men took advantage of advances in naval architecture to chase whales to the far corners of the earth. Even so, people on the Atlantic's shores continued to hunt straggler whales for oil and meat using small open boats launched from cobble beaches or stone bulkheads.

The right whales were nearly gone, but the cod kept coming ashore into Trinity Bay and a hundred other bays and fjords, large and small, that line Newfoundland's folded shores. The vast schools of silver capelin came inshore to spawn, and the cod followed. The cod drew permanent settlers who built modest houses that clung to the steep sides of the bays. With a small boat and a handline, a man could catch enough fish to make a good living. His wife and children helped out by cleaning the fish and drying them on wooden frames called flakes and jigging with small hooks for squid to use for bait. The income from fishing combined with abundant cloudberries and partridge berries, a moose or a caribou, and the produce of a kitchen garden was enough to sustain a family. This way of life supported dozens of generations of Newfoundlanders until Gilbert King's generation saw it come to an abrupt end.

If a young man wanted more money and adventure, he could sign on to a schooner out of Brigus, St. John's, or even Gloucester, Massachusetts, to fish the Grand Banks or Georges Bank. Young men from the Newfoundland outports (remote coastal villages) made able crew, having spent their formative years working in the nearshore fishery.

The pursuit of whales and fishes in the New World made for a seabound link between Newfoundland and New England that endured for half a millennium before being forgotten by many in just a couple of generations. But many a seaward-looking Newfoundlander still remembers and will welcome a mariner from Massachusetts as a kindred spirit.

In fact, Gloucester banks schooners often called at St. John's in bad weather or to provision before setting out for the fishing grounds; Newfoundland schooners often landed their catch in Boston. Occasionally, the two might meet at Halifax in Nova Scotia. Ships that hailed from both regions vied to be the first to make it to buyers, spurring competition that inspired some of the fastest commercial sailing ships ever built.

Over the centuries, the people of Newfoundland extracted their living from the sea in whatever form they could. They enjoyed the great salmon that were once abundant in their rivers and ate every edible part of the cod, including tongue, cheeks, and roe. Many still hunt seals for meat and not long ago also hunted whales for meat and foreign trade. Until cod and other fish in their waters became scarce, they were not averse to sharing the wealth with other nations.

Commercial whaling operations—both homegrown and in coopera-tion with Norwegian and Japanese companies—continued in New-foundland, Labrador, and Nova Scotia until Canada banned whaling in its waters in 1972. According to whale historian and artist Richard Ellis, the preferred targets of the modern Canadian whalers were finback and sei whales, which largely escaped the ravages of the harpoon until the late nineteenth century. Because they have less blubber than right whales and bowheads, finbacks and seis typically sink when dead and don't yield as much oil. But late-nineteenth-century technology provided a way to overcome the problem of sinking. Modern whalers began using har-poons with exploding heads that were launched from a deck-mounted gun. If the gunner were skilled, the exploding harpoon killed the animal quickly, dispensing with the Nantucket sleigh ride. Then the bleeding corpse was pumped full of air to make it float.

According to Ellis, a Norwegian firm opened a whaling station in 1965 at Dildo, a small town at the head of Gilbert King's own Trinity Bay. Then, in 1970, according to Dildo historian Miriam George, a Nova Scotia com-pany opened a whale processing plant at Dildo. The World Wide Whal-ing Company of Tokyo sent a Japanese whale ship, the *Kella Maru*, with a Norwegian gunner, one Captain Bergen, to kill finback whales in New-foundland waters.

George says whales continued to be processed for the Japanese at Dildo even after the whaling ban in 1972. The Japanese ship did not have to go far to reach international waters. Just a dozen miles offshore took them outside of Canadian jurisdiction, though it seems they found their prey in sufficient numbers about 140 miles to the north near Funk Is-land. The *Kella Maru* towed the bloated sixty- or seventy-foot finbacks to port three or four at a time, depositing them at the Dildo plant where, Miriam George says, "the meat would be used for pet food for the United States, the tail for food [for Japan], and the bones and blubber to make oil." Japanese men trained the Newfoundlanders to do the required processing, and the plant remained in operation until 1974.

*　　*　　*

So whaling was a recent memory on the day in 1978 when Jon Lien and his students set out to release a second humpback from a fish net in Trinity Bay. The fisherman who had caught this whale had been shooting at the animal, a tactic commonly used in those days to deal with entanglements. The idea was that when the animal was dead, you could grapple it up or wait a few days for it to bloat and rise to the surface, then take your gear off. The problem with this strategy was that the rifle or shotgun shot didn't penetrate into the whale's flesh far enough to do lethal damage to an organ or a blood vessel. The whale's thick skull could easily stop a bullet. So the whale remained entrapped but had open wounds that became infected. It could take weeks or months before the infection spread throughout the body and finally killed the animal. While the creature suffered, the fishing season passed the fisherman by, leaving him wondering if he would need to leave his family in the outport for the winter while he went to work on an oil rig at sea or a construction crew in Alberta.

As Jon and his students approached, they could see the whale's skin was gray and pocked with bullet holes as it milled slowly where it was tethered.

"It was in terrible shape," says Jon Lien. "But it was kind of neat because as we were releasing that sick whale, another whale came up and tried to stay between our Zodiac and that sick whale. That was very interesting because I didn't know how whales reacted, and here this big thing comes up between and rubs our boat. I said, 'Hmm, I could lose my job at the university because I killed a boatload of students!'" Fortunately, no one was killed.

While Jon and his assistants worked to free the whale, a couple of them held hydrophones in the water and listened for vocalizations.

"Wow, listen to this!" one of them exclaimed.

"And it's the one and only time I heard song phrases in Newfoundland," Jon says. "Mostly up here it's just burps and farts, but the whales were doing song phrases. And I thought, 'God, isn't this amazing?'"

Jon surmises that the entangled whale was a female and her companion a male—only male humpbacks sing, and typically only during the mating season.

They released the whale but could see it was quite sick.

"Uch," Jon shakes his head. "I'm sure it didn't survive after we let it go."

*   *   *

The event on Trinity Bay would change the course of Jon Lien's career.

"I thought it was a terrible way to treat the fishermen and the whales," he says. "So I decided I'd ask around. And everybody said, 'Oh, it's a terrible problem.'"

Jon rented a lecture room in a motel in Whitbourne near the head of Trinity Bay and invited fishermen to come from nearby towns to talk about whales.

"And they all said, 'Jesus, this is a terrible problem. It's the worst problem we have right now. And it's getting worse,'" Jon remembers. "The fishermen all believed that the whales were breeding madly since we stopped whaling in 1972. 'They've been breeding and breeding and now they're thick as shit,' they said."

Jon listened to the fishermen and noted their complaints, then approached the Department of Fisheries and Oceans, telling fisheries officials, "You've got a problem here and you really can't let it go, not from the fishery end and not from the whale end."

The DFO officials responded with their stock answer: "It's a fisherman's problem, and nobody's going to do anything." But when Jon digs his heel in, he is a formidable force. He pestered them until, out of exasperation, someone in the agency told him to write a grant. So DFO funded the first of many grants Jon would receive to begin a program to assess the problem and to devise ways to help both whales and fishermen. Later the provincial government would also put up some funds.

Jon recalls: "At the same time I realized that just doing the whales was not enough; you'd have to deal specifically with the information the fishermen had. Because the fishermen said: 'Well, why don't you just kill them? Just kill them. If you let them go, they're going to come and get me. If you had a bad whale, you'd probably best kill it.'"

The project was clearly going to be an uphill battle, but Jon is a psychologist, a biologist, and, at heart, a Norwegian farmer, a combination that curiously suited him to the task that lay ahead.

"Things just kind of unfolded." Jon says. "I never really decided anything."

* * *

Jon was born in South Dakota in 1939 to Norwegian immigrants. His father ran a tiny corner grocery and was "poor as a church mouse."

"Oh, it was terrible for them, I know," says Jon, his flat midwestern accent getting a little flatter as he speaks about his parents. "I'd get up in the morning and I can remember seeing my mother and father praying that they'd get enough money to pay for a bill that was due that day."

But Jon always found ingenious ways to make money as a kid. His parents had a big barn that sat unused, so when he was in junior high school, Jon started raising chickens.

"I'd raise five hundred at a time, and I'd pick them and sell them special. So by the time I was in high school, I was earning way more money than my father. I'd take the chicken money—I raised a couple batches of chickens a year—and I'd invest it in cattle in the summer. Then I'd pasture the cattle in the ditches because it was free pasture, and then I'd work on a farm besides. Usually I'd get skinny steers and they'd double in weight and the fall prices would go up by at least 50 percent. So for a kid, I had piles of money. . . . I had a very fortunate childhood."

Jon's parents thought raising chickens was a good education for a growing boy, so they rarely pushed him to study or attend school. He was never into dances or hanging out with the other kids—he loved his barn.

"I wouldn't have thought to go to college." Jon remembers. "My dreams all involved huge chicken barns and cows."

He befriended a local veterinarian, and whenever a chicken died or a cow developed a sore, Jon was eager to understand why. The vet recognized a "fire" for solving animal problems and offered to help Jon get through college.

"And I was Norwegian," says Jon, "so I went to a Norwegian college." He attended St. Olaf's in Minnesota, where he met his wife Judy, and graduated in 1962.

Instead of entering veterinary school after graduation, Jon enrolled in the Ph.D. program in clinical psychology at the University of Washington and completed the entire course of study except for the internship before beginning a second Ph.D.

"Really all the time I was in the psychology program I was hanging out with the vets and hanging out with the animal sciences people, and all of my fellowships were with them. So I thought, 'This is crazy, I'm not going to do psychology.' And so I did my degree in biopsychology."

Jon's career in the animal sciences began with a project in which he implanted cow embryos in rabbits, then shipped the rabbits to Africa, where the embryos were removed and re-implanted into cattle so that the Africans could grow larger, more productive beef cows.

"That was the easiest way to ship them," Jon remembers, "as embryos."

Later he raised a flock of miniature pigs for nutrition and radiation research. And he worked for the U.S. government training the astronaut chimps.

Jon and Judy had a great time in graduate school with few worries and plenty of money, but that changed with the advent of the Vietnam War. Jon and Judy joined others in Washington State to organize opposition to the war, but they felt shut out of the democratic process.

"We were really heartbroken and sick and angry. It was a terrible time," says Jon. "So we decided we were getting out of the United States."

In 1972, while Jon was in the process of seeking work at universities outside the United States, he went to New York for a brief stint in the lab of T. C. Snerla, who studied animal behavior at the American Museum of Natural History. Snerla told him about a job opening at Memorial University in Newfoundland.

"That's a pretty out-of-the-way place," Snerla told Jon. "You could do exactly what you wanted."

Jon didn't much care about his academic freedom, but he was curious to see where his Newfoundland dogs came from. So he called the university, and they invited him to visit. He arrived in St. John's, went to the Holiday Inn where the university had reserved a room for him, then called Regina McBride, a local woman who ran a personal tour service. He asked for a tour of the city.

"I decided I was coming here before I met anyone at the university," Jon recalls. "It was just such a marvelous place then and the people were just incredible. At the time the premier was paying university students to go to school. I thought, 'God, this place has got its head screwed on right.' I had come out of this horror of the war—it's still a scar—and this was a simple, good place at the edge of the known world. And it was so different. I can still remember walking down Water Street and looking in windows because the stuff was British and foreign. The people spoke funny.

"I'm still passionate about this place," Jon continues. "You know, the people are very worthwhile. One thing impressed me almost immediately when I came here: The first day we were here, our dog was on CBC television as a native Newfoundland dog. We'd been screaming at the media in the states, and we'd organized the whole state of Washington to take over the Democratic Convention and elect a peace candidate, and they had called the convention a week early and beat us; the feeling was an overwhelming one of not being able to make a difference. That society was just headlong crashing into hell and there was no way to stop it. But then I come up here and my voice is so loud, my dog is on television the next day. And I still have that feeling that you can't get an opera here, but you can sing in the choir yourself. You can't go to the best play in town, but your neighbor is pretty funny at telling stories. It gives you a chance to speak and make a difference in a way that in the United States you couldn't buy with a million dollars."

At Memorial, Jon added other animal subjects to his resume: he began working on squid, then turned to birds, moose, and caribou, before finally settling on whales. At the time Jon arrived, Memorial was very new and very English—some professors still lectured in gowns. A few of those must have looked askance at Jon and some of his colleagues who brought students into their labs and out into the field, but Jon built a successful program in biopsychology that continues to attract graduate students from all over the world.

Jon and Judy bought some land in Portugal Cove outside of St. John's and raised their three children in their adopted home. Judy, the gentlest, most unassuming person I have ever met, has labored for decades to build up the soil on their property and operates an organic farm, selling fresh vegetables to local residents. She hosts young volunteers from all over the world who come to work and learn organic farming. The Liens raise a batch of chickens every year.

When I visited the Liens in the summer of 2001, Jon was on "holiday." The day I arrived, he was in the process of cutting and splitting ten cords of wood. When that was done two days later, he led the three farm volunteers in a charge to tear down the old stockade fence that girded the farm—the fence had been wrecked by the thirty feet of snow deposited on it the previous winter. Then they erected a new fence. The day I left, Jon wore a pair of jeans and a white T-shirt with a Norwegian flag, every inch of his stocky form was smeared with dirt, and sweat dripped from his gray hair and beard. He was delighting in his current project: digging a pond in the yard behind his house where his new golden retriever puppy, Annie, could swim. He smiled for my camera next to Judy, who was neat and self-effacing.

*   *   *

As Jon set out to make a difference for the whales and the fishermen of Newfoundland in 1979, he found his degree in clinical psychology as useful as the degree in animal science. Fishermen believed that the whale population had been burgeoning since the end of the whale hunt seven years before and were swarming inshore and damaging fishing gear in record numbers. The humpbacks comprised more than two-thirds of the documented entanglements, and fishermen told Jon there were "thousands and thousands" of them in the bays of the province. Since they were no longer hunted, the fishermen firmly believed, the whales were no longer afraid of humans and "brazenly approached" people and their gear. Damage to fishing gear could be a major catastrophe to the average fisherman in Newfoundland—the median income of a fisherman at the time was less than $6,500 a year. So the fishermen were understandably concerned, and from the looks of it, the problem seemed to be getting worse. Why it was getting worse was not yet clear.

Jon attacked the problem from several fronts. He established an entrapment assistance program that encouraged fishermen to call for help to release an entangled animal—the goal was to release the whale with minimal damage to the gear. When the fishermen called, he and his students and assistants responded, sometimes driving six hundred miles across the length of the island to release a whale. But Jon spent far less time releasing whales than talking to fishermen, trying to earn their trust and teach them a thing or two about whales.

One day in 1979, a fisherman named Ted Whittaker found a humpback in his cod trap; it was the third whale he had trapped that summer, and he was mad when he called Jon.

"The biggest hardship, the most emotional cases were where the whale actually got caught," says Jon. "If you had a hole in your net, well, you had a hole in your net and you blame God or anybody, but it was probably a whale. But when you had the bastard there, Jesus, you wanted to kill 'em. And you felt like shit because here our peak of the trap fishery was about a week in many cases. So if you're out of the water for that week or two weeks, you've lost your whole voyage, you know, it's over."

Jon drove to St. Vincent's to meet Ted Whittaker, and when he arrived, the whole town was gathered at the pier with rifles in hand, just getting ready to leave the dock. A television crew from the BBC had followed Jon in a van, hoping to film him releasing the whale—a standard heartwarming news story.

"Stay in your van," Jon told the reporter, Richard Brock, and his film crew. "Don't get out. These people are angry and you're not involved."

The film crew did as they were told, and Jon went and stood with the fishermen to discuss the situation. They talked for an hour, shuffling their feet and pointing rifles toward the ground, before they finally agreed.

"Okay, we'll let you try it your way," Ted Whittaker said.

*   *   *

A cod trap is essentially a big box made of fishnet. Each side of the box is ten or fifteen fathoms wide (a fathom is six feet) and as deep as the water at high tide where the trap is set. The top edges of the box are held up on the surface by floats and the bottom is anchored. One side of the box has a pair of doors that open inward and a long leader net, similar to a gill net, that extends away from the box a long distance, often toward shore or some other natural obstruction. The cod, swimming typically near the bottom, chase the capelin toward shore. The tiny silver capelin can slip through the mesh of the leader, but the cod can't. Instead, the cod wander along the leader looking for a way through and are herded between the doors and into the trap. The whale in Ted Whittaker's net had been looking for capelin too.

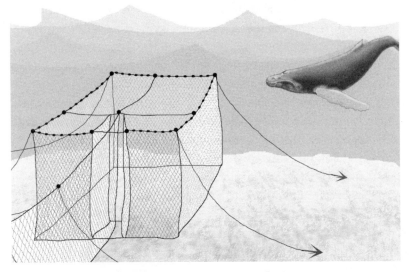

Figure 2.1. Cod trap with humpback whale. Drawing by T. Johnson.

Jon, Ted, and several other St. Vincent's locals made their way to Ted's cod trap on Holyrood Bay, a tiny indentation in the southern shore of the Avalon Peninsula. They simply dropped the top edge of the trap and drove the whale out. No damage. Jon stayed to help Ted and his crew haul the trap up and harvest the fish. First they pulled a line that closed the doors of the box, and then the crew of one boat hauled up the front of the box to concentrate the fish in the back of the net, while the crew in the trap boat used dip nets to scoop the fish from the trap and into the fish hold. Not only did they release the whale without damaging the net, they also got eight thousand pounds of fish.

"And I thought, 'Yes!'" Jon says with a growl. "Over and over again on different shores, there were those kinds of things where it was clear, we were not just getting whales, we were taking care of the fisheries *and* the whales. That had to be a growing trust. The fishermen were not used to that from anyone."

In Newfoundland in the 1970s and 1980s, all conservation groups were called "Greenpeacers." Greenpeace had led the charge in ending the whale hunt and had temporarily interrupted the seal hunt, in part by advocating that 1.5 million harp seals be classified as an endangered species. Regardless of the validity of Greenpeace's claims, to Newfoundlanders their philosophy and their tactics seemed inexplicable, extravagantly impractical, and quite possibly insane. And the Greenpeacers had successfully deprived them of their whale hunt, apparently visiting this plague of whales upon the fishermen of Newfoundland.

If the fishermen had identified Jon as a Greenpeacer, they would have shut him out, the show over. There would have been nothing he could do to help either the fishermen or the whales. So he got another grant to develop educational programs, and in the early 1980s, he and the staff of the newly formed Whale Research Group at Memorial University started a process of communication that Greenpeace had never attempted in the province. First they asked fishermen what they thought about whales, who they respected in their communities, and what they thought of meddling scientists. When fishermen told them there were "thousands and thousands" of humpback whales, they taught the fishermen to identify whales, took them out on aerial surveys, and sent researchers out on their fishing boats to enlist their help in counting whales. Unlike their Cape Cod counterparts, the Newfoundland researchers never attempted to photograph or identify individual whales, much less name them. Their focus was primarily on the humpback population as a whole. Meanwhile, the Whale Research Group blanketed the province with carefully crafted messages about whales and fisheries and did programs in the public schools.

But the problem did seem to be getting worse—each year, more and more whales were colliding with the fishing gear that girded the island. There were times during the fishing season when the Entrapment Assistance Program responded to two and sometimes three calls in a single day. The number of animals caught by fishing gear in Newfoundland peaked in 1991: 137 humpbacks, seven minke whales, two white-beaked dolphins, and one beluga whale were reported to the team, nearly all by fishermen.

Clearly the efforts to educate fishermen were paying off; they were reporting entanglements and, when they could, assisting the team in getting the whales out alive. Even so, in 1991 alone collisions caused almost $1 million in damages and lost fish revenue, twenty-one whales died, and twenty-seven whales swam off towing fishing gear before they

Figure 2.2. Jon Lien (right) with his wife, Judy Lien, and Wayne Ledwell, coordinator of the entrapment assistance program. Photo by Sean K. Todd.

could be released—and remember that Ibis was nearly killed by gear she had carried off. Why was the problem escalating?

During the 1980s, while Jon Lien's whale rescue operation grew, both the United States and Canada were in a frenzy to build up their fishing fleets on both coasts. Newfoundlanders and New Englanders had rejoiced in the mid-1970s when their respective federal governments claimed jurisdiction over a two-hundred-mile zone surrounding their coasts. When this claim was encoded in the U.N. Conference on the Law of the Sea in 1982, the foreign industrial fleets that had been cashing in on Grand Banks and Georges Bank groundfish were finally driven off. Now the North American fishermen geared up to catch the fish that, in their view, rightly belonged to them. Both governments passed out low-interest loans for boats and gear and doled out permits for groundfish. The number of cod traps rose in the Canadian Maritimes, and gill nets and draggers proliferated from New Jersey to Labrador.

Says Jon: "Oh, it was a politician's dream. Money to be made! Get all the fish the foreigners had been catching! So we grew up to twenty-eight thousand fishing enterprises. Jeez, it was crazy. Then as the effort increased, the stocks started to decline, so the fishing effort increased. Where one guy used one cod trap in the past, now he had three. And the government was subsidizing this. There was not a brain in the whole fishery."

There were more nets in the way of the fish and the whales.

"So the number of whales getting caught kept going up and up. And there was no measure of inshore effort. We didn't have it. My reports always speculated on what was the fundamental issue. Was it just increased effort or were the whales redistributing?"

Even a doubling in fishing effort didn't explain the 375 percent rise in trapped and tangled whales between 1981 and 1991. The humpback population had risen somewhat since the whale hunt had ceased, but scientists were seeing their numbers rise even more sharply in the near-shore waters of Newfoundland in summer and a corresponding *drop* off-shore. The implications of this trend were dire.

Both the whales and the cod depend upon the tiny silver capelin as a primary food source. Before the two-hundred-mile limit was imposed, the Russian fleet had begun scooping vast schools of capelin from the rich waters around the Grand Banks with seine nets. After laying their two-hundred-mile claim, the Canadians took up the capelin fishery, an inconceivably wasteful endeavor given that the main product made from capelin was fish meal for fertilizer and fish food. They were engaging in an infamous practice known as fishing down the food chain: When the top predators were fished out, they fished for the prey, thus guaranteeing that the predators couldn't come back.

The year whale entanglements and entrapments peaked in the waters of Newfoundland—1991—was a bad one for whales, fishermen, and cod. That year, few capelin came ashore, chased by a few young skinny cod and what seemed like a horde of desperate humpbacks. The ground-fisheries—both nearshore and on all of the region's ravaged banks—were closed in 1992.

*　*　*

Ten years later, in 2002, I rode with an old Newfoundland gill-netter into the harbor at Calvert on the eastern shore of the Avalon Peninsula. He told me what the harbor had been like in his youth, with children running about and the shores lined with fish flakes covered with drying cod.

He described the beaches of his youth, ankle-deep in summer with a spongy gel—the eggs of spawning capelin. Then he paused, looking ahead, turning the wheel. The motor throbbed, and I could see the muscles of his jaw working under his ruddy cheeks as he regarded what was left of his town.

"Too much greed," he said. "Too much greed."

He pulled the boat alongside the pier to offload two hundred pounds of cod, a meager amount compared with the eight thousand pounds Ted Whittaker had extracted from his net after letting a whale go in 1979.

*　*　*

When Jon talks fish, he has a lot to say.

"Now northern cod is at 3 percent of historical biomass, and we're fighting over who's catching the last of it. They set a quota for fifty-seven hundred tons for 'information,' blah blah blah. Bullshit! It's a political fishery." Jon nods at the word "political." "There's a sentinel fishery we have now for information, and they take less than five hundred tons, and they give us great information. So we don't need any more information."

As the cod crisis brewed, Jon had been recruited to sit on the newly formed Fisheries Resource Conservation Council because, after more than a decade of work on their behalf, fishermen trusted him. The FRCC had the unenviable task of closing down nearly every groundfishery on the Atlantic coast.

"I got calls from two fishermen this week," Jon continues, raising his voice. "They were trying to sell me the idea that there's still plenty of fish and they should catch it. And they're pissed off about it because DFO's putting restrictions on gill nets. We haven't learned anything. And the managers say, 'We're in a position now where we're so cautious that we could never have a collapse again.' But then when crab really started showing signs of being bad, we kept fishing."

3 Sarda

The Right Whale in the Wrong Sea

It is because whales are such grand and glowing creatures that their destruction degrades us so. It will confound our descendents. We were the generation that searched Mars for the most tenuous evidence of life but couldn't rouse enough moral outrage to stop the destruction of the grandest manifestations of life here on earth. We will be like the Romans whose works of art, architecture and engineering we find awesome but whose gladiators and traffic in slaves are loathsome to us.

Roger Payne, *Among Whales*

While Jon Lien fought to protect fisheries and humpback whales in Newfoundland, Stormy Mayo and his American colleagues were just beginning to understand that fishing gear was a major hazard to the world's most endangered large whale—the North Atlantic right whale. In the late 1990s, just when scientists thought the right whale was finally moving away from the brink of extinction, their numbers began to dwindle anew, prompting a frenzy of studies, lawsuits, and regulations. As scientists pick apart the threats to the right whale, they are making important discoveries about the ecology of the North Atlantic as a whole. Now they say that the fates of fishermen and whales may be linked by more than monofilament net and polypropylene line.

*　　*　　*

The whale the Basques called *sarda*—the right whale—has been threatened by humans for a millennium. Though whalers would eventually discover and decimate right whale populations in nearly every one of the world's ocean basins, the first population they discovered and decimated was in the North Atlantic. Beginning around 1000 AD, the Basques worked their way from east to west on the Atlantic, harvesting this most prized leviathan.

The same characteristics that had made the right whale persistently successful for eons made it the "right" whale for man to kill. Right whales are strong but slow swimmers, so they were easy for whalers to apprehend under sail or oars; like all whales, they must breathe air from the surface, bringing them within the sights of the harpooner waiting at the bow of a whaleboat. And once dead, the right whale proved enormously profitable.

A well-fed right whale is absolutely corpulent, weighing up to one hundred tons, with twenty-eight to thirty-five tons of oil-rich blubber. A single individual can yield more than three thousand gallons of oil for light and lubrication. And because fat is lighter than water, right whales float when they are dead, so the whalers could kill the animals without losing them to the depths when they finally succumbed to harpoon and lance. The baleen plates that hang from the right whale's upper jaw are designed to strain minute plankton from the water and are unusually flexible and long—up to ten feet, yielding fine "whalebone" for stiffening corsets and making numerous items we now make from plastic.

Powerful and stubborn, the right whale was by no means easy to kill, and before the days of exploding harpoons, killing them was a gory endeavor. One modern researcher calls right whales "pugnacious," and some early whalers dubbed them "devilfish." Once struck with a harpoon, right whales struggled tenaciously; they writhed and dove, often towing a whaleboat for hours at a time while men tried to penetrate the thick blubber with a lance to sever an artery or a lung. Blood poured from the animal and turned the sea red. The whale flailed, churning the water

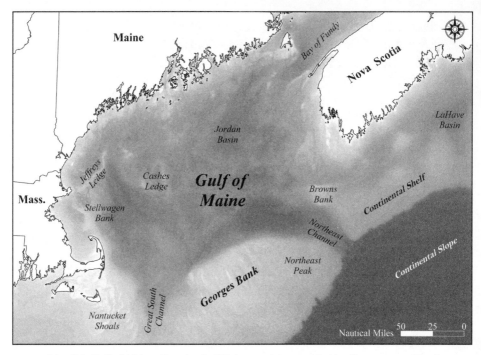

Map 3.1. Gulf of Maine. Drawing by T. Johnson; data provided by Commonwealth of Massachusetts and GIS Data Depot.

with flukes and flippers, soaking men in gore. Its desperate spouts spewed blood into the air.

It seems that the Basques were exceedingly efficient at killing right whales in spite of their pugnaciousness, taking hundreds and perhaps thousands per year during the 1500s. It is difficult to say how many right whales roamed the North Atlantic before whalers roamed the sea. In any case, North Atlantic right whales likely numbered in the thousands, possibly tens of thousands. But by the time the Basques moved on to other fisheries, the Yankee and European whalers that followed found *sardas* to be scarce in the North Atlantic.

Scientists have been using newly developed genetic techniques to peer into the past and estimate the size of the population that gave rise to the extant individuals. Piles of whale bones at remote, long-abandoned tryworks along the Atlantic coast provide DNA from whales killed by the Basques and other whalers. Geneticists can extract and analyze this centuries-old DNA to determine species, sex, and the composition of the whalers' harvest. Information gleaned from logbooks left by the whalers themselves adds to the body of evidence the scientists are considering. These forensic techniques are still being refined, and geneticists are still debating their results, but they do agree on one thing: the North Atlantic right whale population has been very small for a very long time, at least half a millennium. Right whales may have been relatively uncommon even before the concerted Basque whale fishery reduced their numbers yet further. And the persistent whalers who followed the Basques kept the population at dangerously low levels. In 1900, the population probably included fewer than one hundred individuals.

Even so, modern whalers killed right whales whenever they came upon them, and this practice continued well into the twentieth century. In the 1930s, most whaling nations adopted an international ban on killing the world's most endangered large whale, but several countries did not comply. Experts now believe that right whales are no longer hunted.

After the ban in the 1930s, the population of right whales in the North Atlantic slowly increased, apparently peaking at between 300 and 350 in the late twentieth century. Recently, however, four separate studies have shown that the northern right whale population is again on the decline. There are probably many causes of this decline, and scientists are scrambling to sort them out, but two human activities now account for at least one-third of the deaths in the North Atlantic right whale population. As ships have become larger and faster, slow-swimming whales—which often sleep and feed at the water's surface—can be hit and killed by passing ships. Also, with the advent of plastics (ironically the same material that replaced whalebone in many products), fishing gear has become stronger and more durable, far more capable of fatally entangling whales. More than two-thirds of all right whales bear scars from encounters with fishing gear, and a study by scientists at the New England Aquarium estimates that between 10 and 28 percent of the entire population becomes entangled in fishing gear every year. In other words, out of the population of three hundred, as many as eighty-four may be entangled in any given year.

The North Atlantic right whale must indeed be tenacious to have endured a thousand years of killing without finally succumbing to oblivion. Now three hundred individuals, the ragged remnants of a vast tribe, are the legacy left by our profligate forbears. And even though hunting has

presumably ceased, the future of the North Atlantic's right whale population is not assured. Scientists warn that even one human-caused death of
a reproductive female could tip the balance in favor of oblivion.

*   *   *

Much of the food chain in the North Atlantic, including the right whale
and the cod, hinges on a tiny planktonic animal called *Calanus finmarchicus,* a creature so minute and unassuming it doesn't merit a common
name. As an adult this shrimplike creature—one member of a group
of crustaceans called copepods—is considered gargantuan by copepod
standards: they can reach lengths of up to four millimeters. This copepod
is nearly transparent and torpedo-shaped with a single red eye-spot and a
pair of long antennae tipped with tufts of hair. Scientists believe that *C.
finmarchicus* is the most numerous animal on the planet. As such, it
forms a critical link in many oceanic food chains.

During the summer, swarms of these copepods float along with the
currents in shallow, productive nearshore waters. As winter weather
settles over the Atlantic, *C. finmarchicus* enters diapause; it arrests its
development in a pre-adult stage and sinks to the bottom to wait out the
dark cold winter. When spring rolls around, cool currents sweep the pu-
bescent crustaceans up the Great South Channel, over the Grand and
Georges Banks, and into the Gulf of Maine and the Bay of Fundy, where
they graze on phytoplankton—tiny floating photosynthetic organisms
that bloom under the sun in the nutrient-rich waters. The most numerous of these photosynthesizers are diatoms, single-celled organisms that
make themselves tiny and ornate pill-box shells out of silicates—glass
houses that scientists call frustules.

When I was peering once into a microscope at a plankton sample
taken from the ballast water of a ship, I saw a very small copepod eating
a very large diatom like it was a sideways sandwich. The diatom was disc-
shaped with whorls of markings on its clear frustule. I could see the
golden brown chloroplasts through the frustule, which was at least half
the size of the copepod. The copepod held the unwieldy meal with awkward hairy legs, much the way you might grasp a couch cushion with a
hand on either side. With its mouthparts, the copepod worked at the
edge of the frustule until the glass house had been breeched and cyto-
plasm began to leak out of the diatom. The copepod's mouthparts waved

and gathered the juices as best they could, and some of the brownish gunk from the diatom entered the copepod's transparent stomach. After a few seconds of slurping, the copepod left the leaking diatom and moved on, perhaps bothered by the bright light shining on the dish in which it now resided.

Overall, it was a very messy affair and not at all what I had imagined this second link in the food chain to entail. Perhaps when the size difference between predator and prey is more in the predator's favor, the operation is neater, with the copepod able to swallow the diatom whole. Messy or not, the critical role of copepods in the food chain is clear. They gather the sun's energy in the form of sugars and fats stored in diatoms and make them available to the rest of the food chain in the form of big fat copepods.

So when spring currents carry the pre-adult *C. finmarchicus* onto the banks and into the relatively shallow bays, they are met by a prairie of diatoms on which they graze and flourish. If you are looking for a meal in the Gulf of Maine during the warm months, *C. finmarchicus* would be a good bet. They are concentrated into vast crowds wherever currents run together carrying plankton into windrows. The swelling multitudes of copepods, each with a droplet of fat for food storage and buoyancy, draw hundreds of other animal species, which feed on them and in turn are fed upon. The humble little creatures are so critical to the North Atlantic's fisheries that when scientists observed a dip in the *C. finmarchicus* population during the mid-1990s, the species became the focus of intense study looking at the effects of climate and nutrients on their numbers. In August 1999, ninety-three scientists convened for three days in Tromsø, Norway, to discuss the population dynamics of this keystone species.

Believe it or not, the minute and multitudinous *C. finmarchicus* is the principal food for the right whale, known to reach weights of one hundred tons and lengths of sixty feet—more than six thousand times longer than the largest copepod. More commonly, though, adult right whales are fifty feet long and weigh fifty or sixty tons. Imagine subsisting on a diet of hamburgers that are so small you could fit five or six of them on the head of a pin. You would need some pretty specialized silverware. Right whales have their baleen, specially adapted to take advantage of the dense swarms of copepods they find where favorable currents meet.

Unlike the humpback, the right whale has no pleats on its throat, so it doesn't feed by gulping huge sections of ocean. Instead, it gathers food by slowly straining swathes of sea.

The right whale's upper jaw, sometimes called the *rostrum*, is long and narrow with the patches of rough light-colored skin that scientists call callosities. The underside of the rostrum is hung with long plates of fine baleen. The lower jaws, also marked with callosities, curve upward at either side of the mouth, forming a groove into which the upper jaw fits. This curve—some call it a frown—gives the whale an expression that those given to anthropomorphizing might call grim or resolute. Herman Melville, an unrepentant anthropomorphizer, devoted a whole chapter in *Moby Dick* to a description and contemplation of the right whale's head in comparison to that of the sperm whale. The chapter ends: "See that amazing lower lip, pressed by accident against the vessel's side, so as firmly to embrace the jaw. Does not this whole head seem to speak of an enormous practical resolution in facing death? This Right Whale I take to have been a Stoic; the Sperm Whale, a Platonian, who might have taken up Spinoza in his latter years" (Melville 1930, 485).

*   *   *

You also might think of these resolute right whales as gap-toothed. The left and right rows of baleen plates don't meet at the front of the right whale's cavernous maw, leaving a space where plankton-laden water can enter as the whale swims forward. The water passes through the plates at the back of the whale's mouth where the copepods gather on the baleen's fringes. Occasionally, the whale swallows the catch of a trillion or so copepods and then opens its mouth again and swims on. Scientists call this strategy skim feeding. Right whales will consume copepods wherever they find them in concentrations that make it economical to open their mouths and expend the energy required to plow through the water. They are often observed in Cape Cod Bay swimming with their upper jaw above the surface and their lower jaw below, straining swarms of plankton. In the Great South Channel east of Cape Cod and in the cold waters of the Bay of Fundy, the whales apparently feed near the bottom. Scientists have seen whales blowing at the surface with mud on their snouts, having grazed hundreds of feet below where the copepods and other planktonic organisms are gathered.

Figure 3.1. North Atlantic right whale. Note stout body, light-colored callosities, narrow upper jaw (rostrum), and absence of dorsal fin. The largest right whale on record weighed over one hundred tons, though weights of sixty to eighty tons are more common. Drawing by T. Johnson.

The following excerpt from *Moby Dick* describes right whales skim feeding on concentrations of plankton so dense they change the color of the water:

> Steering north-eastward from the Crozetts, we fell in with vast meadows of brit, the minute, yellow substance, upon which the Right Whale largely feeds. For leagues and leagues it undulated round us, so that we seemed to be sailing through boundless fields of ripe and golden wheat.
>
> On the second day, numbers of Right Whales were seen, who, secure from the attack of a Sperm Whaler like the Pequod, with open jaws sluggishly swam through the brit, which, adhering to the fringed fibres of that wondrous Venetian blind in their mouths, was in that manner separated from the water that escaped at the lip.

As morning mowers, who side by side slowly and seethingly advance their scythes through the long wet grass of marshy meads; even so these monsters swam, making a strange, grassy, cutting sound; and leaving behind them endless swaths of blue upon the yellow sea. (Melville 1930, 396)

This skim-feeding strategy allows right whales to feed very low on the food chain where the most energy is available because it hasn't been used up by passing through other creatures first. So in a summer of straining the sea, they can grow extremely fat, storing calories for their southward migration and a winter of snacking off the coast of Florida. A right whale thus fattened presents a wide black back to the whale watcher, with a smooth powerful momentum that reminds me of a freight train, immense and unstoppable.

But all too often, skim feeding at the surface puts the right whale in the path of oncoming ships, the only thing in the sea with power and momentum to match the mighty creature. Also, a right whale can hook a fishnet or a rope as it plows forward with its mouth agape, a disaster that can prevent the whale from feeding and leave it withered, sick, or dead.

*   *   *

Not surprisingly, the world's most endangered large whale population is the focus of intense scientific scrutiny as researchers try to sort out and address the factors that have kept the North Atlantic right whale from recovering as quickly as other whale species. Dozens of people are testing whale-safe fishing gear; trying out whale detection devices for ships; counting whales and warning ships away; testing every tissue and bodily fluid a right whale can produce; writing reports to Congress, Parliament, and the International Whaling Commission; and conferring and arguing over ways to protect the species.

So intense is this scrutiny and so small is the population that scientists see and photograph the majority of the individuals every year. Whenever weather allows, researchers fly in search patterns over right whale habitat, locating and counting whales. Scientists watch when right whales plow through summer blooms of plankton in Cape Cod Bay or the Bay of Fundy. They watch when right whales form mating groups. They peer at mother/calf pairs lolling in the warm waters of their Florida calving grounds. Whenever scientists observe a right whale defecating, they swoop in to collect the sample for tests on hormones and diet. When a dead right whale washes up on a beach, veterinarians and biologists perform elaborate autopsies on the reeking carcasses. People have been known to test new disentanglement equipment on dead beached whales.

Using special hollow darts fired from crossbows, scientists have collected small plugs of skin from more than two-thirds of all North Atlantic right whales for DNA analysis. With these, the scientists can determine the gender of the animal; they can sometimes tell who is related to whom; and they can assess the population's genetic diversity, which may be a measure of the resilience of the population.

Not one, but two major databases are maintained on right whales. The New England Aquarium research team has the job of managing identification data, tracking calving and DNA information, and matching photos of the unique pattern of callosities on each whale with those taken in previous sightings. The nearly constant flyovers and reported sightings generate distribution and sighting data that Bob Kenney manages at University of Rhode Island.

In the fiscal year 2001–2, the U.S. National Oceanic and Atmospheric Administration (NOAA) budgeted $5 million for research and protection of the North Atlantic right whale; that's almost $17,000 per whale. Given the energy and money spent on the right whale, it is truly astonishing how little we really understand about right whales and how ineffective protection measures have been. In fact, about one-third of the population does not frequent the summer feeding grounds in New England and the Bay of Fundy. Scientists are not sure where these whales go in the summer, but they know they exist because the whales return to the southern wintering grounds once in a while.

In 1998, researchers were distressed when the herd of three hundred right whales produced only five calves. The next year saw only four births. Then, to their horror, researchers saw only one calf in 2000. Right whale calving rates normally go through boom and bust cycles, but this trend was nothing short of alarming. Also, researchers began to notice that many females in the population had never calved, even though they were of reproductive age and had often been seen in mating groups on the Florida mating grounds. Suddenly it became clear that the factors that contribute to the whale's reproductive success were little known.

So, in April 2000, the National Marine Fisheries Service (NMFS) convened a group of about forty people in Woods Hole, Massachusetts, to share what they knew about right whale reproduction and to confer on how they should focus their research in the future. The group, composed of whale biologists, conservationists, veterinarians, population experts, and others, agreed that nutrition was likely to be important in the calving equation, but almost nothing was known about the caloric intake of right whales, beyond a little work by Bob Kenney at the University of Rhode Island on energetics and prey requirements.

A few days after the Woods Hole workshop, Stormy Mayo stood in his lab in Provincetown talking to his assistant, Amy DeLorenzo, while she peered into a microscope counting copepods in a plankton sample.

"Some people from outside whales are asking a lot of questions about nutrition," he told Amy. Some scientists at the workshop had said reproductive success in terrestrial species is often tied to nutrition. Maybe that was true for the right whale too.

Amy looked up from her scope and said, "Well, if that's true, next year's going to be a good year for calves."

Stormy and his colleagues at the Center for Coastal Studies had been interested in the productivity of Stellwagen Bank and Cape Cod Bay, especially since the city of Boston began constructing a sewage outfall pipe that extends nine and a half miles into the bay; CCS had collected data on plankton concentrations for the past fifteen years. Amy was analyzing the latest of these samples when she made the prediction about right whale calves, setting off a cascade of ideas in Stormy's mind. If calving success was indeed linked to the populations of copepods in Cape Cod Bay, then monitoring the copepods could allow scientists to predict calving success. It was a compelling thought, and he pursued it right away. With the help of Richard Pace, a statistician at NMFS, Stormy analyzed the fit between right whale calving and the amount of food available in Cape Cod Bay over the previous fifteen years.

When statisticians talk about "fit," they are referring to a very specific, mathematical definition for establishing cause-and-effect relationships. In brief, goodness of fit is determined by the size of a particular number—probability, or "P" for short. This number tells you whether the cause-and-effect relationship could be real or whether it's probably all in your head. The higher the P value ($P > 0.05$), the more likely that there is no cause-and-effect relationship; the two phenomena are probably unrelated. The lower the P value (P < 0.05), the more likely that there is a cause-and-effect relationship; the two phenomena probably have something to do with each other.

Stormy watched over Richard Pace's shoulder as he ran the data through the statistics program on his computer. The first test, checking the fit between plankton and calving in the same year, produced no correlation. So Stormy and Richard surmised there might be a time lag in the effect of nutrition, especially given that cows are pregnant for the year preceding the birth of a calf. With a one-year lag time, the P value was just under 0.05, just barely statistically significant.

Then they tried the fit with a two-year time lag. When Stormy saw the results, he got goose bumps.

"The P value," he said, "was vanishingly small." Less than 0.01.

The fit was even tighter when they looked only at the calving rates of the subset of the right whale population that feeds in Cape Cod Bay and the Bay of Fundy.

You don't need a Ph.D. to see the correlation between the food and the calves. In the report that Stormy, Amy, and CCS biologist Ed Lyman gave to the Marine Mammal Commission in October 2000, a figure shows the two graphs—calves born and calories available to the whales in Cape Cod Bay—with the two-year time lag. The two lines rise and fall together. Such a certain result is an extreme rarity in science. The precipitous drop in North Atlantic *Calanus* populations in the mid-1990s—the same drop that had spawned the meeting of ninety-three concerned scientists in Norway—had caused three dismal years of right whale reproduction in the late 1990s. And as Amy DeLorenzo had predicted, 2001 and 2002 were good years for right whale calving. Thirty-one calves were born in 2001, though four died before reaching the summer feeding grounds; at least two of these four were killed by the slicing propellers of passing ships. In 2002, right whale researchers counted twenty-six right whale calves on the calving grounds, though one has already died of unknown causes. Though this finding does not explain all the problems with the population, there is absolutely no question: calving success is directly linked to food availability. But what determines food availability?

I traveled to the University of Rhode Island (URI) in the spring of 2002 to ask Dr. Robert Kenney that question. Bob Kenney has been staring at right whale data on computer screens since the late 1970s. When he first arrived as a graduate student at URI, Bob worked on a project funded by the federal government. It seems the Bureau of Land Management had hatched a plan to lease oil rights in Baltimore Canyon and Georges Bank, and the law required them to do an environmental impact statement. Howard Winn, Bob's advisor, won the grant to do surveys of the protected species along the eastern seaboard that would be affected by the proposed oil rigs.

Bob spent many hours peering at the ocean surface through the window of a small plane, looking for whales, dolphins, porpoises, sharks, and sea turtles. He also worked with technicians who counted these creatures by bumming rides on fishing boats, ferries, commercial vessels, and Coast Guard buoy tenders. The plan for oil leasing never came fully to fruition, but the surveys yielded reams of comprehensive data from which many scientific careers were built, including Bob Kenney's. He stayed on as a postdoctoral researcher and eventually joined the research faculty at URI.

Nowadays Bob spends about half his time managing the right whale distribution database. The rest of his time he ponders and probes the mysteries of right whale populations and their reliance on the populations of *Calanus finmarchicus* and other Calanoid copepods in the North Atlantic. Recently he has teamed up with Cornell physical oceanographers Charles Greene and Andrew Pershing to determine why *Calanus* populations fluctuate the way they do and how this might figure into the future of the right whale species.

When I visit Bob Kenney, we sit in his lab, one room in a temporary modular building that has apparently been here for at least twenty years. We are surrounded by computers of various vintages and bookcases filled with disks, computer tapes, books, and papers. Bob is a frank and practical guy known among his colleagues as having an incisive intellect. He is a little cynical, perhaps jaded by thirty years of banging his head against government and university higher-ups who make inexplicable decisions. When I ask a question, he pauses for several long seconds before answering, as though carefully sorting pieces of information. While thinking, he shifts in his squeaky chair; he doesn't stroke his graying beard. When he finally speaks, his answers are startlingly clear.

Bob wasn't at all surprised by Stormy's findings about the tight fit between plankton and calving with a two-year lag time.

"We see a two- to three-year lag also," Bob says, "but it's not between the food and the reproduction, it's between reproduction and the North Atlantic Oscillation." Bob had already been looking at the problem but from a slightly different angle: he was studying climate.

"I went to an International Whaling Commission workshop on whales and climate change in Hawaii in 1996," Bob remembers. At this workshop, several researchers who studied penguins and seals in Antarctica presented data showing that fledging and pupping were directly linked to El Niño events. El Niño is a periodic warming of the Pacific, known by scientists to be connected to the Southern Oscillation, a naturally oscillating weather pattern in the South Pacific Ocean.

"They kept putting up graphs of the Southern Oscillation," says Bob. "But every time I saw that graph of the pressure index, it just looked familiar to me. It looked like the shape of the long-term annual fluctuations in right whale calves. So when I came back, I started going out on the web and trying to find Southern Oscillation index data and did some correlations, and it's significantly correlated."

Bob found that one year after an El Niño in the Pacific, right whale calving tended to decline. Then he started looking at the oscillating climate patterns in the North Atlantic, aptly named the North Atlantic Oscillation (NAO). He found that the calving rates correlated closely with the NAO, especially for the individuals who belonged to the lost population that rarely visits known congregation areas in the Bay of Fundy, Cape Cod Bay, and the Great South Channel. Then two colleagues at Cornell found that the populations of *Calanus* in the region are largely determined by climate that undergoes cyclic fluctuations similar to those in the Pacific. Another piece of the puzzle fell into place. Scientists believe there must be some connection between the Southern Oscillation and its smaller counterpart in the Atlantic, but the mechanisms are not understood.

Of course, it seems logical that if it's warmer or sunnier, then there will be more photosynthetic diatoms for the copepods to munch, but sunshine has only a little to do with it. Those savvy about ocean ecosystems might think that changing ocean currents lead to differences in the amount of nutrients carried up from the bottom, a phenomenon scientists call upwelling. The currents do change with the NAO, but nutrients are only part of the story. In fact, the whole story uncovered by Bob and the Cornell oceanographers is far more interesting and surprising.

Remember the trick *Calanus* has for waiting out the winter? They arrest their development and sink to the bottom. So the deep water off the edge of the continental shelf hosts hordes of waiting copepods. Come spring, the tiny crustaceans will be carried over the banks to mature in the floating meadows of diatoms near shore only if the whims of wind and water allow. If the currents have weakened—as they do when the NAO index is low—the copepods will not appear in the Bay of Fundy or off the Cape in nearly sufficient numbers to sustain a herd of fifty-ton behemoths.

"*Calanus* is not really a full-grown species in the Gulf of Maine. It comes in from offshore. It's reseeded every year, and the strength of the North Atlantic Oscillation is correlated with the strength and volume of the Labrador Current," Bob says, referring to a cold current that flows down from the far North Atlantic. "It's also correlated with the average north/south position of the Gulf Stream in a given year, and all those things affect circulation and intensity of circulation in the Gulf of Maine. And that's what controls how much new *Calanus* is brought in and how active the currents are that are sweeping it around and shoving it into places where it concentrates for right whales. There's a lot more physics involved in it than just plain old food chain biology.

"The phytoplankton that all the *Calanus* have been feeding on is someplace upstream. That's where all that productivity is; it's all being swept in on the currents that concentrate it there. The reason that the Great South Channel is such a great feeding ground is the shape of the basin and how currents come in. The same thing is probably true in the Bay of Fundy."

So right whales depend on favorable currents to bring the food into their feeding grounds. But the story doesn't end there. It seems that the temperature of the water flowing into the Gulf of Maine determines whether the copepods will be large enough for the whale's baleen to strain them out of the water. To understand this, you must know that copepods, like all crustaceans, grow in stages by molting their hard exoskeletons.

Right whales, Bob says, "like *Calanus* because they're big and they're rich in oil, so they've got a ton of calories. But the size class of *Calanus* that they can filter really well doesn't happen until they get to the fourth-stage juveniles. So the sizes that they really like are the fourth- and fifth-stage juveniles and the adults. The threes are a little bit too small. And the copepods are cold-blooded, so their growth rates are controlled by temperature; if water temperatures are cold, they grow slowly. So if they're coming in on a cool current, the time when they molt and grow to that fourth stage happens farther downstream."

In a cold year, the right whales must travel farther east in the Great South Channel to find copepods of sufficient size. In a warm year, they can feed farther west.

When Bob, his former advisor Howard Winn, and a colleague at University of Washington compared the historical sightings of feeding right whales with temperature profiles, "it matched up perfectly."

Most impressive were the results for 1992, a year when only a few right whales appeared in the Great South Channel. Whale researchers were at a loss to explain their absence until these scientists found that in 1992 the water in the region was especially cold. The whales had apparently traveled through the area looking for large copepods, and finding none, left to search elsewhere.

To us it may seem very risky for the right whale to hang its reproductive hopes on such a fickle phenomenon as the NAO, but when the climate of the North Atlantic swings in their favor, they really hit the jackpot. According to Bob's calculations, the concentrations of copepods available to right whales in a good year offer an extremely efficient source of food. In just nine minutes of continuous skim feeding on a thick soup of *Calanus*, a right whale can eat enough to supply its daily caloric needs. It can consume a year's supply of calories in just a few days of intense feeding. And a right whale can wait a very long time for a good meal when it is blanketed in twenty-five or thirty tons of blubber; remember that entangled whales can apparently live for many months without feeding at all. But calving is energetically expensive, and nursing a calf that gains about one hundred and twenty-five pounds a day can leave a mother lean and hungry. So when times are lean, it seems that many right whales forgo calving while they wait for the NAO to oblige.

If this is a natural pattern and the NAO has held sway over right whale calving since long before a Basque harpoon ever sank into skin and blubber, why are North Atlantic right whales so slow to recover? Their South American counterparts, the southern right whales, are increasing by 7 percent a year, while the northern right whale population is now in decline. Why?

To answer this question, Bob reminds me that the Basque whalers concentrated their efforts on the right whales in the high latitudes around Greenland and Labrador. The few animals they left were on the southern end of their range—precisely where today's right whales live.

"I think of right whales as big fat Carolina wrens," Bob tells me. "I'm also a birder and I like Carolina wrens—they live in my backyard. When we have nasty winters here in Rhode Island, the Carolina wrens get knocked way down. Back in the mid-1990s we had a couple of bad winters in a row and the next spring, during the Rhode Island Audubon Bird-a-Thon, nobody saw one Carolina wren. But they came back. It's a southern species, but between bird feeders and warming temperatures, they've all moved up here. So they're on the periphery of their range where conditions sometimes are good and sometimes are bad. The range contracts and expands with changes in conditions.

"I think what happened with right whales," Bob continues, "is the Basque whaling—and the Yankee whaling that followed it up—wiped them out in the core of their range. And there aren't any up there any more. It must have been the best habitat because that's where they were. So I think we're looking at the remnant of the population that's living on the edge of the original range where sometimes it's good and sometimes it's bad. The difference between right whales and Carolina wrens is that right whales are not very good at recolonizing habitat because whales go to the place that mom took them and they're very slow at exploring and moving into new habitat.

"So the Basques wiped them out, the Yankee whalers helped it along toward the end of the Basque whaling, and then they weren't a target of the fishery, but the sperm whalers still took one when they saw it. The shore-based whalers on Long Island took them right into the twentieth century. There was low-level whaling that kept them from recovering. So they go through this boom-and-bust cycle as the climate varies on a decadal scale. They have good sets of years and bad sets of years in terms of reproduction.

"But then there's this human-caused mortality overlaid on the natural mortality." Bob raises a finger to punctuate the point: here's where entanglement comes in. "We thought we finally got rid of that human-caused mortality; we finally stopped all the whaling. But instead now, we've replaced whaling mortality with ship strikes and entanglements. There's still this baseline mortality laid on top of this environmental variability.

"So," he nods, "the only hope for the right whale is to get rid of the human-caused mortality. Then they could make it through those low times."

The current genetic studies of the whalebones scattered along the shores of Atlantic Canada and new studies of whalers' logs will help to determine the original range of the right whale and the size of the population when the Basques arrived. So Bob's theory about the restricted range of right whales may be confirmed or refuted in the next few years.

"What about the frequency of the climate oscillations like NAO and El Niño?" I ask Bob. "What do the long-term climate models predict when they figure in global warming?"

"Well, the modelers say that it looks like they're coming faster," Bob says. "Atmospheric modeling is still more art than science, but a lot of the long-term models say that if you raise the temperature of the Atlantic you will increase El Niño frequencies." That means conditions in the North Atlantic will be unfavorable for right whale calving more often.

"It's still too tenuous to predict what the long-term impacts of global warming will be on right whales, but my gut feeling is that it isn't going to be good." Bob adds, "If it changes—no matter which direction it changes in—they're just not very good at adapting to change. It's not going to help them out."

We are both quiet for a moment, absorbing the implications of this last statement. Bob's chair squeaks.

I heave a sigh. "Well, that's depressing."

*   *   *

But hopelessness is a luxury we don't have when it comes to the future of right whales. If the fate of the world's most endangered large whale is a game of probability, then the best we can do is try to stack the odds in their favor. We cannot bring back the whales killed by the Basque and

Yankee whalers, and global warming may well keep some swarms of copepods from gathering where the whales can find them, causing calving to fall. However, most scientists believe we can change the other end of the equation. Recall that at least a third of right whale deaths are caused by ship strikes and fishing gear.

And whales are not the only member of the Atlantic ecosystem caught between climate and human-caused mortality; the future of Atlantic fish stocks hangs in the balance too. Copepods serve as a staple for the capelin, sandlance, and other baitfish that feed the larger fish. Copepods fatten the tiny larvae spawned by the Atlantic's stocks of cod, hake, haddock, mackerel, herring, and flounder. Even the sea's top predators—the torpedo-shaped tuna, the deep-diving swordfish, and the stony-eyed sharks (blue, great white, hammerhead, mako)—all derive their sustenance third- or fourth-hand from the calanoid copepods. So fluctuations in climatic conditions will inevitably affect every thread on the Atlantic's food web. The only thing we can control is the number of the fish or whales we kill. So where do we start?

* * *

These new revelations about the role of climate-driven currents in the North Atlantic's ecosystem suggest that it behooves ecologists, fisheries biologists, and environmentalists to completely revamp their ideas about how to manage commercial fish stocks and protect endangered species. But such holistic thinking is rarely embraced in these circles.

During our lunch at Napi's in Provincetown, Stormy Mayo tells me he is frustrated with the narrow focus of most whale research.

"My colleagues are consistently missing the point that these are living animals in an ecosystem. I mean, Jesus Christ, we all call ourselves biologists and most of us don't know anything about geostrophic flow or Eckman spiral or the complexity of processes that make plankton patches," Stormy says, referring to key principles of physical oceanography. "It's the whole reason that right whales exist. It's the whole reason that they hang by the thread. It's the reason that they go the places they go and tangle as they tangle and get run over by ships. And these people are coming to it like it isn't an ecosystem. They forget that there's water around these animals. There is a large and not well understood complex of stresses forcing these animals in a direction that looks, by all accounts, desperate." He shakes his head in disgust.

"You know," I say, "that just triggered a sudden understanding: the reason there is so much settlement around Cape Cod Bay is the same reason that the whales are here. It's the plankton."

"Absolutely," Stormy says. "That's an ecosystem. And, you know, if you want to be poetic, you can say that if you save the whales, you save us. We've heard that in a larger global context, and it certainly is true here. In the extreme, if you blighted the ocean and killed the food that forms the base for the right whales, you would kill the humans. If that ocean stopped producing what it produces unseen for right whales, then you would cease to have people on this earth. It's that important. The right whales would be gone. The ocean would certainly die. The right whales are working at that level, directly, in fact, and it's not by chance. They have picked—speaking teleologically—that level of the system to work with because it is the richest that exists on earth. Unfortunately it also is the most finicky of all the portions of the world system—the plankton. So they are feeding at the right level. They are making a living in the most calorically rich part of the earth, but they also are confronted continually with the question of where it is and what it is, because it doesn't grow with roots, season by season. It's always neat as hell, but it's always different. That's why plankton to me is a lot more interesting than right whales."

4   There Ought to Be a Law

Searching for the Smoking Gun

It's a rare thing for one fisherman, but it's a very common experience for one whale.

Bob Bowman, Center for Coastal Studies whale rescue team

"I've been fishing these waters since I was a kid, and I have never seen an entangled whale." This is a statement I have heard again and again from fishermen all over New England as they try to deflect criticism and regulations.

Given the tumultuous decade fishermen in New England have had, it's not surprising that they would rather not deal with the whale problem. All the tumult has spawned a new breed of fishermen who spend more time in meetings and hearings than they spend on the water. The whales represent another excuse for meetings and hearings—all for a problem that many fishermen think does not even exist. They don't dispute that whales sometimes get caught in fishing gear, but they just don't think it happens often enough to endanger a whole species or justify the enormous expenditure of time, money, and effort that U.S. federal law requires.

"Deer get hit by cars all the time," a lobsterman told me, "but we're not going to ban all the cars."

A Cape Cod gill-netter said the entanglement issue came out of the blue. "We never had an inkling that the whales were going to be a problem for us. I think it's over-exaggerated, by far. I think the green groups are using it as a fund-raiser."

Fishermen often continue by quoting an old statistic. Until recently, scientists believed that one-third of all right whale deaths were caused by ship strikes, less than a tenth of the deaths were caused by collision with fishing gear, and the rest resulted from natural or unknown causes.

"Do something about the ship strikes," said one man from Maine, "then come after us lobstermen!"

"That's the *real* problem," said another fisherman. "They [the government and the environmentalists] are just picking on us because we're easier to get to the table, easier to regulate."

As with almost any issue relating to fish, whales, or fishermen these days, the truth is far more complex, and the solutions are not so black-and-white.

* * *

There is no question that ships collide with and kill whales, especially when whales cross shipping lanes where big fast boats with tight schedules hurtle toward their ports. In fact, every so often a cargo ship will tie up to the dock after an ocean crossing to find a dead whale draped over its bulbous bow, evoking ire among whale lovers watching the news. In the fall of 2002, over the course of just eight weeks, three vessels arrived at Pacific Northwest ports, each with a fin whale—the second-largest animal on earth—dead on its bow. Not only big cargo ships but also navy vessels, Coast Guard vessels, and even high-speed whale-watch boats have clobbered whales at sea. But new studies are showing that fishing gear most likely kills far more whales than anyone, even the fishermen, could have guessed.

To come up with the old figures of anthropogenic (human-caused) mortality, scientists had looked at the dead whales they had on record and added up the ones they could attribute to a specific cause. For right whales, this came to about a third from ship strikes and less than a tenth for entanglements—but that was only for the right whale deaths they knew about and could attribute to a specific cause.

Scientists maintain two North Atlantic right whale catalogs: Bob Kenney keeps one catalog at the University of Rhode Island to track population trends and distribution, and the right whale team at the New England Aquarium keeps another catalog of identification photos. In the early 1990s, Scott Kraus from the aquarium began examining the photos of right whales more carefully for evidence of entanglement.

Having seen entangled whales in the wild and talked with people on the rescue teams in the United States and Canada, Scott could recognize the characteristic scars of an entanglement, especially those left by wraps of rope around the tail stock. The results of this scar study were appalling. The majority—more than 60 percent—of all the right whales in the catalog showed entanglement scars.

These startling results prompted David Mattila and Jooke Robbins at the Center for Coastal Studies to look at their catalog of humpback whale photos for the same trends, and the results were equally disturbing: fully 88 percent of the humpbacks in the catalog had entanglement scars.

When the whale scientists statistically compared the number of whales that were reported with the numbers of scars, they discovered that just about 8 percent of entangled right whales and a mere 3 percent of entangled humpbacks get reported. In other words, not only were more whales colliding with fishing gear than we had thought, but rescue teams have a crack at disentangling only a small fraction of the whales that run afoul of fishing gear. This was bad news for fishermen who believed the problem really lay with the shipping industry.

*　*　*

I visit Scott Kraus at his home north of Boston on a wet spring day. We sit in his living room for hours, sipping tea and talking about why right whales die, a subject he has spent countless hours pondering as head of New England Aquarium's whale research team.

In probing the right whale database, Scott has recently discovered several individuals that were last seen tangled in fishing gear and then were never seen again. This, combined with the scar studies, has led him to believe that collisions with fishing gear are far more common and lethal than anyone had previously believed.

"We know that ship strikes account for over a third of all right whale mortalities. And the interesting thing right now is that we have five mortalities from fishing-gear entanglements, but we have a *dozen* animals that have disappeared after being entangled and are presumed dead. So if you add those numbers up, if you decided that that all those whales died, then fishing and shipping are about neck and neck. So, fishing probably accounts for about another third of the total mortalities in right whales."

"And the other third is . . . ?" I ask.

"It's natural mortality, mostly calves, some juveniles, some old animals. Generally, I tend to include natural and unknown causes of mortality into one category, all as natural, because animals certainly die of disease and mistakes and old age and things that happen to them." He shrugs. "We are pretty good about taking animals apart now, so evidence of an entanglement is obvious on the outside, and evidence of a ship strike is obvious when you take them apart—you know, skeletal damage or big hematomas, those sorts of things."

Part of Scott's job on the aquarium's whale research team is to be on call to perform necropsies on dead whales. Since it is typically impossible to move the whale to a more convenient location, this is usually done wherever the whale happens to be. I imagine Scott's lanky form clad in gory foul-weather gear, knee-deep in the surf, hacking open a gargantuan stinking carcass with oversized knives.

Scott and his colleague Amy Knowlton have gone on to compare photos of right whales in multiple years and found that several have been entangled more than once. They also found that younger right whales were more prone than older whales to both colliding with fishing gear and getting hit by ships.

"The anthropogenic mortality does appear to have a little bump in two and three year olds," Scott told me, his feet propped on an enormous drum with an animal-skin head that serves as his coffee table. "It's also somewhat understandable; those would be the teenage drivers, basically wandering around getting entangled and getting hit by ships. They haven't figured out that this is a dangerous place to live."

"So do you think that they learn to avoid entanglements as they get older, or are they capable of avoiding them?" I asked.

"That's a good question. I don't know. We have had one whale who got entangled three times and is now dead, or we presume it's dead. So that one had a little trouble, or else very bad luck. There is a fairly high percentage of animals that have repeat entanglements. We document entanglements and we monitor the population all the time, so we see when entanglement scars are added. A measurable percentage of the population has been entangled at least twice."

Amy Knowlton and Scott (2001) concluded in an article in *Journal of Cetacean Research and Management*: "The data show that ship strikes are more immediately lethal, but entanglements can result in long term deterioration of an animal and may be responsible for higher levels of mortality than previously thought. Considering that some animals become entangled, drown and never return to the surface, even these levels may be underestimated."

Clearly, laying the whale problem at the feet of the shipping industry is not going to be a way out for fishermen.

*   *   *

Both whales and fishermen depend on the same set of complex processes to produce food in abundance enough to satisfy gargantuan appetites. And the broad Atlantic obliges them only along its narrow margins in places where the whims of sun, wind, nutrients, and currents concentrate the animals they seek. In these places—the curving offshore banks and the curling eddies between powerful ocean currents—whales and fishermen meet. The nature of these encounters has changed as the devices that people use to pull fish from the sea become more and more efficient at catching fish (and whales), eventually outpacing even the whale's voracious maw in the effort to extract sustenance from the sea.

When the Europeans first settled widely in the New World more than four hundred years ago, they fished for the superabundant groundfish with weighted handlines from small open boats. But handlines were quickly supplanted in the offshore commercial fisheries by longlines, prodigious lengths of twine bearing baited hooks. These were some-times called tub trawls because they were set from tubs where the lines were carefully coiled.

Tub trawls served much of the Northwest Atlantic's groundfish fleet until late in the nineteenth century; the only radical technological ad-vances in the fishery in the nearly five hundred intervening years were in naval architecture. Faster and bigger boats allowed fishermen to get the catch to market faster, but most still caught fish in the same old way and nearly all of the cod catch was salted and dried for export. The infamous Atlantic triangle trade of codfish, slaves, and rum (or molasses to make rum) rose on the backs of the codfish, the African people, and the people and lands of the Caribbean.

In this venerable fishery, men (and they were nearly all men) launched dories from shore or ships and hauled the tub trawls by hand, a slow, grueling, and perilous job. They wrestled the great fish aboard with gaffs until men sat waist-deep in cold slimy fish. Water slopped over the gunwales. Then the men rowed for the ship or home, where they spent long hours cleaning and salting the catch. Fathers, sons, and broth-ers spent more than half their lifetimes at sea. The possibility of death, disappearance, and dismemberment shadowed everyday life in coastal communities of New England and the Canadian Maritimes, insinuating itself into the psyche and culture like a skulking, unpredictable family member.

By the late nineteenth century, technology and necessity had begun to transform the Northwest Atlantic's fishing industry. Centuries of exploi-tation had finally made a dent in the Atlantic groundfish populations, but with a burgeoning human population, demand continued to grow. And as fish became harder to find, resourceful fishermen invented new ways to search out and catch them.

People along shore had begun using seines and gill nets, but in the mid-1800s, a Newfoundlander named Captain William H. Whitely in-vented the cod trap for use in the Labrador inshore cod fishery. Accord-ing to one Canadian government history, the design worked so well—allowing a small crew to intercept so many fish—that by 1911 Labrador was girded by more than six thousand cod traps, and Newfoundland fish-ermen were avidly adopting the technology.

In the offshore fishery, with the advent of powerful and reliable engines, fishing boats became bigger and faster and required fewer people to operate. Stout power boats began fishing with otter trawls, great cone-shaped nets that bumped along the sea floor devouring whole schools of fish. And larger boats could tow larger nets at greater depths, so as the twentieth century progressed, catches grew and fishermen plied new grounds.

What did all this new fishing gear mean to whales in the early 1900s? At the time, no one thought to ask. The biggest threat to whales was still whaling, and just a handful of people were agitating for international cooperation to regulate the whaling industry. The International Whaling Commission met for the first time in 1949 and then presided over three decades of profligate commercial whaling until the moratorium in 1982 slowed the slaughter to a couple of hundred whales killed for "scientific purposes" each year. Until the late 1960s, the only comprehensive scientific studies of whales focused on the corpses of the animals killed in the fishery.

Certainly whales got caught in cod traps and gill nets in the early twentieth century. Older fishermen in New England and Canada have told me that they remember seeing or hearing about whales caught in fishing gear, but no one regarded entanglement as a widespread or serious problem for either the whales or the fishermen. In the latter half of the twentieth century, that would change. After centuries of intensive fishing, fish in the Northwest Atlantic were becoming ever more scarce. So fishermen and fish-eating whales had to change the way they hunted for food.

As offshore capelin in their countless trillions succumbed to seiners, humpbacks wandered toward the shores of Newfoundland to search for food. Right whales did what they had always done, roaming about the Gulf of Maine, Bay of Fundy, or over the continental shelf in search of patches of copepods. Meanwhile, collisions with fishing gear became more deadly due to the advent of synthetic rope and twine and more likely because of burgeoning fixed-gear fisheries that used traps or nets left unattended in the water for days at a time.

In the 1960s, synthetic fiber rope and twine began to replace the traditional manila rope and cotton or linen twine in fishing gear. These new-fangled fibers were a boon to fishermen since they were more durable than natural fibers and could be chemically engineered to suit the task at hand: nylon will stretch under a heavy load without parting; polypropylene floats so it lifts clear of the bottom and doesn't chafe on rocks or debris; and polyester (also known as Dacron) sinks out of the way of a turning propeller and is extremely strong and durable. Better, stronger rope also meant larger nets.

But rope that strong and durable will also last for months or years wrapped around the tailstock of a whale or jammed between plates of baleen. A very large whale may be able to wrench free, even from thick, strong synthetic lines, but in doing so the whale may pull the lines so tight that they cut into flesh or restrict circulation. And the bigger the line, the harder the animal must pull to part the line. Many whale scientists believe that this results in more grievous injury when the animal writhes and struggles to reach the surface to breathe.

In the summer of 2002, the CCS whale rescue team encountered a grisly example of the damage whales can sustain in such a struggle. On the morning of June 17, they responded to a call from the harbormaster in the Cape Cod town of Dennis regarding an entangled humpback near the beach on the north side of the peninsula. When the team arrived in the Zodiac, they found the animal in grave condition. The young adult had more than a dozen wraps of synthetic line around its flukes. The rope was embedded in deep gashes in the leading edge of each fluke, where swollen red flesh bulged around the wounds. Worst of all, the whole tail was twisted into a vertical orientation (whales' tails are normally oriented horizontally). Apparently, the whale had writhed and pulled so hard on the tangling gear that it had dislocated its tail, leaving it permanently, and most likely painfully, deformed. In photographs and underwater video documenting the event, I could see the stricken creature was emaciated as it waved its maimed flukes listlessly.

The team easily cut away the twining white and green lines, leaving just a bit of rope embedded in the gashes at the leading edge of the flukes, but they held little hope that the whale could survive its injuries. There was a shadow of hope, however. According to the team's Maine coordinator, Bob Bowman, one other humpback whale in the North Atlantic population had already lived many years with a twisted tail, most likely caused by entanglement. But given the sickly condition of the whale off of Dennis and the possibility of infection from the deep wounds, it was unlikely that this animal would recover.

In the days before synthetic line, whales could often swim right through gill nets made of cotton twine, leaving behind a big hole and a frustrated fisherman. Now whales collide with monofilament nylon gill nets strung between polypropylene lines, which they twist into tangled wads in their panic, then swim off trailing plastic floats in their wake.

Grave injury may befall a very large whale caught in strong synthetic gear, but not all whales have the strength to wrench themselves free. Those that are smaller and less able to drag the gear to the surface to breathe are more likely to die immediately when they collide with gear. And the larger the gear, the less likely a smaller whale will have the strength to haul it to the surface. So, juveniles and members of smaller whale species like the minkes tend to drown more often when they get caught, and they may be drowning in larger numbers as fishermen use stronger, heavier gear. Scientists have barely begun to ask how many.

In the 1990s, when the transition to synthetic fishing gear was complete, the groundfish stocks crashed and tens of thousands of fishermen from New England and the Canadian Maritimes had to look for another way to put food on the table. Many quit fishing for good, but others turned to new fisheries. In the decade after the cod crash, fishing operations that used gill nets, cod traps, and bottom trawls declined radically, and the same decade saw an enormous growth in pot fisheries, which use small baited wire traps that rest on the sea floor. Fishermen mark traps by tethering buoys to them, using a length of line stretching from the surface to the bottom, where they can catch a flipper or a fluke.

Lobster and a few species of crab are the most common target of the burgeoning pot fisheries, but fishermen also set traps for some fish such as hagfish and scup. And as traps have become larger and more effective, the fisheries have been creeping seaward to exploit previously unharvested resources, placing traps in more and more of the whales' habitat.

In New England, the offshore lobster fishery has become the mainstay. In Massachusetts, Maine, and New Hampshire, landings of lobsters from traps set offshore have more than tripled since 1990. Because the price of lobster has risen by about 60 percent, the tripled landings translate into a fourfold increase in the value of the offshore lobster fishery. The rapidly growing offshore industry allows fishermen to extend their seasons, too, by following the lobsters into deep water when they migrate with the seasons.

Offshore trap fisheries tend to place fewer buoy lines in the water because fishermen tend to use long strings of traps. However, the traps in long strings are linked using a heavy, usually floating, groundline. Floating groundline lifts free of the bottom so it doesn't chafe on rocks and debris, but it forms loops in the water column where whales may encounter the line.

In Massachusetts, the inshore lobster fishery has actually declined over last decade, and fishermen have turned their attention to offshore lobsters, which now account for half the value of their $55 million industry.

Lobster reigns supreme especially in Maine, where in many coastal communities over half of the residents work in the fishery or in fishery-related jobs. The landings from offshore traps still only account for less than 2 percent of Maine's lobster catch, but they have increased fivefold since 1990 and are increasing further every year.

The story in the Canadian Maritimes is much the same: explosive growth in trap and pot fisheries. But here the queen crab reigns, supplying a $400 million (Canadian) industry. The crab industry grew so rapidly and so profitably in the 1990s that the value of Atlantic Canada's fishing industry has nearly *doubled* from $950 million to $1.7 billion between 1990 and 2001. In spite of the crash of the groundfish stocks, more modest gains in other fisheries, and a *decrease* in the number of pounds landed in all fisheries, Atlantic Canada is raking in more money from fisheries than ever, largely because of the crab fishery.

With all that heavy fixed gear offshore, the whale entanglement problem has gained a new dimension. In the summer of 2000, Jon Lien got a call from a Grand Banks crab fisherman who had a humpback caught on his string of traps 190 nautical miles offshore. The fisherman had tried and failed to free the whale and get his traps back, so he steamed back to port and called for help. Jon boarded the fifty-five-foot crab boat for the long steam to the fishing grounds. While Jon and the crew of the crab boat worked to free the whale, the skipper chatted with his colleagues on the radio, explaining that he had Jon aboard to help with the whale. At that, two other skippers—one a crabber and the other a turbot gill-netter—asked if Jon could help them with entangled whales too.

"That's where the fishery actually is now," Jon says. "The inshore stuff is trivial. And the program I ran fit the fishery at the time. The program now fits the fishery of yesteryear." The disentanglement programs relying on inflatable outboards and small inshore support vessels like *Halos* can't hope to help whales and fishermen 150 to 200 miles offshore.

"We may have been unaware of the extent of entrapments that the distant water fleet is experiencing," Jon wrote in an email to the U.S. disentanglement network about the incident. "Finding two additional entrapments in the area on a single day might just be a queer sample but we will have to do some checking with this fleet to be sure."

By some estimates, there are currently over a million crab and lobster pots dotting the surface of the sea off New England alone. Early European settlers used to joke that one could walk across the waters of the Northwest Atlantic on the backs of the cod. Now they make the same joke about the lobster pot buoys, and the Northwest Atlantic, including the offshore banks, has become an obstacle course for feeding whales.

Enter the feds.

*   *   *

In the United States, two federal laws protect whales—ostensibly. The Endangered Species Act of 1973 (ESA) covers the species in the greatest peril. Of the whales that frequent the banks and bays of the Northwest Atlantic, these species include the right whale, of course, but also the humpback and the fin whale. Basically, the provisions of the ESA forbid the federal government from engaging in or granting permits for any activity that would place an endangered species in jeopardy. The ESA calls for federal agencies to prepare and execute recovery plans for listed species, establish critical habitat areas, and report to Congress periodically on the progress of the efforts to wrest each of the listed species from the brink of extinction. In the case of endangered marine mammals, these tasks fall to the National Marine Fisheries Service (NMFS, usually pronounced "nymphs"). If NMFS doesn't enforce the ESA, then citizens can sue them, and many have.

Because of a political and popular groundswell of sympathy toward whales, the United States granted marine mammals special status under a unique law in 1972. Ironically, the Marine Mammal Protection Act of 1972 (MMPA) offers all whales, even nonendangered whales, more protection than the ESA. The MMPA put an end to all but traditional subsistence whaling in the United States. It also gave NMFS greater authority to regulate human interactions with marine mammals, including a stringent definition of what it means to "take" a marine mammal.

Under MMPA, to "harass, hunt, capture, or kill, or attempt to harass, hunt, capture or kill any marine mammal" constitutes a take. This in itself is similar to the definition of take under the ESA, but the MMPA goes further—it defines harassment as "any act of pursuit, torment, or annoyance which

(i) has the *potential to injure* a marine mammal or marine mammal stock in the wild; or

(ii) has the *potential to disturb* a marine mammal or marine mammal stock in the wild by causing disruption of behavioral patterns, including, but not limited to, migration, breathing, nursing, breeding, feeding, or sheltering." (emphasis added)

Taking a marine mammal without a permit to do so is against federal law, so under this definition, anyone who causes a whale to change its breathing pattern or the direction in which it is traveling could get hauled into federal court. What's more, engaging in an activity without a permit that could *potentially* cause the whale to change its breathing pattern or the direction in which it is traveling is against the law.

This strong wording seems to put teeth into the law, but in practice, because it is virtually impossible to enforce, many critics of the law say it leaves both whales and fishermen open to harm. If a feeding whale veers to avoid colliding with a gill net, has the owner of the net broken the law? Under this definition, fishing, shipping, recreating, or doing anything around whales is likely to result in harassment of whales.

For these practical reasons, the MMPA allows the feds to pass out permits to fishermen for "incidental take" of marine mammals—commercial fishing can proceed, even if it means some whales will be harassed, injured, or even killed as a result. But how many of these permits can you dole out until you're allowing the industry to "take" too many whales? Even fishermen are asking.

Obviously, allowing too much incidental take could potentially harm whales, but many argue that taking too many whales could also hurt fishermen. Aside from the fact that whales damage and destroy fishing gear when they collide with it, fishermen must also worry about the future of their fisheries as a whole.

Consider the case of the right whale, the most critically endangered large whale in the world. The National Marine Fisheries Service is charged with protecting whales through regulations and deciding when to grant permits for commercial fisheries and incidental take. But what happens if NMFS's regulations don't work? What if right whales continue to die from collisions with fishing gear?

If the MMPA cannot protect the right whale, then the ESA will have to do it. And the ESA (at least in some cases) has brought down billion-dollar hydroelectric projects, halted construction of commercial buildings, and changed the paths of highways. Under the ESA, the feds cannot issue permits for any activity that could place an endangered species in jeopardy. If NMFS continues to issue permits for fisheries that kill whales, a federal judge could order them to revoke the permits and shut down the fisheries. So as long as the whales are in jeopardy, the fishing industry is in jeopardy too.

More than enough evidence exists right now—in the form of right whale carcasses wrapped in fishing gear—to legally justify shutting down the lobster and gill-net fisheries along the eastern seaboard. Several times over the past ten years judges have faced the choice, and each time they have chosen to grant a reprieve to the industry. Massachusetts fishermen were the first to be blindsided by a federal judge's 1996 ruling against the Commonwealth of Massachusetts, forcing the state to develop a plan "to restrict, modify or eliminate the use of fixed-fishing gear" in right whale critical habitat. The judge left the decision to the state whether to close the fisheries (they did not), but he had included the chilling word "eliminate" in his ruling. Settlements in several subsequent lawsuits also granted the fishermen a reprieve, but how long will the courts' patience last? I have posed this question to nearly everyone involved with the issue of whale entanglement.

"The political will does not exist to shut down the fisheries for any reason," was the mantra I heard again and again. "Besides, that was not what Congress intended when they passed the MMPA."

This conviction seemed to wane in 2002, however, when a federal judge, in an unrelated case, ordered NMFS to impose draconian regulations on the groundfish fisheries. Environmental groups sued the Fisheries Service, charging that the fish stocks were not recovering quickly enough after the crash in the early 1990s.

This judge's ruling was later diluted, first by a settlement agreement, and again when NMFS revealed that they had been using flawed equipment to count groundfish, but fishermen understood this ruling as a shot across the bow. If a federal judge could all but shut down the almost-sacred, time-honored groundfishery, then other fisheries might be vulnerable too. The will to shut down the fisheries to protect the environment, whether for whales or groundfish, may be rising.

* * *

The Fisheries Service was formed in 1970 when an act of Congress brought the Bureau of Commercial Fisheries under the newly formed National Oceanic and Atmospheric Administration, which itself is part of the Department of Commerce. In addition to enforcing the MMPA and the ESA for marine organisms, NMFS is also charged with enacting and enforcing a couple of federal laws that are supposed to keep our fisheries and fishing communities healthy and productive: the Magnuson-Stevens Fishery Conservation and Management Act of 1976 and the Sustainable Fisheries Act of 1996 (which also amended the Magnuson Act).

On top of all these federal laws, NMFS officials must coordinate fisheries management with individual states and keep us in compliance with the myriad international treaties on fisheries to which the United States is a signatory. NMFS scientists conduct research and make recommendations, the regulators promulgate regulations and issue fishing permits, and the lawyers defend the agency against lawsuits. If the Fisheries Service does not enforce these various laws and treaties, citizens and organizations can sue them. As I write, NMFS is defending itself against about a hundred lawsuits.

Congress added a new item to NMFS's already full plate in 1994 when they reauthorized the MMPA. The new amendments called for NMFS to identify strategic stocks, those most needing help to avoid the danger of extinction. Section 118 of the act is called "Taking of Marine Mammals Incidental to Commercial Fishing Operations" (that's government-speak for commercial fishing killing, injuring, or harassing marine mammals) and includes provisions to address the growing problem of marine mammal by-catch (marine mammals caught in fishing gear by mistake).

NMFS scientists use two main criteria for choosing strategic stocks: They are listed under the ESA and/or have human-caused mortality that exceeds a number called the "potential biological removal" for that population. "Potential biological removal," or PBR, is a euphemism for the number of whales people can kill per year without putting that population in jeopardy.

Under Section 118, NMFS was to devise and implement a Take Reduction Plan (TRP) for strategic stocks of marine mammals. With characteristic abandon, Congress set lofty goals for the TRPs. They were to reduce mortality and serious injury caused by fisheries to below the PBR within six months of implementing the plan and "to insignificant levels approaching . . . zero" within five years. All of this had to be accomplished within seven years of the enactment of Section 118. Section 118 was another seemingly toothy congressional mandate that, by virtue of being practically unattainable in some cases, would undermine its own strength, spawning discord and lawsuits rather than practical solutions.

To attain this lofty goal, the overworked staff in the Protected Resources Division of NMFS was to convene Take Reduction Teams (TRTs), groups of the various stakeholders from industry, government, science, and environmental groups. The TRTs were to advise NMFS on management strategies for reducing take as prescribed by Congress.

In 1996, two years after Congress had reauthorized the MMPA, when NMFS showed no signs of getting a TRT together for Atlantic large whales, the first spate of lawsuits on the issue forced NMFS to convene the Atlantic Large Whale Take Reduction Team. The team, hard-pressed by deadlines and conflict, never reached full consensus on the best way to reduce whale entanglement in fishing gear. Congress had foreseen that eventuality, however; Section 118 said NMFS should look at all the choices the team considered, then choose for them.

* * *

The seven-year deadline for the salvation of America's large whales came and went: April 30, 2001. And in spite of the efforts of literally hundreds of people, several lawsuits, and four incarnations of the Take Reduction Plan, the right whale is still inching closer to the brink of extinction; the vast majority of humpbacks carry scars from colliding with fishing gear; no one knows or even knows how to find out how many minkes die from entanglement every year; and fishermen are waiting for the other shoe to drop.

The Atlantic Large Whale Take Reduction Plan, as it stands now, covers many trap and gill-net fisheries and has four main components. General ideas for the plan did come from the TRT, but nearly all the specifics came from NMFS lawyers and regulators choosing options from among those the TRT debated in their marathon two-day meetings. NMFS has nearly always made these choices under pressure from the courts to comply with the MMPA and the ESA.

The plan, now in its fourth incarnation, includes:

- *Gear modifications,* including specially designed weak-links, smaller line diameter, and changes in the type of line used in fishing gear;
- *Area closures and restrictions,* including a veritable jigsaw puzzle of polygons where certain gear modifications are required at certain times of year, or where fishing is prohibited for some part of the year;
- *Disentanglement,* a network of rescue teams, veterinarians, scientists, and government officials from Florida to Maine who have caches of special boats and equipment. They are charged with saving whales, or trying to save whales, after they have collided with fishing gear;
- *Gear research and development,* funding NMFS researchers, academics, and private entrepreneurs in their search for the Holy Grail: "whale-safe" fishing gear.

Who keeps watch to be sure NMFS is keeping all these balls in the air? The key stakeholders—fishermen and environmentalists—generally take that task upon themselves. But each uses slightly different tactics.

The fishermen lobby and harangue while the environmentalists sue and nitpick; and in their worst clashes, each casts the other as the villain.

*   *   *

"Shut the lobster and gill-net fisheries down!" some conservationists are quick to say. "No fixed-gear fishing industry, no dead whales. Right?"

True enough. But in the grand scheme of things, abolishing the trap fisheries would have environmental and social consequences that reach far beyond the whales—in many places, fixed-gear fisheries are the only thing keeping small fishing communities fishing. As long as the price and the stocks hold out, these communities are living well on lobsters and crab, putting off the tourism juggernaut, at least for the time being. If small individual fishing enterprises went the way of the dinosaur, many communities would either be deserted or consumed by vacation development.

Many fishermen insist that, when (and if) the groundfish stocks finally recover, fixed-gear fisheries such as traps and gill nets in the hands of many fishermen will present a more sustainable alternative for harvesting fish and shellfish than large-scale trawling operations. Fleets of big boats employ fewer people and drag big nets across the bottom that can damage habitat and devour every living thing in their paths.

For now, with the groundfish stocks beginning a very slow and sporadic climb, gill-netters are a rare breed and getting rarer. That leaves many communities dangerously dependent on a single trap fishery such as lobster or crab, with no safety net if those stocks fail due to the whims of climate or human error.

*   *   *

Bill Look of Beal's Island, Maine, started gill-netting for groundfish— cod, hake, and haddock—in 1985.

"I went into gill-netting to give me a diversity in the summer, so I didn't need to rely on fall lobsters."

Bill's story is typical of fishermen in Maine's rural ports. In the past, groundfish represented a seasonal supplement to lobstering. In recent years, however, fishermen in small New England ports have been squeezed out of supplementary fisheries such as groundfish, scallops, and urchins.

He says that in the late 1980s, gill-netting accounted for 75 percent of his income, but by 1998 it was bringing in only about half of his yearly earnings. In the spring of 2001, he gill-netted for groundfish for just two days. He reported his landings—140 pounds of fish—and divided the catch among his crew. It was too little to sell; he went back to lobstering.

Fifteen years ago, Beal's Island and Jonesport—two tiny communities nestled in the rocky convolutions of the Maine coast—had fourteen gill-netters, but today Bill's boat is one of two. In the same period, a frenzy of urchin fishing led to a crash. In 2000 and 2001, scallop landings were dismal.

"Now we're using lobsters for 90 percent of our income, and lobstering might not be that good in five years," Bill told me after his two-day attempt at catching groundfish in 2001. "I'm one of the few that still has a number of permits, and I don't know if I can make it, even with all the permits I have. We've got all our eggs in one basket."

In many of Maine's rural ports, more than half of the population makes its living on lobstering. Because they now lack a safety net, fishermen in New England's small fishing communities have been pressuring U.S. fisheries officials to give them more access to the groundfish stocks that are, according to the feds, rebounding too slowly from their dramatic crash ten years ago. Fishermen argue that the future of their communities and their way of life may depend on higher groundfish quotas. Rather than getting the additional quota they wanted for the 2002 season, they got stringent restrictions on groundfish after environmental groups successfully sued the NMFS.

Moreover, fishermen in rural ports all over New England accuse federal fisheries regulators of favoring urban ports in their management of groundfish over the past decade. They say NMFS should consider the social and economic impacts of fisheries regulations on their small communities.

Urban ports like Portland, Maine, tend to have large trawlers that can fish for days at time far offshore. Since the groundfish crash in the early 1990s, a few owners have been buying trawlers from those selling off and getting out of the game, consolidating these large boats into fleets of two to four. The boats in the Portland fleet fish almost exclusively for groundfish, only occasionally dragging for scallops.

New England's few remaining rural groundfishermen tend to have smaller boats and use gill nets, small otter trawls, and, in a few cases, hook and line. These small operations fish near shore, usually for a day or two at a time. These smaller boats can't travel long distances to fish in the patchwork of closures the Fisheries Service uses to try to manage the fishery.

Fishermen from small ports also point to measures aimed at eliminating "latent effort"—vessels and fishermen that could reenter the fishery once the stocks return—as another example of a policy that favors large boats in urban ports. NMFS plans to distribute groundfish permits in the future to vessels that have fished a minimum number of days during a qualifying period. This may mean that people with small boats who are unable to fish during inshore or rolling closures may lose their permits. As a result, they may be more tempted by NMFS's multimillion-dollar permit buy-back program.

"You've got a lot of old men here holding permits who haven't fished in ten years," Bill Look says, "so they're going to sell."

While necessary to decrease the pressure on the groundfish stocks, the buy-back programs have been most successful in decreasing latent effort by pushing fishermen in small communities to sell out. This has a net effect of concentrating the fishery in urban ports and in few hands, so if and when the stocks recover, small communities will land a much smaller share of the catch. From Bill Look's perspective, every retired permit brings his community closer to relying entirely on the lobster fishery.

If a federal judge decides to shut the lobster fishery down because lobster gear is killing right whales, the small New England fishing community will be a thing of the past, a quaint motif on a postcard sold in a gift shop overlooking a harbor full of yachts. This is constantly on the minds of the fishermen who take time from their fishing to attend meetings and conferences about whales.

5 Churchill

Dancing with Eternity

*The Great Spirit . . . made a special time each spring, when the ice of
the ocean would break apart to form a road where the whales would
swim. In that whale road, the Open Lead, the whales would come to
the surface and wait there to be struck by the harpoons of the Inupiaq.
They would continue to do so every year as long as the Inupiaq showed
respect . . . as long as the Inupiaq only took the few whales that they
needed in order to survive.*

*But the Great Spirit decided this also. At that time each year when
the Open Lead formed, when the whales came to the surface to be
hunted, the Great Spirit made it so that a heavy cloud of thick mist
would hang just above the ice, just above the heads of the whales and
the Inupiaq. That thick mist would hang there between the sea and the
sky. "Though I give you permission to kill my most perfect creation,"
the Great Spirit said, "I do not wish to watch it."*

"The Gift of the Whale," as told by Michael J. Caduto
and Joseph Bruchac

At about 4 p.m. on a Friday in early June 2001, a small survey plane
circled a group of right whales that were feeding in the Great South
Channel, a divot in the ocean floor at the southwestern end of Georges
Bank. These aerial surveys are conducted by the U.S. National Oceanic
and Atmospheric Administration (NOAA) to keep track of the endan-

gered animals, to warn approaching ships of their presence, and to look for entangled whales. One of the right whales in the group looked unusually light in color, its skin "gray and mottled"—a sure sign of sickness in right whales. In light winds and partly cloudy conditions, the survey team in the plane could see the whale gliding ghostlike beneath the water. A light green rope led from the left side of its mouth and trailed a few feet behind its wide flukes. This sighting of the whale later dubbed "Churchill" marked the beginning of a slow-motion nightmare that would unfold over more than three months while the world watched.

By this time, David Mattila had been working for the Center for Coastal Studies (CCS) for twenty years, researching humpback whales in New England and the Caribbean. He had begun disentangling whales seventeen years before, when he and Stormy Mayo had rescued Ibis outside of Provincetown Harbor in 1984. A soft-spoken and affable man with a bushy gray-blond beard, David had been a commercial fisherman and a marine technician before getting involved with whale research in the West Indies in the 1970s. Stormy invited David to join CCS in 1981.

"Stormy asked me to be the director of Caribbean Studies," David recalls. "I said, 'Whoa, what are you doing down there?' And he said, 'Nothing, but you are.' And that was back when the center was a very young place and nobody was getting paid. Some people were working as waiters in town. Some were naturalists on whale-watch boats. But some of us would get little grants to do our little projects."

David's responsibilities grew with the center, and by 2001 he was dividing his time between directing the disentanglement program and directing humpback whale research. NOAA's National Marine Fisheries Service (NMFS) had—and still has—a contract with CCS to keep, train, and equip a disentanglement team and a network of responders who can help in large-whale emergencies from Maine to Florida.

When Churchill was spotted in June 2001, NOAA contacted David Mattila that afternoon.

"From their description," David remembers, "it didn't sound like a complicated entanglement, but it was a little unnerving that the animal was very light colored. That was not good. So the next day, we did something that we don't usually do."

The chances of finding a particular whale just by going out and looking are generally pretty slim. The whales are big, but the ocean is vastly

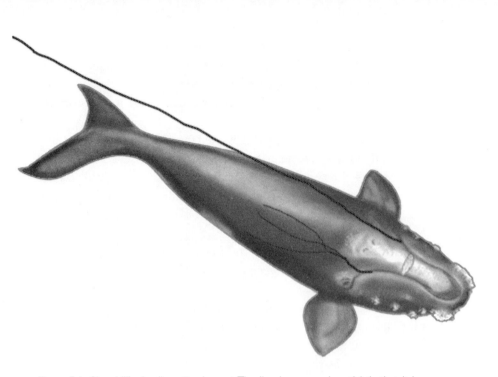

Figure 5.1. Churchill's deadly entanglement. The line is wrapped so tightly that it has become embedded in the flesh of the rostrum. A frayed end trails from the right side of the mouth, and the other end exits the left side of the mouth and trails behind the flukes. Drawing by T. Johnson.

more immense. Also, right whales commonly swim more than forty miles in a day and often don't follow predictable routes, so you usually can't expect to find them where you left them last. Typically, when an entangled whale was spotted, David and his team would prepare to set out at a moment's notice and then wait for word that a whale-watch boat, a fisherman, a research vessel, or an aerial survey had resighted the animal. If the whale was spotted again nearby, the center's thirty-nine-foot research vessel *Shearwater* could be on the scene in a matter of hours, depending on where the whale was sighted.

But the weather on Saturday June 9 was predicted to be calm and clear, and if this whale was still in the area—a good bet since right whales seemed to be taking advantage of concentrations of copepods in the Great South Channel, it should be easy to spot because of its light color. And given the whale's condition it seemed urgent that they attempt to relocate the animal. So early the next morning *Shearwater* made her way toward the area where the whale had last been seen, about eighty nautical miles west of Provincetown. An aerial survey plane also searched the area, looking for the whale in nearly flat calm seas under scattered clouds.

Against all odds, the plane's crew spied the whale at about 1 p.m. and guided *Shearwater* by radio to its position. The CCS rescue team donned life vests and climbed into the Zodiac. The first thing they did was use the time-honored technique of kegging; they threw a specially designed grapple hook to catch the line trailing behind the whale and attach a big Norwegian float.

"We put a buoy on it to see if it could keep the whale at the surface, and it did," David Mattila says. "Then we started to try to assess it, to see what we were dealing with."

Now that the whale was not diving, David could see an eruption of white, bumpy tissue in a line across the whale's narrow upper jaw, which scientists call the *rostrum*. Light-green rope trailed from both sides of the whale's mouth. David could finally make out that the green line entered the right side of the mouth, wrapped around the rostrum, and exited the left side of the mouth, trailing past the flukes. The wrap around the rostrum was so tight that the line had cut into the flesh, possibly to the bone, and was completely embedded in the upper jaw.

"Putting it all together we realized we had never seen an entanglement quite like this. We also felt that we wouldn't be able to pull it out."

David remembered trying to disentangle another whale in which the rope simply passed through the mouth and jammed between the plates of baleen. The team attached the oversized tooth floss to the larger vessel standing by and pulled.

Says David: "With the line jammed up into the baleen and lips closed on top of it, we parted the line; I think it was about a four-thousand-pound breaking strength. We parted the line before we could pull it out of the mouth. So that's what we're up against with baleen whales when the rope gets jammed up in the baleen. And we realized that this one wasn't just a straight shot through; it went up and over, deeply embedded, and then back through again—so it was jammed in four places in the baleen, not two. We said, 'Okay, we're not going to be able to pull this out. We can't cut it because we can't even see it; it's embedded in the

Figure 5.2. Close-up taken June 26, 2001, of Churchill's rostrum with the wound caused by the embedded rope. The twin blowholes are to the left, and the lower right lip curves up from the bottom of the picture. The light-gray encrustation across the rostrum is granular tissue healing around the rope, and the dark area surrounding the wound is an infestation of cyamids (whale lice). Note the light-colored, peeling skin. Photo courtesy of the Center for Coastal Studies and taken under the authority of Scientific Research and Enhancement Permit No. 932–1489–04/PRT009526, issued by the National Marine Fisheries Service and U.S. Fish and Wildlife Service.

head.' So we knew that this was a candidate for something that we had been planning for."

The art and science of disentanglement was about to take another technological leap, one of many such leaps David Mattila had witnessed in his tenure as a whale rescuer.

* * *

During the 1990s, as the whale entanglement issue came to a head in the U.S. Congress and the courts, fishermen, feds, and environmentalists became more and more desperate for a solution. Fishermen worried that the next dead right whale could prompt the courts to shut down the lobster and gill-net fisheries under the Endangered Species Act. Environmentalists pointed to recent population studies that warned that losing even one reproductively mature right whale could eventually spell the demise of the species. The feds were stuck in the middle. With stakes this high and no easy way to prevent entanglement, the fishermen, feds, and environmentalists turned to disentanglement—and to the team at CCS—as one solution on which they could all agree. The only problem with relying on disentanglement is that, at least in the case of right whales, it's not all that reliable.

Of the twenty-four entangled right whales reported to CCS between March 1999 and June 2003, the team was able to disentangle seven (about 30 percent), and at least one of these seven died anyway. Three animals shed the gear themselves, and two had minor entanglements that didn't require the team's intervention. The remaining twelve—half of the entangled right whales reported to the center—either remain entangled, have died, or have not been seen again.

Given the complexity and danger involved in wrestling fishing gear off of whales, 30 percent is not a bad record. But when you consider that a single dead whale might doom the population to oblivion, a dozen lost, dead, or dying entangled whales is pretty alarming. This thought plagued David Mattila, Stormy Mayo, and the other members of the team as they considered what to do with the sick whale.

They recalled right whale #2030, a female first reported entangled in May 1999. This whale had run afoul of a gill net and had wraps of line and netting around both flippers, across her back, and, the team later learned, across her belly. The tightest of the wraps across her back cut through the skin and several inches into the blubber. The team and NMFS veterinarians agreed that #2030 would die if they did not remove the gear.

When #2030 was spotted again in the Bay of Fundy in September, a rescue team was able to cut away the loosest wraps of line and netting by grabbing the line with a specially designed hooked knife at the end of a long pole. The tightest and deadliest wrap remained embedded in the wound across her back, impossible to reach with a hooked knife or a grapple. In order to gain access to this line, the team would need to approach very close to the whale, forcing them into the "danger zones"—within striking distance of the tail or the head.

Over a week in mid-September 1999, with help from a variety of organizations and agencies in the United States and Canada, CCS focused an enormous amount of effort on attempting to slow #2030 down and restrain her enough to approach in relative safety. The team attached a motley collection of buoys and sea anchors, all to no avail.

"We had been working with that whale for several days," David Mattila says of the efforts to help #2030, "and at one point we thought we had it almost stopped; we had all kinds of buoys, a big sea anchor, and we had the whale just swimming slowly in a circle. We were just trying to move the sea anchor closer to try to reduce the circle size, and that whale whacked its tail at us, dragged everything under water for eight to ten minutes, came up a mile away. But the gear had almost sawed through the blubber at that point."

The tail swipe had narrowly missed the inflatable and had yanked a sea anchor off the boat and into the water.

The CCS report on #2030 reads: "At one point, five medium sized buoys, one large buoy, and two six-foot diameter sea anchors [essentially underwater parachutes] were attached to #2030. This was the most kegging gear the disentanglement team had ever attached to a whale. Unfortunately, even this amount of drag and buoyancy was not enough to slow her down or keep her at the surface. Because the whale's tail was not restrained, #2030 was able to tail slash, which created a dangerous situation for the rescuers."

The team attempted many times to capture #2030's tail in a specialized tail harness designed to tether the whale's deadly flukes to a large boat that could slow the animal and prevent tail slashes. If the larger boat could tow #2030 backward by the tail (a tactic that often works with humpbacks), then the crew in the inflatable could approach the whale from the front relatively safely. But #2030 was skittish, and the tail harness was untested and needed tweaking, so the team never captured her tail. They also had antibiotics to inject into the whale to try to stem the infection in her wounds, but they were never able to administer the shot.

On September 13, with bad weather coming and the surly whale avoiding them, the team decided to wait for another opportunity to approach #2030. That opportunity never came; the whale soon left the Bay of Fundy heading south. Five weeks after she took a violent swipe at the disentanglement team and then dragged a cluster of big floats beneath the surface, #2030 was found dead, floating five miles east of Cape May, New Jersey.

David Mattila was part of the team that traveled to New Jersey to perform the necropsy on #2030. On the beach in Barnegat, New Jersey, where the whale had been towed ashore, David saw the extent of the damage to the fifty-ton whale. Ropes cut several inches into the leading edges of her flippers, and she had wraps of line tight across her belly, in addition to the line slicing into her back. In his report, David wrote, "All wraps were so tight that the lines literally 'popped' when cut."

After they had failed to save #2030, CCS joined with the New England Aquarium and the Woods Hole Oceanographic Institution to gather biologists and veterinarians for a workshop to brainstorm ideas for addressing untenable cases like that of #2030. They sought to improve restraint devices such as the tail harness and to develop methods to administer drugs such as antibiotics and sedatives.

"We talked about both chemical and physical restraint, drugs, sedatives, and harnesses that we had developed, seines and floating dry docks," David says of the medical intervention workshop. "All kinds of methods were brought up, potential methods for trying to restrain the whale so we could deal with a difficult entanglement. But what we had thought best and most practical was a combination of chemical sedatives and getting something on the tailstock so we could restrain the tail."

The right whale that David saw from the inflatable in the Great South Channel in June 2001 reminded him of #2030: a difficult, probably lethal entanglement on a right whale that only extraordinary measures could remove. Not only would disentangling this animal require approaching close enough to be within striking range of the flexible tail or the massive head, it would also involve cutting into the flesh of the rostrum to sever the embedded line. Causing pain would only make the whale more likely to lash out. Therefore, this sickly whale was a candidate for both medication and a modified tail harness.

So, rather than attempting to remove the line on their first visit to the whale, the team attached a satellite telemetry buoy to the trailing line. This device sends signals to satellites, which can detect the whale's position whenever the buoy is at the surface. The buoy also transmits a radio signal so searchers on planes and boats can use a radio direction finder to home in on the whale. In this way, the team could keep track of the whale while they prepared their next rescue attempt. They also hoped that the additional steady drag on the line would help to pull the line out as it had done for some previously tagged whales. *Shearwater* left the whale late in the afternoon and headed back to Provincetown.

David notified NMFS veterinarian Teri Rowles that this whale was a candidate for drugs and a tail harness, and Teri began to assemble a team of advisors. She brought in veterinarians who worked with captive whales, experts in veterinary anesthesiology, several whale biologists, and technicians who could make ballistic devices to administer drugs. Over the next two weeks, NMFS officials and the CCS team had meetings and conference calls almost continuously, while following the whale's movements via satellite.

The right whale research team at the New England Aquarium matched the photos of the entangled whale to an animal in their catalog known as right whale #1102. Generally researchers refer to right whales by their number in the catalog, but they often give a whale a name if they have occasion to deal with the whale more often. The aquarium researchers dubbed #1102 "Churchill" after the stalwart British prime minister who uttered the famous words: "never give in, never give in, never, never, never, never—in nothing, great or small, large or petty—never give in except to convictions of honour and good sense" (Churchill 1941).

Churchill the whale was first seen in 1980, so he was at least twenty-one years old in 2001. As right whales go, Churchill had been something of a wanderer. His record in the right whale catalog showed that he had been photographed intermittently over two decades in the Bay of Fundy, Cape Cod Bay, Browns Bank, and the Great South Channel. Based on this pattern, David Mattila surmised that Churchill was among the segment of the right whale population that didn't stick to specific haunts but rather made the rounds to several different feeding areas at different times in different seasons. Whale researchers are only now discovering that many more right whales make these far-flung peregrinations than previously thought. Over the second week in June 2001, while the rescue team scrambled to organize a high-tech mission to save him, Churchill temporarily abandoned the roving lifestyle and remained in the Great South Channel, describing a zigzag path indicating that he was most likely feeding.

During this time, a right whale calf died when a ship ran it down off New Jersey. When the carcass was dragged ashore, David Mattila, Stormy Mayo, and two veterinarians went down to gather information that might be pertinent to their efforts to help Churchill. The group must have been a curious sight to onlookers on the New Jersey beach. They practiced dropping an enormous weighted syringe into the carcass to see what kind of force they would need to penetrate the blubber and inject the sedative into muscle. They also did a careful dissection of the baby whale's rostrum so they could understand the structure of bone and flesh surrounding Churchill's wound. They practiced cutting an embedded rope with various cutting tools.

Meanwhile, the story of Churchill hit the press worldwide. Before the team could mount the second attempt to disentangle the whale, the press had gathered at their doorstep—literally. CNN, Fox, and ABC had television crews in Provincetown to report on the story, and a team from the National Geographic Society followed the situation closely and filmed segments for a television special. Many news outlets in the United States, Canada, and Europe picked up the story from newswire services. Cape Cod and Boston papers ran major features on the whale and the CCS disentanglement program. And as leaders of the rescue effort, David Mattila and Teri Rowles bore the brunt of the press's attention.

"The T.V. coverage has been outrageous," David told me soon after. "They give you thirty seconds, and they're asking questions that are just totally off the wall. And it's amazing to see the variability in the accuracy and what people choose to lead with. For some news outlets a balanced story isn't always what sells a paper."

News coverage generally included the same set of basic facts: The team was waiting for a weather window to try the unprecedented techniques in rescuing Churchill; the right whale as a species had been hunted nearly to extinction and the population now numbered around 350; and scientists believed entanglements in fishing gear were contributing to the right whale's continued decline. Though David and Stormy mentioned the need for prevention whenever they got the chance, this information rarely made it into stories about Churchill. The press focused instead on the story that sold papers: the heroic team's perilous mission to save a suffering and endangered whale. The worries of New England fishermen were also absent from the press coverage.

The media frenzy prompted hundreds of well-meaning, but often naïve e-mails and phone calls with suggestions on how to rescue Churchill. One man somehow acquired David Mattila's private cell phone number after seeing him on television and called to offer a proposal:

"I know what you have to do," the man shouted into David's ear. "You just get the Navy Seals—they'll do it."

When David asked the man, "What will the Navy Seals do, exactly?" he had no answer.

One woman called to say, "You just need to communicate with it and it'll stop. I've been communicating with it. It's in pain."

Another person suggested using trained porpoises to befriend the whale and calm it. Someone else told them to put a woman in the water with the whale because the whale will be calmed by her presence.

The Sea Shepherd Conservation Society—a California-based environmental advocacy group founded by radical whale advocate Paul Watson and now most noted for its efforts to stop traditional gray whale hunts by the Makah tribe in the Pacific Northwest—offered the Fisheries Service the use of their 187-foot vessel *Ocean Warrior*. According to *Cape Cod Times* reporter Emily Dooley, Sea Shepherd's information director, Andrew Christie, outlined the organization's plan as follows: "*Ocean Warrior* would approach Churchill . . . and release a large mesh net to slow the animal down. A system of attached lines and onboard winches would hoist up the whale so his flukes, or tail, are out of the water to prevent dangerous thrashing. A veterinarian would then inject antibiotics into a spreading infection while a diver would hit the water and remove the line" (2001).

A similar proposal came from an ocean engineer on the team assembled by the Fisheries Service for the Churchill effort. But the idea of wrapping a whale with any kind of net was rejected for several reasons, not least because it could be dangerous to the would-be rescuers, and if the plan went wrong it could leave the whale in an even worse entanglement situation. Also, if the team could get close enough to the whale to enclose it with some kind of net, they would probably be close enough to attach a tail harness and inject the sedatives.

As the media's attention to Churchill reached a fever pitch, some CCS staff members had to take time away from research activities to help field questions from the press and the public. Several people who were working as naturalists on Massachusetts whale-watch boats at the time told me that passengers bombarded them with questions about Churchill, and that many passengers expected to see Churchill on their two-hour whale-watch cruises. Churchill's plight had apparently captured the imagination and the sympathy of the public, and the meager sound bites provided by the press did little to slake their curiosity.

Then, as if Churchill's situation were not complex and bizarre enough, environmental advocate Richard "Max" Strahan decided to request a court injunction to stop the rescue attempt. He told Federal District Judge George A. O'Toole Jr. that the Fisheries Service and CCS were conspiring to kill Churchill.

* * *

Whales and fisheries seem to attract colorful characters, but none more colorful than Max Strahan, who called himself the "Prince of Whales." For nearly twenty years, Strahan had been a fixture in Boston public places: He approached tourists in Quincy Market clutching a clipboard with pictures of dead entangled whales, asking for donations to his environmental organization, GreenWorld. In the early 1990s, he began setting up a card table in front of the New England Aquarium's whale-watch fleet to collect signatures and donations. With his bushy mustache, shaggy ponytail, and forceful approach, Strahan inspired many of the people he canvassed on Boston sidewalks to retreat in fear. Since Strahan lacked the appropriate permits for solicitation, police often questioned him or chased him off. And Strahan spent quite a lot of time in the halls of justice, either pressing legal cases on behalf of whales or answering to petty criminal charges.

He may have looked more like a vagrant than a shrewd environmental activist (and at times he was apparently homeless), but by all accounts he elicited more action on behalf of New England's endangered whales than all the well-heeled and well-intentioned environmental groups combined. Using a barrage of largely successful lawsuits, Max Strahan had been a thorn in the sides of the National Marine Fisheries Service, the U.S. Coast Guard, and state fisheries agencies since the early 1980s, when he first began agitating on behalf of whales.

In the mid-1990s, Strahan sued the state of Massachusetts for endangering right whales by issuing permits for commercial gill-net and lobster fishing in state waters. Strahan's abrasive style (he commonly interrupted and harangued the judge), not to mention his improper attire, did not go over well in court, but U.S. District Court Judge Douglas P. Woodlock could not deny that his case had merit. Fixed fishing gear was killing endangered whales, and killing or even injuring those whales was prohibited under the Endangered Species Act and the Marine Mammal Protection Act. Judge Woodlock ruled in Strahan's favor in 1996, ordering the state of Massachusetts to convene an Endangered Whale Working Group and develop a plan "to restrict, modify or eliminate the use of fixed-fishing gear" in right whale critical habitat. Fishermen were horrorstruck by the ruling, which in practice did not close the fisheries entirely but acutely restricted fixed-gear fisheries in state waters where right whales commonly congregated.

When he sparred in the courts with the state of Massachusetts over right whales, then Attorney General Scott Harshbarger threatened to press charges against Strahan because his nonprofit GreenWorld had not filed the appropriate tax forms in a decade, but these threats were never realized.

Max Strahan's case against the U.S. National Marine Fisheries Service was already on Judge Woodlock's docket when he ruled in the case against the state. So as Massachusetts moved to comply with their court order, federal officials took the hint and began to step up the timetable on their whale protection plan. In May 1997, Judge Woodlock dismissed Strahan's case against NMFS, saying the Fisheries Service had made substantive progress toward implementing a plan to protect the endangered whales. But the judge also berated the federal government because it took a lawsuit to spur them into action.

Strahan next set his sights on the state of Maine, where thousands of fishermen cultivated ulcers dreading the advent of the Prince of Whales. Strahan himself gave interviews to Maine papers warning that the end was near for New England's fisheries. This lawsuit never got off the ground, however, as Strahan missed a deadline for filing the suit. The state of Maine's Department of Marine Resources did begin to take the whale problem a bit more seriously thereafter, mostly because they were legally compelled to take part in the federal plan. But Strahan's high-profile posturing had certainly made an impact.

By all accounts, Strahan's suits were effective. Even people within the government agencies sued by Strahan admitted that court orders were necessary to force them to fulfill their obligations under federal law in a more timely manner. But many people in all camps believe his belliger-ent, uncompromising style polarized the debate over whale entangle-ment.

David Mattila told me soon after the Churchill affair that he was troubled by Max Strahan's divisive tactics.

"I may agree with a few things he says, especially the ultimate goal of protecting right whales from extinction," he said. "But it just runs com-pletely against my grain to be combative, abusive, insulting. And it wor-ries me a little bit, in a much bigger picture, nothing to do even with whales: How do you get things done in life? I have always believed that you do it by working together. Yet you see this squeaky wheel or sue-'em-till-they-move sort of stuff, and you see them having short-term suc-cesses. Do I have it all wrong? Is this what life has to be like, just combat between everybody? I really don't want to believe it."

Government agencies weren't the only ones who found themselves in the crosshairs of Strahan's litigious aim: he also battled the New England Aquarium and the Center for Coastal Studies. With his black-and-white convictions and his far-fetched conspiracy theories, Strahan targeted nearly everyone involved with the whale issue. The notion that CCS and NMFS were conspiring to kill Churchill illustrates clearly the edge on which Strahan operated, sometimes pulling off brilliant legal coups with pro bono help from top environmental lawyers, and at other times repre-senting himself in court, ranting at the judge about whale-killing con-spiracies.

While Max Strahan was pursuing lawsuits against federal and state agencies in the mid-1990s, folks at the New England Aquarium began to tire of his strident sermonizing in front of their institution. Strahan had targeted the institution because he opposed whale-watch vessels.

"They're killing baby whales," a *Boston Globe* reporter heard Strahan tell a woman outside the aquarium (Cullen 1993).

After he was arrested in front of the aquarium, Strahan filed a lawsuit, charging that aquarium employees had violated his civil rights, depriv-ing him of his right to free speech in a public place. After a week-long trial in 1996, the jury voted in favor of Strahan, though the judge later threw out the verdict, saying that Strahan himself was guilty of harass-ment. A woman had testified at the trial that Strahan had threatened her life when she refused to make a donation to GreenWorld. The judge ordered the aquarium to give Strahan's attorney five thousand dollars to cover legal costs, and he ordered Strahan to stay away from the aquarium. Strahan's attorneys passed the money on to him to buy a computer.

Strahan told the *Boston Globe*: "They were such jerks and stupid. We got everything and they got nothing. Now I get to write lawsuits on my laptop" (Allen 1996).

Strahan had long been opposing whale watches, saying they harass whales and could cause collisions. He won key victories in the late 1980s and early 1990s when first the state of Massachusetts and then NMFS implemented regulations forcing boats to stay at least five hundred yards away from right whales. But his temper flared again in 1998, two years after the aquarium case, when a Boston Harbor Cruises boat struck and injured a humpback whale, and then, in the same year, a Cape Cod whale-watch boat hit and killed a minke whale. Neither boat was directly associated with the New England Aquarium.

Scott Kraus, who heads up the aquarium's research team, was named personally in the lawsuit and in Max Strahan's sidewalk ranting.

"He's a total pain in the ass," Scott said of Strahan in a recent interview. "He calls me Satan. He was telling people for a while that I was killing whales. He said I was using the research vessel to drive whales into the paths of big ships."

More recently, Strahan has threatened to sue the Fisheries Service if they grant permits for research activities that he believes will harm whales. Scott has had to wait for NMFS to conduct an environmental assessment of whale research activities before he could get a permit to test small lights and fluorescent line for warning whales away from fishing gear.

"He's just a unique piece of work," Scott observes of the Prince of Whales. "I think he's well-intentioned, but I think he's actually harming whales more than he's helping them because he's holding up needed research and impeding progress in analyzing data. It's really frustrating."

"Have you said that to him?" I ask.

"Oh, yeah."

"And how did he respond?"

"He's very defensive. He says basically, 'No you're the one that's been killing whales.' It's not a rational conversation."

Of course the press loved Strahan's quixotic, quotable diatribes and bold legal maneuverings. The *New York Times, Boston Globe, Cape Cod Times,* and a few of the Maine dailies ran features about him and kept readers abreast of Strahan-related events. The stories were rife with terms like "belligerent," "abrasive," "combative," "shrewd," and even "genius." Many described his aggressive fund-raising tactics and shady past.

For a January 13, 1997, feature about Max Strahan, the *Boston Globe*'s Scott Allen dug into Strahan's history. In his story "Devil Doing the Angels' Work?" Allen wrote that Strahan had

> at least 20 criminal convictions and occasional jail time. . . . Strahan's lifestyle has brought scores of clashes with the law since 1970, mainly charges of trespassing, illegally soliciting money, writing bad checks and using GreenWorld funds improperly—for a membership at a health club and courses at the University of California at Berkeley, for example. Strahan's criminal record shows that he served brief jail terms in the late 1980s for trespassing, larceny and driving a car without a license or insurance. He has received suspended sentences, fines or community service for other charges. . . .
>
> Remarkably, Hollywood has put a fictional version of the Max Strahan story on the big screen. The homeless street prophet played by Joe Pesci in the 1994 box-office flop *With Honors* apparently was based on Strahan, who occasionally stayed with a group of sympathetic Harvard University students, including screenwriter Alek Keshishian. In the movie, Pesci's character teaches the students valuable lessons in life, revealing a depth of character lacking in some faculty members.

In real life, recalls one of the Harvard roommates, Jeffrey Rosen, Strahan was unpredictable and sometimes scary, although he could also be charming. "He went on a mad joyride in my rental car, threatened me with an antique scythe and rampaged around the dorm, shattering Victorian lamps," wrote Rosen in the *New Republic* in 1994. At graduation, Rosen added, "he interrupted an emotional farewell in our suite and denounced us as pigs."

In 2000, Strahan granted an interview to Dexter Van Zile of *National Fisherman*, a monthly magazine for U.S. commercial fishermen. The piece, titled "Prince of Whales," was illustrated with a picture of Strahan holding up a clipboard plastered with pictures of whales. Superimposed on the photo are a crown and a staff.

"[Expletive] the fishermen, I'd rather eat chicken," Strahan told Van Zile (2000).

Over the two decades Strahan advocated for the whales, he seems to have alienated nearly all his potential allies. He claimed to be the national campaign director for GreenWorld, which was a "small but legitimate environmental group in the early 1980s," according to Allen's article, but at the time of his writing consisted of only Strahan himself (1997). Though whale advocates privately applaud the progress Strahan has produced, they publicly distance themselves from him and his tactics, wishing to avoid political suicide. Distancing themselves was usually pretty easy because he often bristled when other environmental groups filed briefs in his court cases or spoke to the press about issues in which he was involved.

In the 1990s, while his various lawsuits were wending their way through the federal judicial system, Strahan appeared in court with a series of lawyers from Boston firms specializing in class action cases, including Jonathan Ettinger of Foley and Hoag, and Thomas Sobol, then of Brown, Rudnick, Freed, and Gesmer. He also got help from law students and professors at area universities. As time went on, however, he acted alone more and more often, though he had no formal legal training.

In the Churchill case, Strahan appeared in court wearing shorts and sneakers, representing himself.

*　　*　　*

On June 19, ten days after the CCS rescue team had relocated Churchill and attached the telemetry buoy, Max Strahan filed a request in U.S. District Court for an injunction against CCS and NMFS to stop the unprecedented rescue attempt. He named David Mattila specifically in the civil action. That same day CCS sent an aerial survey plane to check on Churchill, and they found him still zigzagging around the Great South Channel. The flight crew took photos of the whale, clearly showing that the additional drag from the buoy had pulled the line some distance through the wound. The rope on the right side of Churchill's mouth was much shorter, and the buoy attached to the rope trailing from the left side had dropped back about twenty feet.

The judge heard arguments from Strahan and a gaggle of NMFS and CCS lawyers on June 21.

"This whale is going to be murdered by these people with a carelessness that is in total violation of everything the Endangered Species Act stands for and what conservation is supposed to be all about," Strahan told the judge (Kibbe 2001). They intended to kill the whale, Strahan averred, to accomplish their ulterior goal: shutting down the lobster and gill-net fisheries. The dead whale would give them the political cover they needed.

The suitably attired lawyers for the defendants argued that their mission was urgent, and they presented the required permits and evidence of proper procedures. The following day, Judge O'Toole issued a ruling denying Strahan's request for an injunction, saying Strahan had not produced any evidence that the Fisheries Service or CCS was acting outside the law.

So with clearance from the courts, a new tail harness and injections of sedative ready to go, a passel of veterinarians and technicians on hand, and a Coast Guard cutter standing by, the cast of thousands waited for a weather window while the press fed on any tidbit they could squeeze from the harried rescuers and pundits.

Finally, on June 26, after fog lifted to reveal a clear morning, a small flotilla and two planes converged on Churchill in the Great South Channel. At 5:30 a.m., *Shearwater* and the Coast Guard Cutter *Monomoy* motored out of Provincetown Harbor. *Shearwater* carried the disentanglement team, several veterinarians, a couple of technicians, and representatives from NMFS. The CCS plane—a Cessna Skymaster—and a NOAA aerial survey plane began searching for the whale where he had last been detected via the satellite buoy.

At 9:20, the Skymaster found Churchill and guided the vessels to his position. Once again, David Mattila donned his lifejacket and climbed into the inflatable with Dave Morin and Stormy Mayo. The sea lay calm under clear skies and light winds. While dozens of people watched and planes circled overhead, they motored up to the whale, carefully avoiding the dangerous flukes, then grappled the trailing line and attached a large additional buoy. Again, the buoy kept Churchill at the surface. The next step was to assess the state of the whale, his wound, and the entangling gear.

They circled the whale, noting that Churchill was still light-gray and mottled, a result of skin sloughing and an indicator of illness. David also noted that the whale now had wide orange patches of cyamids, tiny crustaceans commonly known as whale lice, which feed especially on dead tissue. When they had seen him on June 9, cyamids had covered just small patches around the wound on Churchill's rostrum, but now the orange patches covered much of the upper jaw and infested the curved lower lips.

In preparation for this effort at disentangling Churchill, David and the team had constructed a cantilever pole mounted on a bitt at the bow of the inflatable. The butt end of the pole was weighted and bore handles; the other end reached some thirty feet forward of the bow. They now attached a video camera to the end of the pole and maneuvered the inflatable so that the camera hung over the wound on Churchill's rostrum. The camera caught a close-up of the cyamid-infested wound; the line was completely buried in the scarified, cyamid-covered flesh.

Veterinarians aboard *Shearwater* timed Churchill's breaths, assessed his activity level, and squinted at the whale's mottled back and wound through binoculars. They noted a depression behind the twin blowholes. In a well-fed whale with plenty of blubber laid on, the area at the back of the skull—what you might call the whale's neck—is flat, but Churchill was apparently emaciated, so this area showed a curved depression where the skull met the spine. It was impossible to tell whether Churchill was emaciated because the rope interfered with his feeding or because of an infection raging in his rostrum. Either way, it did not bode well for his prospects of surviving the lean winter, even if they could remove the rope.

The planes circled overhead, snapping pictures of the whale and the inflatable. Low clouds hung on the horizon. As David and the team assessed Churchill, they did note some encouraging signs. Churchill appeared to be swimming vigorously throughout the encounter, and the satellite buoy had indeed placed enough drag on the rope to pull it through the baleen, unfortunately not all the way. The short end of the entangling rope that protruded from the right side of the mouth originally bore frayed loose ends that trailed half the length of the whale. Now the frayed ends were in a tangled ball that lay against the animal's right lip. The tangle was preventing the rope from pulling all the way through the baleen, and until they sedated and restrained the whale, there would be no safe way to get close enough to cut the tangle away. As clouds began to move in on a light breeze, the team decided to attempt to administer a sedative.

David Mattila felt a twinge of trepidation about sedating the whale while the world watched. Sedating a large, free-swimming baleen whale had never been attempted and bore certain grave risks. Most marine mammals are voluntary breathers, so if they are rendered unconscious they will not breathe, even if they remain at the surface. Members of the team knew whales sometimes died because they were too fearful or confused to surface and held their breath until they lost consciousness. A whale biologist has told me he rarely finds inhaled water in a dead whale's lungs.

So the veterinarians needed to gauge the dose of sedative to calm the whale without allowing him to lose consciousness. And since no one had ever attempted such a procedure, the biologists and veterinarians had to make some educated guesses in Churchill's case. First, they had to make an estimate of the whale's weight; the background for this came mostly from whaling records. Based on this information and their experience sedating captive and beached whales, they had to choose a dose and concentration that would produce the required effect without killing the whale. For the first attempt, they decided to start with a very conservative dose given in multiple shots, if necessary. They also had to determine how long the needle should be to penetrate the blubber and inject the sedative into muscle, and they settled on twelve inches.

"You can imagine all of us thinking, 'We're dealing with chemicals in marine mammals . . . what if we do go out and kill this right whale by accident?'" David Mattila shakes his head, remembering. "So we had antidotes and several different plans for how we could get it out if it did go too deep. We went through all sorts of ideas; we considered monitoring the heart."

As an added precaution, the team had arranged for the Coast Guard cutter to stand by in case they needed additional help dealing with the whale if he reacted to the drug unpredictably.

After assessing the whale, the team returned to *Shearwater* to don helmets and attach a syringe to the end of the cantilevered pole, and then they motored toward the whale and grabbed the trailing green line. They shut down the outboard motor and lifted it out of the water to avoid fouling the propeller in the line and to minimize the noise. Dave Morin and Stormy knelt along the port side and hauled the inflatable up toward the wide flukes. Churchill pumped his tail up and down, driving forward in spite of his sickly condition and the added weight of the inflatable on the rope wrapping his rostrum. David Mattila worked the cantilevered pole, pulling down on the handles to lift the syringe as they drew up behind the whale. From the air, with the pole poised to give the shot, it was easy to see that the fully grown whale was more than twice the length of the inflatable.

When Churchill's back parted the surface and rolled into view just ahead of the inflatable, David Mattila lifted the handles on the pole, and the weighted needle at the other end dropped into the whale's back. The delivery mechanism forced a liter of Midazolam into Churchill's back muscle. Now the team and the onlookers waited and watched for some sign that the sedative was working.

Nothing changed. The whale continued to tow the inflatable at a steady clip of five knots (just under six miles per hour), breathing at regular intervals. So they rigged up another shot and injected him again.

"And that was it," David Mattila shrugs. "It didn't do anything."

Apparently the conservative dose was too conservative. The next stage of their plan, attaching the tail harness, depended on the whale being sedate enough to approach from behind. So under gathering clouds and a setting sun, the team cut about twenty feet from the trailing line and moved the satellite buoy closer to Churchill's flukes. They returned to Provincetown to face the press and the drawing board.

"All through this process, we're learning," David Mattila says, remembering the meetings they had after the first attempt to sedate Churchill. "The vets are learning about what we do, and we're learning about the drugs and what they do. We learned, for instance, that the primary drug we were giving him had to get into the animal before he got excited, because if the animal is excited it wouldn't work. We also learned that it didn't really make him stop feeling any pain and wouldn't necessarily prevent him from doing anything; it would just make him feel more okay about what's going on. In other words, we learned that once we went to stick a knife in the head, he was going to react. We said, 'Hold on a second, haven't you got something a little more potent?'"

Midazolam, the drug they administered to Churchill, is a sedative used commonly in humans in conjunction with general anesthetic. It helps to calm the patient's nerves prior to surgery. The veterinarians had chosen to use it on Churchill for several reasons: it had an antidote that they could inject if the whale seemed to be too lethargic or disoriented, it could be concentrated and administered in doses appropriate for such a large creature, and it was readily available. Unfortunately, it wasn't an anesthetic. So for the next attempt, the veterinarians prepared a mixture of Midazolam and an opiate to diminish pain. They also prepared a local anesthetic to apply when the team attempted to cut the line.

The weather did not allow another opportunity to try the new concoction until mid-July, though the world followed Churchill by satellite as he meandered around the Great South Channel. Pilot Chan Lofland, flying the Skymaster, located Churchill on July 3 and observed him making six- to seven-minute dives punctuated by short stints at the surface. On July 10, the *Shearwater* and the Coast Guard cutter *Ridley* located the whale, but sloppy seas and fog prevented the team from attempting their plan. The *Boston Globe* and the *Cape Cod Times* both ran stories about the media frenzy over Churchill and the array of suggestions pouring in from well-wishers.

Winds abated and fog cleared by early morning on July 14, so the flotilla set out for Churchill once again. The whale had obligingly remained in the Great South Channel, and the vessels were with him by midday. In the two and a half weeks since the last rescue attempt, Churchill's condition had deteriorated. His skin was "nearly white" and peeling off in sheets. Following the procedure of previous attempts, the team attached a big float to keep Churchill from diving and injected him with two shots of the latest drug cocktail. This time the injection mechanism failed to deliver the whole dose because it couldn't accommodate a larger volume. Churchill showed no signs of sedation.

Figure 5.3. July 14, 2001. David Mattila uses the cantilever pole to inject Churchill with sedatives while other members of the CCS team keep the line clear of the Zodiac. Others look on from the deck of the U.S. Coast Guard vessel *Ridley*. Photographed from the CCS research vessel Shearwater. Photo courtesy of the Center for Coastal Studies and taken under the authority of Scientific Research and Enhancement Permit No. 932–1489–04/PRT009526, issued by the National Marine Fisheries Service and U.S. Fish and Wildlife Service.

The team attempted twice to attach the tail harness but failed both times. Finally, they attached two six-foot diameter sea anchors to the trailing line. With this added resistance, Churchill slowed down enough for the team to pick up the trailing line and pass it to *Shearwater*. With the thirty-nine-foot boat hanging on the other end of the line, Churchill slowed to less than a knot (a knot is about 1.15 miles per hour), but not for long. In spite of his sickly condition and the enormous weight on the line around his rostrum, Churchill drove forward, pumping his flukes to resist the strain. Concerned that they might cause additional injury if he continued his driving resistance, they released the trailing line with the satellite buoy attached.

Another attempt had failed. The rescuers set out for Provincetown. Churchill, on the other hand, made a beeline for Canada. Perhaps his latest encounter with humans was the last straw, or maybe the copepods in Great South Channel were getting scarce, but Churchill made his way northeast. Now the person most attuned to the wayward whale was Bob Bowman, who observed the whale's progress, hour after hour, day after day, at his home office on Mount Desert Island, Maine.

Bob, who is my brother-in-law, is CCS's Maine disentanglement co-ordinator. Beginning in the late 1970s, Bob ran one of the first whale-watch businesses in New England, and he later did research with the Center for Coastal Studies and Allied Whale, a research center at College of the Atlantic in Bar Harbor, Maine. His scientific investigations focused on Maine finback whales and humpbacks in the Dominican Republic. He began disentangling whales in Maine on his own, responding whenever he got a report about an entangled whale.

In the mid-1990s, when Max Strahan was goosing the states and the feds into action, Bob was drawn into the fray. He had begun training a network of Maine fishermen to help with reporting and rescuing entangled whales. However, as the political climate heated up, fishermen in Maine stopped reporting entangled whales. Bob is relentlessly frank and a consummate devil's advocate. These are traits that fishermen generally appreciate, but I have seen Bob's style render government employees speechless.

Bob joined the CCS disentanglement team in 1998, working out of his home on Mount Desert Island. His job at the time Churchill held the attention of the world was in part to manage and distribute information about entangled whales. He created and maintained a comprehensive private website and an email list for members of a network of professionals involved with whale entanglement. He also received and mapped data from the satellite tags on entangled whales.

At his computer in his home office, Bob plotted Churchill's position as it was relayed from the satellites. Using this information, he could determine roughly how much time Churchill was spending at the surface and note any major changes in his behavior. When planes or boats needed to relocate Churchill for their disentanglement efforts, Bob provided them with recent coordinates and predicted, as best he could, the whale's position in the near future. While the team worked with Churchill, the buoy continued to transmit, so Bob "watched" as the whale towed the team at a steady pace for several hours straight.

Now, as Churchill made his way toward Canada, Bob Bowman formed the connection between the whale and the rest of the world. On the morning of July 17, Bob updated the Network Website with this information:

> We have done a little analysis of the satellite data and here are the basics. At approximately 19:00 last night #1102 [Churchill's catalog number] crossed The Hague Line into Canadian waters. As of 07:20 this morning #1102 was 75 NM from Yarmouth, NS—nearly the closest point of land. During the previous 8 hours or so the whale was traveling at an average speed of 2.9 knots. During the previous 24 hours (at least) the buoy has been at the surface for 100% of the time. This indicates that either the whale is always at the surface or is swimming probably not much more than 20 feet down (the buoy is approximately 100 feet behind its attachment to the whale). The general course of travel has been [northeast], heading more or less straight for Yarmouth [Nova Scotia]. While we are awaiting another weather window of opportunity, new equipment is under research and development and logistics are being planned for the next attempt. . . . We got a note from Jon Lien in Newfoundland last night saying, "Welcome to Canada!"

The Canadian weather would not accommodate another attempt, however. Over the next two weeks, Churchill towed his buoy along the southeastern shore of Nova Scotia, then at Halifax took a right. After making a loop off the edge of the continental shelf, he passed through Cabot Strait between Cape Breton Island and Newfoundland. Fog and wind followed the whale and frustrated all plans for additional rescue attempts. All this while, the CCS team and NMFS officials kept in constant contact with Canadian biologists and fisheries officials, making daily plans for action if the weather cleared.

Upon entering the Gulf of St. Lawrence, Churchill lingered near the Magdalene Islands long enough to allow a Canadian Department of Fisheries and Oceans plane to locate him on August 2. Canadian biologist Jerry Conway was aboard the plane and reported that Churchill was making dives of twenty minutes or more, with short intervals at the surface. From this behavior it seemed Churchill was diving to the bottom to feed on deep concentrations of copepods. The photos taken of Churchill in this fly-over were blurry because of poor weather conditions, but they showed that his skin was now very white, and that cyamids lent an orange tinge to his head. With the wind and seas picking up, the plane left the whale in the gulf.

I was in Newfoundland with Jon Lien while Churchill swam around the Gulf of St. Lawrence, and we perused the pictures and agreed that the whale looked horrible. We found it difficult to imagine that Churchill could survive, even if there were a way to remove the entangling line. We began to discuss euthanasia.

"If that wasn't an 'American' whale," Jon told me, he would probably be arranging some way to kill the whale and end its suffering. We discussed various ways one might accomplish such a thing. I'll spare you the unpleasant details, but Jon knew firsthand from his experience in ending the suffering of doomed beached whales that whales are not easy to kill.

I later asked David Mattila whether the team had considered euthanizing Churchill and ending his suffering.

"That was brought up, but we believed that given the status of the species, we couldn't ever intentionally kill one," David answered. "In our minds, anyway, the animal welfare issue was outweighed by the extreme danger that the species was in. We felt our mission was to try to save the genes."

But David was touched by the whale's suffering.

"It just makes you more and more convinced that this whole entanglement issue has got to stop. We need a preventative solution. They shouldn't have to go through that kind of thing, from an animal welfare point of view. It's horrible."

"How much hope did you hold for Churchill's survival, even if you were able to beat the odds and remove the line?" I asked him.

"It's an important point. In almost every conference call, we always brought up the question, Is this a lost cause? We knew from the get-go that it had a low likelihood of success. This was all new stuff and a very simple but difficult entanglement. But given the status of the population, we felt that as long as there were some chance of success and as long as we didn't reach the point where everybody said this animal has no chance, we were obligated to continue to try to do it. People have seen some pretty amazing healing in marine mammals."

The day after he was spotted by the plane in the Gulf of St. Lawrence, Churchill decided, for reasons known only to him, that it was time to return south. By this time, Churchill had been towing his satellite buoy for eight weeks, traveling more than 2,500 zigzagging miles. Now, under Bob Bowman's watchful eye, he made his way back through Cabot Strait and headed along the coast of Nova Scotia. During this time he was tantalizingly close to shore, but fog, wind, rough seas, and Churchill's rapid pace forced the rescue team to keep any disentanglement efforts on hold. After making a few stops along the canyons of the continental slope, Churchill crossed the Hague Line in the early morning hours of August 18, then wandered around Georges Bank.

The Canadian press made a halfhearted attempt to follow Churchill's progress while he wandered Canadian waters, and as he returned to the United States, the American press greeted him with brief asides. Their attention had waned when the story dragged on without providing them with a neat happy ending.

By late August, Churchill was back in the Great South Channel and within reach of the team in Provincetown. The weather cleared enough to allow another attempt. So early in the morning of August 30, *Shearwater* left the dock to find Churchill once again. The Skymaster left Chatham Airport at 10 a.m. and, guided by information from Bob Bowman, found the whale within an hour. Cyamids now covered most of the whale's body, and the depression behind his blowhole had grown deeper since he was last photographed by the team in July. After the third dose of the sedative/opiate mixture, Churchill finally showed signs of slowing down. The new syringe mechanism had worked.

Now that they had succeeded in sedating the whale, the team attempted to capture his tail with two experimental models of the tail harness. Unfortunately, the whale held his flukes well below the surface; apparently this was an unexpected effect of the sedative. The tail harnesses were designed to capture the tail near the surface, so the team was never able to immobilize the tail. And after a short time, the sedative began to wear off. After tying a fresh satellite buoy to the trailing line, the team returned to Provincetown, planning to rework the tail harness in time for the next weather window.

Over the first week of September, Bob Bowman began to see a change in Churchill's progress. He now spent nearly all of his time at the surface and seemed to be wandering aimlessly, neither feeding nor traveling. Bob suspected the whale's condition was worsening, so he and CCS asked the Coast Guard to fly over the whale and assess his condition. On September 9, a Coast Guard Falcon jet located the whale at the southern end of Georges Bank. The jet's crew observed the whale remaining nearly motionless just below the surface. It seemed that Churchill was dying.

Then, suddenly—a day after the jet had visited the whale—he began to swim again, moving southwest with bursts of speed punctuated by periods of slower travel. On September 11, 2001, while Churchill made halting progress to the south, the world's attention turned away from the wandering whale. All planes were grounded in the days that followed September 11th, so nobody visited the whale as he made his way slowly southeast over the next few days. With only Bob Bowman and a handful of others watching, Churchill moved off the continental shelf.

Then, on the afternoon of September 16, Churchill was about four hundred nautical miles east of New Jersey when his satellite buoy stopped transmitting. Given his condition and his recent behavior, he had most likely died and sunk, bringing the buoy down with him. Though right whales normally float when dead, Churchill may not have had enough blubber left to buoy him to the surface. In the one hundred days since the CCS team first attempted to help him, Churchill had traveled more than 4,900 nautical miles in spite of his mortal wound and gaunt condition. Like #2030 and other right whales the team had worked with, Churchill had shown astounding tenacity and strength, even when he was at death's door. Such endurance had surely served the species well over evolutionary time, but it was also the one thing the rescuers could not overcome in order to save him. He endured months of suffering, and his genes were lost.

After waiting a couple of days to be sure the transmitter was no longer working, CCS and NMFS announced to a somber and distracted press that, although there was no way to be certain, Churchill was almost certainly dead. Many national and international news outlets ignored the news or gave it a brief mention. New England papers devoted more room to summarizing the whale's story.

Many things changed that September. No one has tallied up the price tag for the effort to save Churchill, but CCS spent tens of thousands of

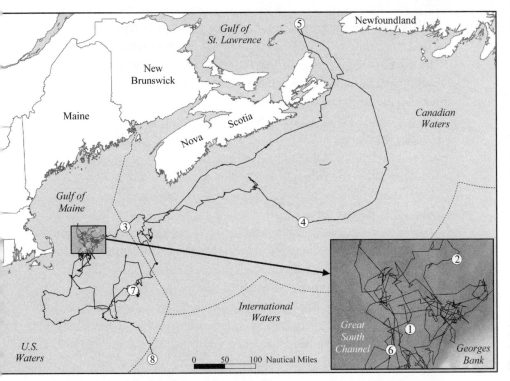

Map 5.1. 2001 satellite telemetry track of right whale #1102, "Churchill": (1) Right whale with rope trailing from his mouth is sighted June 8 in the Great South Channel by an aerial survey team; (2) Center for Coastal Studies team administers two doses of sedative on July 14 with no discernible effect; (3) Churchill crosses the Hague Line and enters Canadian waters on July 16; (4) Churchill swings east and away from land on July 26, still traveling at approximately four knots; (5) Canadian flight finds Churchill just east of the Magdalene Islands on August 2; (6) Center for Coastal Studies team administers four doses of sedative on August 30 but is unable to capture Churchill's tail in a harness; (7) on September 10, a Coast Guard Falcon jet locates and films the whale as he remains nearly motionless just below the surface; (8) satellite telemetry signal stops on September 16. Churchill is presumed dead after traveling over 4,900 nautical miles in one hundred days. Drawing by T. Johnson; data provided by Commonwealth of Massachusetts, GIS Data Depot, and Center for Coastal Studies.

dollars, and hundreds of thousands came out of the taxpayer's pocket. The Fisheries Service worked hard to put a positive spin on the failed rescue effort, telling the press that the things we had learned would likely save whales in the future, but many people involved with the issue wondered if the effort had been worth it. As more than one person observed, you can buy a lot of whale-friendly fishing gear with half a million bucks.

Even Max Strahan, the Prince of Whales, seemed to lose heart. Soon after Churchill was lost, Strahan stopped haranguing people at Quincy Market and on the sidewalk in front of the New England Aquarium. When I tried to contact him for an interview, no one, friend or foe, could tell me how to find him.

In November 2003, *Right Whale News*, a newsletter for those concerned with right whale recovery, ran this brief and rather bizarre update: "Max Strahan of GreenWorld, a frequent litigator over right whale issues, has enrolled in a graduate program in astrophysics in San Francisco" ("People").

After the Churchill drama ended, the disentanglement team at the Center for Coastal Studies agreed as a group that they needed to work harder to put themselves out of the business. They vowed to push harder for measures that would prevent whale entanglement. Since then, every time I have heard members of the CCS team speak in meetings, working groups, presentations, and interviews, they have said pointedly: "Disentanglement is not a solution to the entanglement problem. We need to find ways of preventing entanglements without destroying the fishing industry."

By the end of the Churchill saga, David Mattila felt drained and burned out. He had endured months of attention from the press, juggling a million details, gauging risks, and making plans. After decades of disentangling whales, David struggled to remain optimistic, to believe that someday whales wouldn't have to suffer, fishermen wouldn't have to worry, and scientists could get down to the business of learning about whales rather than scrambling to save them. He was ready for a break.

For the last three or four years, the disentanglement program had been taking up most of David's time. "It was supposed to be fifty-fifty, but it's been more like eighty-twenty," David told me.

Wanting to get back to his humpback research, David had been grooming Ed Lyman, another member of the disentanglement team, to take over the program, but Ed had accepted a job elsewhere. The center's search to find someone to take on the program did not yield a suitable candidate. Finally, the Hawaiian Islands Humpback Whale Sanctuary offered David a position that would take him away from the Center for half the year. He accepted, but not without some reservations.

"I'm using that to back out of the directorship," he said. "I'm very torn about it because it is a big challenge. You know this is the single most important conservation issue that most of us in the whale world will ever face, and we have an opportunity to solve this. If we can solve it here it will have global applications. If we can solve it here, it can hopefully be exported, it could save whales all over the place—and save gear."

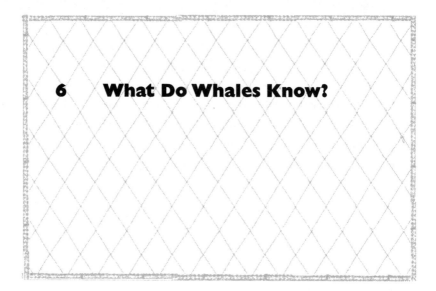

6　What Do Whales Know?

. . . To embrace a sea ethic we need not idealize or distort the ocean's creatures. Indeed, up to now our view of the sea's living inhabitants can hardly have been more distorted. Instead, we have the opportunity to see them fully for the first time, as wild animals in their habitats, confronted with needs and dangers, equipped by evolution with the capacity and drive to manage and adapt and survive.

Carl Safina, *Song for the Blue Ocean*

The notion that whales are gentle and spiritual—commonly blended with the idea that whales are extremely intelligent—was something I often heard from people involved with the Save the Whales movement as I explored the links between whales and humans. The aggression exhibited by entangled right whales when people attempt to help them, though understandable given the circumstances, did not fit with the image of whales as gentle, wise giants. I began to realize that our ideas about whales and fishermen are colored by the myths and shibboleths to which we cling. Where did this image of whales come from, I wondered, and how realistic was it?

I have heard many stories about the gentleness and altruism of all kinds of whales, and most specifically about the baleen whales. Remember Blizzard, who stood by Ibis and trumpeted nervously while Stormy Mayo and David Mattila cut the lines away from her tail and mouth? Recall the humpback that sang to his sick and entangled companion in Trinity Bay while Jon Lien and his students freed her from a gill net? Some people, even a few who study whales, go so far as to suggest that whales may be more intelligent than humans, endowed with a transcendent understanding of abstract concepts about the living world. On the other hand, baleen whales are apparently also capable of aggression and violence.

So which is it, wise and gentle giant or brutish beast? It's a compelling question from an intellectual standpoint but a very important one from the perspective of the whale's well-being. If we are to help whales avoid entanglement, we need to have some understanding of how the whale perceives and makes sense of its environment. If we are to disentangle them, we need to know how they will respond to the ministrations of humans. Finally, much of the Save the Whales movement has been based upon the purported extraordinary intelligence of whales. Do they merit saving if they fail to live up to our myths?

* * *

Myths about whales are certainly nothing new. In his book *Men and Whales*, writer and artist Richard Ellis reviews the history of humanity's relationship with the leviathan. According to Ellis, in the centuries before technology allowed Europeans to go after the whale in its own element, people knew of them only from specimens that had stranded or washed ashore and from the tales of terrified mariners who had wandered into perilously unknown seas that afforded only rare and fleeting glimpses of living whales.

In medieval Europe, when men traveled and traded by sea, these fantastical creatures snarled from the corners of the nautical charts depicting the watery regions where men ventured only with trepidation. Mariners of the fifteenth century, according to Ellis, did not look upon the whale as an object of discovery or curiosity. "There was no science for the sake of science," Ellis writes, "and if men found whales, they took them for what they believed them to be: huge, mysterious, threatening creatures. On their early maps, they figured them as large, scaly animals with a frightening array of unlikely appendages: horns, fringes, crests, armor, lumps, bumps, ridges, horrific dentition, and often twin pipes gushing water into the air" (Ellis 1991, 36).

A plate in Ellis's 1996 book *Monsters of the Sea,* under the chapter title "Leviathan, or, The Whale," depicts an imposing dragonlike creature emerging from the surface of the sea with long sharp teeth jutting from its lower jaw, a frilly tail, four stubby legs equipped with curving claws, and scales along its back. The only things vaguely whalelike about this sea monster are the two tubes emerging from the top of the creature's head spewing water (whales blow warm moist air from their blowholes, not water). Two of the monster's young swim by its side. This terrible image seems to be a manifestation of the artist's fears and desires rather than any attempt at realistic rendering. The scene is something the artist could only have witnessed in a dream or gleaned from an embellished account. In looking at it, we learn far more about the artist's worldview than we learn about whales. This is the mythic whale of the medieval mind.

Europeans were not the only culture to produce early images of whales. Many of the scattered peoples encircling the Arctic depended upon whales for sustenance and even building materials, often carving representations of whales that were far more accurate than those of the early Europeans, owing presumably to their direct and intimate experience with their subject. Some of the natives of North America's Pacific Coast—for instance, the Tlingit and the Haida—made stylized renderings of killer whales, which held a revered place in their religions. For many other cultures, both European and non-European, the immense and mysterious creature of the deep played a powerful role in their myth or religion. The mythic whale was endowed with great and mystical powers and regarded with a mixture of terror and awe.

Encountering whales at sea, I can understand why they might seem at once terrifying and awe-inspiring. When we set out across the glinting surface of the ocean, try as we might, we cannot see into the deep. The interface between water and air seems featureless and terrifyingly vast. We know that whole worlds populated by cold and mysterious creatures exist below, but they are inaccessible and dangerous. We are not equipped to visit them. The startling appearance of a whale's black back with a rush of air and mist only accentuates the things you can't see or know beneath the waves. The whale's immensity reflects the unfathomable immensity of the sea itself. Whales, Richard Ellis has told me, "might as well be living on Europa," Jupiter's icy moon. They inhabit another world.

*   *   *

The whale's mythos, honed and embellished over the centuries, haunted the psyche of Europeans and later Americans as they began to roam the seas to kill whales. It was as though they hunted two whales, the real flesh-and-blood whale and the whale of their dreams, the one formed from biblical stories, from yarns passed from one sailor to another, from the crazy figures in the uncharted corners of their maps.

Even as they came to know the whale more intimately, their wonder at the creature only deepened and grew more specific. It was indeed a fantastic being, apparently formed from a grotesque and ungodly combination of features, unimaginably immense and mighty. The whale thrived in the cold waters of the sea, and it knew the secrets of the shadowy deep. The whalemen came to understand that the whale had warm blood, breathed air, and suckled its young, but this only made the whale's lack of the other standard mammalian features and its complete independence from land that much more inexplicable. Whalers must have been haunted by the dinosaurian bellows of dying whales.

Of course, Herman Melville understood all of this. In building the character of Moby Dick, he devotes an enormous amount of text to evoking the mythic whale of dreams, while at the same time revealing the other whale, the flesh-and-blood whale, by dwelling on anatomy and the mechanics of whale killing. The sermon delivered by Father Mapple from the ship's-prow pulpit of the whaling church in New Bedford recounts the biblical story of Jonah and the whale. Recently I acquired a copy of a 1930 edition of *Moby Dick* illustrated with drawings by Rockwell Kent in which Kent's rendering of Jonah, the "God-fugitive," bears the same bleak and tortured countenance as Ahab, the monomaniac who barters with the devil. For both Ahab and Jonah, the whale represents the hand of God.

Some months into my study of whales, whale rescuers, and fishermen, I reread a passage in *Moby Dick* with new understanding. Melville describes the *Pequod*'s second encounter with the White Whale, in which the harpooneers of three whaleboats have pierced Moby Dick's hide and their three lines have been twisted together by the writhing monster:

But at last in his untraceable evolutions, the White Whale so crossed and recrossed, and in a thousand ways entangled the slack of the three lines now fast to him, that they foreshortened, and, of themselves, warped the devoted boats towards the planted irons in him; though now for a moment the whale drew aside a little, as if to rally for a more tremendous charge. Seizing that opportunity, Ahab first paid out more line: and then was rapidly hauling and jerking in upon it again—hoping that way to disencumber it of some snarls—when lo!—a sight more savage than the embattled teeth of sharks! Caught and twisted—corkscrewed in the mazes of the line, loose harpoons and lances, with all their bristling barbs and points, came flashing and dripping up to the chocks in the bows of Ahab's boat. (Melville 1930, 800)

Like a whale twisted in a mess of lobster gear, Melville's White Whale carries with him the rope and iron from previous encounters with men. Ahab deftly cuts away the tangled lines and harpoons Moby Dick again:

That instant, the White Whale made a sudden rush among the remaining tangles of the other lines; by so doing, irresistibly dragged the more involved boats of Stubb and Flask towards his flukes; dashed them together like two rolling husks on a surf-beaten beach, and then, diving down into the sea, disappeared in a boiling maelstrom, in which, for a space, the odorous cedar chips of the wrecks danced round and round, like the grated nutmeg in a swiftly stirred bowl of punch. (800)

After surfacing again and capsizing Ahab's boat, Moby Dick stirs the punch again with his flukes:

he now lay for a moment slowly feeling with his flukes from side to side; and when ever a stray oar, bit of plank, the least chip or crumb of the boats touched his skin, his tail swiftly drew back, and came sideways smiting the sea. (801)

When I first read this passage years ago I wondered how far-fetched this characterization of the whale was, but in light of what I had learned about aggression in whales, Melville's White Whale seemed both more vivid and more plausible. A whale could indeed have the physical means to endure harpoons embedded in its flesh for years, as whales today endure entangling rope for months or years. And a whale does seem to have the intelligence to mount a directed attack against a perceived foe.

Every professional whale rescuer can tell stories of whales striking out by slashing or smacking with their tail flukes, slapping with their flippers, or ramming with their heads. Even when she was near death with rope sawing into her flanks, right whale #2030 was aware enough of her surroundings to place her blows with impressive accuracy when the disentanglement team attempted to help her. I myself have come under attack by a panicked humpback during a disentanglement attempt.

Before writing *Moby Dick*, Melville met and was, at least in part, inspired by a surviving member of the Nantucket whaleship *Essex*, which was stove and sunk in 1820 by an immense raging sperm whale when two of the whale's companions had been harpooned by *Essex* whaleboats in the tropical Pacific. In his compelling 2000 reconstruction of the *Essex* story, Nathaniel Philbrick writes:

> With its huge scarred head halfway out of the water and its tail beating the ocean into a white-water wake more than forty feet across, the whale approached the ship at twice its original speed— at least six knots. . . . the force of the collision caused the whalemen's heads to jounce on their muscled necks as the ship lurched to halt. (84)

Melville's White Whale, though inhabiting a fictional story, is a composite of factual tales and observations from Melville's own experience with both whales and whaling men; in the novel, Moby Dick only attacks when provoked, and Melville goes to great lengths to show that the sinister mythic stature of the whale is as much a construction of the whaling men's fears and fables as a product of the whale's actual deeds. From this perspective, I came to understand the climax of the novel as a clash between the flesh-and-blood Moby Dick and Ahab's dream whale, the sea monster that haunted his sleep and moved him to sell his soul for revenge. Melville leaves us to wonder where the mythic whale ends and the flesh-and-blood whale begins. Perhaps we each carry mythic whales with us. If so, is the whale in my dreams the same as the whale in yours?

* * *

When people speak of "whales," they commonly use the term to mean all members of the mammalian order Cetacea. But the cetaceans split into two distinct groups very early in their evolution some thirty million years ago. This split gave rise to the baleen whales—such as humpbacks and right whales—and the toothed whales, such as killer whales, sperm whales, dolphins, and porpoises. Given that the two groups eat, reproduce, and avoid predators in radically different ways, it makes sense that they would differ in characteristics such as intelligence, gregariousness, aggression, and awareness of their surroundings. Similarly, the pleat-throated rorquals—such as humpbacks—have very different feeding strategies from other baleen whales, such as the right whale, presumably giving rise to additional differences. In other words, sperm whales, right whales, and humpbacks probably know and understand different things.

Whale biologists are quietly divided on the matter of whale intelligence and the question of gentleness among the various whale species. I say "quietly" because whales enjoy protection, especially in the United States, in large part because the public has been sold on the notion that whales—all whales—are extraordinarily intelligent and gentle. If some species are revealed to be less intelligent than others, some biologists fear, perhaps these protections will be relaxed. Nearly everyone who studies whales, whether or not they see them as wise and gentle giants, believes they merit and require protection.

Roger Payne, president of the Whale Conservation Institute in Lincoln, Massachusetts, has studied right whales and humpbacks and has served as a scientific advisor to the International Whaling Commission since the late 1960s. He is perhaps best known as the first scientist to suggest that the mating vocalizations of humpback whales should be technically classified as songs. Payne asserts that the baleen whales he has studied are highly intelligent, even by human standards. And though capable of terrific violence if attacked, he says, whales are sensitive, gentle, even considerate. As evidence for whale intelligence, he points to things like the relatively large size and complex anatomy of whales' brains and their social behaviors including play, learning, and reciprocal altruism. Most scientists agree with Roger Payne that whales of all types are extraordinarily sensitive creatures. As Stormy Mayo has put it, "They have a solid command of their near field."

In the 1960s and 1970s, divers began for the first time to observe whales in their own element; both Roger Payne and Richard Ellis were among these pioneers. They discovered that the immense creatures could and would carefully avoid touching or harming the divers who visited them beneath the waves.

In his memoir, *Among Whales*, Roger Payne recalls his early dives with whales. The chapter entitled "Making Friends with Whales: Laying Our Fears to Rest" begins:

> When you stop to think about it, going swimming with a whale ought to be the scariest thing you could imagine doing. Talk about vulnerable! . . . having pulled alongside a creature that could kill you with a single swipe of its tail (the way we might casually swat a fly), you then get into the water with it. . . . To make matters worse, you put on a heavy wet suit and strap on a lot of cumbersome gear. . . . When I first did it, it seemed rather like putting on a straight jacket and rolling around on the ground in front of a polar bear.
>
> . . . The wonderful thing, of course, is that the whale does not take advantage of your condition. It doesn't blunder into you, or smash you against the bottom, even when it is in fifteen feet of water and you are below it. Instead, it maneuvers with consummate skill—sometimes missing you only by inches with its flippers or tail. (Payne 1995, 212)

Many of Dr. Payne's colleagues do not agree with his conclusions about baleen whale intelligence, however.

"Well, despite what Roger Payne says, I don't think baleen whales are all that bright," says Bob Kenney at the University of Rhode Island. "Intelligence is an adaptation just like any physical anatomical structure, and it doesn't take a lot of smarts to open your mouth and graze. It's just basically what a cow does. So they're not hunting down something that's trying to get away from them; they're not living in extended social hierarchies where they have to have a lot of intelligence or computing power to remember who's who and keep all the hierarchical relationships and dominance straight. So why would they be intelligent?"

Payne also asserts that whales know when they are being helped by disentanglement teams. In the same chapter, he talks about the work of Jon Lien helping fishermen and whales in Newfoundland. He recounts an event in which Jon released a humpback from fishing gear that had cinched tight around its body. The rope passing over the animal's twin blowholes had cut several inches into the sensitive flesh and become embedded. Jon had cut away the gear on either side of the blowhole, but the embedded rope remained, and the only way to get at it was to reach into the blowhole and pull it out.

When Jon told me the same story, he showed me with a motion of his hand how he had grabbed the rope and pulled.

"God!" he flinched as he remembered the incident. "That musta hurt something awful." The whale twitched and writhed.

What struck Payne, however, was that the whale did not clamp its blowhole shut on Jon's hand and drag him under or and capsize his boat with a swing of its head. Payne insists that even in its desperate condition, the whale would have had the wherewithal to deliver such a blow. Payne writes:

> I want to be clear on one point: Jon does not believe he has some sort of mystical rapport with the whales. He simply feels that of the two most likely interpretations of his behavior available to the whale, the whale apparently chooses to believe that Jon is there to help. (215)

When Jon had told me the story about pulling the rope from the whale's blowhole, he never implied that the whale knew he was trying to help. In fact, Payne's interpretation of these events did not match my experience of Jon at all. As a biopsychologist and a consummate pragmatist, Jon seemed careful not to read too much into the actions of the whales. After puzzling over the passage, I sent an e-mail to Jon to ask him what he thought about Payne's interpretation of the whale's behavior.

> My question to you is do you believe that the animals know you are trying to help them? If so, what exactly do you think they understand? I have heard many accounts in which a whale actually pokes its head out of the water, making the gear more accessible to the disentanglers, but I really don't know how to interpret this. In my own experience, I have seen whales behave in ways that seem to

indicate that they are relating to the boat, specifically. But in a couple of other instances, and only with humpbacks, I have seen behavior that seems to indicate that they see and understand the humans as separate from the boat (i.e. repeated spyhopping to look at us on the deck of a ship). Could the whale think that the boat is the thing trying to help? Or do you think baleen whales can cognitively separate the person from the boat? Or are these stories just coincidence?

Jon responded:

Roger is very romantic and I like that, but I'm not that way. Animals sometimes do exactly the wrong things when you try to help them. Other times they do the right things. I have worked on a variety of wild animals in trouble. When they should be stressed—hurting—often they allow remarkable contact. Perhaps it's just endorphins? But I've had dogs stand still when pulling glass from a paw when they could just as well have run—things like that cause pause. But some of those are with domestic animals who have gotten used to parent humans getting them out of trouble (tangled leads, dog fights, whatever). With wild animals I've certainly had cases where animals had wounds and seemed to tolerate human intervention. Once I put my hand, initially inadvertently, but later to check, in the wound of a wolf and it was tolerated even though the animal flinched in pain, etc.

A very basic survival skill is learning to predict what others (species included) are going to do (recall the zebras laying around with well-fed lions about, etc.). By its approach I think a boat can certainly indicate to a whale if it is coming to chase or to watch, for instance. Habituation is a big part of the response of an animal in trouble and I believe it occurs quickly. When you initially approach an entrapped animal you are a big deal. But if nothing happens it quickly focuses on the big deal—the gear holding them, and you become pretty insignificant quickly. There are species differences here (e.g. right vs. humpback whales). I've always wanted to do a bunch of right whales my way. You stop them. Calm them down and then go to work. I've only done one and could not calm him down over three days. But I've had some humpbacks that way, too.

In other words, Jon can neither prove nor disprove that the animal knew he was trying to help, and there are plenty of other plausible explanations.

In a phone call, I posed the same question to Stormy Mayo: Do whales, even sometimes, know you are trying to help them?

"They don't make that decision," Stormy said. "Generally they never stop. They either run or make it hard. I haven't seen a single example when I can scientifically say they knew they were being helped."

But even those who disagree with Roger Payne's conclusions about what whales know are quick to point out that his work has been good for whales.

Stormy says, "I think what Roger has done, and Cousteau—the eloquent ones—is to show that these animals are next to us in sensitivity and intelligence. How intelligent? Well, they're better than we are at what they do. Others told me in the beginning of my work that whales are 'as dumb as cows and goats.' If we had taken that . . . we have to anthropomorphize them in order to save them. For me, whales are unreasonably amazing creatures, but for me clams are amazing."

Those who trust that whales know they are being helped may suffer dire consequences. In June 2003, Tom Smith, a thirty-eight-year-old charter fishing captain in Kaikoura, New Zealand, donned scuba gear and entered the water to free a humpback that had run afoul of crayfish pots. While his family and a boat full of whale watchers looked on, Smith swam around the whale to assess the entanglement. Then, as he passed within reach of the flukes, the whale lifted its tail and struck the would-be rescuer. He never surfaced.

While the search for Smith's body was still underway, the *New Zealand Herald* ran a background story that said, in part:

It was not the first time Mr. Smith had attempted to rescue whales, and it was almost two years to the day since Mr. Smith was photographed freeing another humpback whale tangled in crayfish-pot ropes.

At the time, he told the *Christchurch Press*: "I was pretty scared."

Mr. Smith said he believed the whale knew it was being rescued.

"The first thing I did was make eye contact with its dinner plate–sized eye. It let out a roar of distress. . . . It started whistling as I started to cut the loop of rope from around its head. I dumped the scuba gear back on the boat and hopped back in to cut the other tangled rope from the tail. . . . When it stopped moving, I approached. The whale dropped its head and raised its tail, waiting for me to do the cutting. They talk about how whales know you are going to help them—I believe it."

All whales are prone to becoming entangled in fishing gear, though apparently some do so far more frequently than others. Of course, how often a particular species becomes entangled depends in part on whether they happen to be where fishermen have put their gear and how much gear the fishermen put in the whale's way. Also, though large baleen whales can be surprisingly agile, their agility is nothing compared to that of smaller whales, porpoises, and dolphins. Once you get sixty tons of bulk moving through the water, it's very hard to stop. Whales can't just put on the brakes and can't really swim backward. So even if a large baleen whale wants to avoid a collision, it would need plenty of advance notice to veer in time. Sean Todd, a whale biologist at College of the Atlantic in Maine who did his doctoral work with Jon Lien, believes many of the whales that are tangled by the tail get caught as they are trying to swerve around fishing gear as it looms suddenly ahead.

Also, baleen whales have enormous mouths that comprise as much as a third of their length. To feed, they must swim forward with their mouths open. Their relatively tiny eyes are far back on the sides of their bodies near the corners of their mouths. To gaze at something closely, they must do so by turning to one side or the other. So it is very unlikely that they can see what's ahead of them when they are feeding. To get an idea of what it may be like for a right whale to swim among the lobster buoys in Cape Cod Bay, try taping an index card to your forehead so it hangs in front of your eyes and allows you to see only to your left or right. Then try trotting across a crowded room with your mouth gaping without bumping into anyone. No wonder they collide with fishing gear.

You might think that the baleen whales' strategy for acquiring its food is maladaptive, akin to hunting rabbits with an index card taped to your forehead. But think about it: before people started spreading fishing gear around the continental shelves, the only things in the path of the whale's advancing maw were either food or something that could get out of the way.

In addition to all of these variables—size, agility, and methods of feeding—some scientists suspect that intelligence and possibly temperament play a role in whether the animal can (or even attempts to) avoid getting caught in fishing gear. As I mentioned earlier, entanglements are typically deadly for the smallest whales, including porpoises, dolphins, and often minke whales. But for those that are large and strong enough to survive the initial entanglement and carry off the gear, both intelligence and temperament may influence whether the whale ultimately survives the encounter.

* * *

Unless we figure out a way to give whales IQ tests, we will never be able to quantify whale intelligence—even if we could agree on what constituted a smart whale. But there are a few clues to how and how well an animal assesses and interprets its world. If we apply Bob Kenney's calculus that predation and complex social systems imply intelligence in the whales, then we would expect the toothed whales like the sperm whale, killer whale, and pilot whale to be the most intelligent of the whale species. They are predators that prey upon predators, and many live in large groups and have complex social structures. They all echolocate and must therefore process very complex auditory information in their relatively enormous brains. Adult sperm whales like the one that sank the *Essex* possess the largest brains in the history of life on earth. Fortunately for them, sperm whales are a pelagic lot, rarely venturing near land or into shallow water where they might encounter nets and traps. Even so, Newfoundland fishermen have been known to catch a sperm whale upon occasion. Even the largest brain in the world doesn't always prevent collision.

Of the baleen whales, humpbacks do occasionally need to outsmart their prey, which are mostly small fish. They sometimes feed in cooperating groups, lunging in formation from below through glittering schools. Their open maws burst through the surface in a carefully timed and oft-repeated ballet as their pleated throats balloon out with fish and seawater. Humpbacks will also blow bubbles in a slowly rising spiral around a school of fish, forming a barrier that corrals and confuses their prey until they can charge up through the bubble net and scoop them up.

And if you're looking for complex social interactions, perhaps the mating songs of male humpbacks are an indication of intelligence. Why they sing—whether to attract females or to challenge other males—is a matter of debate, but the songs that male humpbacks sing in their warm-water mating grounds are intricate, constantly evolving, and by some human definitions, musical. The males pass the songs from one whale to another, even between different breeding grounds, until all the whales in the same ocean basin are singing some version of the same song.

Humpbacks may get themselves into trouble by simply being curious. Is curiosity a sign of intelligence? Who can say? Either way, however, humpbacks are nothing if not curious. They are well-known and loved for their tendency to approach whale-watching boats when they have nothing better to do. Once, in a boat on the Atlantic, I came upon a juvenile who was so curious about the strange object in its midst that it spy-hopped several times, poking its head high up out of the water to steal a glimpse of the deck of the ship. I have heard many accounts of humpbacks circling and eyeing strange objects in the water such as buoys, divers, and research equipment. They may be just as curious about a gill net or a lobster buoy, occasionally catching a knobby flipper or a fluke on a vertical line, though this would not explain why so many are caught by the mouth. In the 1980s and 1990s, Jon Lien tested noisemakers designed to scare whales away from nets, but rather than shying away, many humpbacks came over to investigate the source of the obnoxious beep.

Eighty-eight percent of all humpbacks carry scars from tangling with fishing gear. So, whatever the cause, the North Atlantic's humpbacks apparently collide with fishing gear quite often. Does this higher rate of scarring mean that humpbacks are less intelligent, less lucky, or curious to a fault? Perhaps. But it could also mean humpbacks are very good at getting themselves out of fishing gear.

Very little is known about how whales react when they are entangled, because few people have ever seen it happen, but those who work with humpbacks call them "wimps." They have little tolerance for pain and tire easily, so after an initial panic (which may last hours or even days) they typically lapse into morose docility.

"They get that sad-sack look," says Stormy Mayo, "like the picture of John Walker Lindh being captured in Afghanistan."

Once a humpback is morose and docile, it is usually fairly easy to disentangle—if you can find it.

*   *   *

I'm told that minkes, slender whales that rarely reach lengths over twenty-eight feet, are also "wimpy" whales. They are the most common baleen whale in the world and the main target of Japanese "scientific" whaling, which kills a few hundred every year. Because they are so common, quietly haunting the coastal waters of the eastern seaboard, they often become entangled in fishing gear, and because they are small, scientists believe collision with fishing gear kills them outright more often than humpbacks and right whales.

Though minkes often pursue the same prey as humpbacks, as far as anyone knows they do not employ the clever tactics that humpbacks have developed. They are unobtrusive loners with little interest in boats. And they are not much to look at from a whale-watch boat, offering only a fleeting glimpse of a curved fin, no flukes, no spy-hopping, and hardly ever a breach. This might place minke whales a notch below the humpbacks on our (albeit arbitrary) intelligence scale.

Scott Kraus of the New England Aquarium once "disentangled" a minke with a small loop of net draped over the end of its pointy rostrum. The animal, apparently unable to decide what to do, had simply stopped and floated quietly at the surface. In describing to me how he performed the disentanglement, Scott mimed with his thumb and forefinger daintily lifting the loop of net off the nose of the whale.

This whale was lucky. If a minke becomes tangled far below the surface, it may not have the strength to haul the gear up to take a breath. In this case, it may panic. Several people have told me that entangled minkes tend to roll over and over, wrapping themselves up further in the gear, sometimes picking up more lines, until they are anchored and hopelessly snarled. If they are lucky enough to reach the surface, and if a rescuer reaches them before they drown of exhaustion—two big ifs— then they can be pretty easy to work with owing to their relatively small size. To untangle a minke's tail, Jon Lien typically hauls the tail in question onto the Zodiac, where it flaps fecklessly in the air.

Most entangled minkes that are reported are dead. But how many minkes become entangled is completely unknown because few are reported, especially since entanglement has lead to stricter regulations for fisheries. Several fishermen, especially on the coast of Maine, have told me in private that on the rare occasion that fishermen find a whale in their gear, they quietly handle the situation themselves (these are likely to be minkes because larger whales usually carry the gear off). When the whale is dead, they simply cut it loose and go on their way. When the whale is alive, many say they have simply done their best to set the whale free. This action is technically against federal law in the United States, and some whale rescuers insist that fishermen botch the job, leaving the most dangerous loops and wraps on the whale when they cut it loose.

*   *   *

Then we come to the other baleen whale we are concerned with here, the right whale. Right whales are near and dear to Roger Payne's heart, and he believes them to be quite clever and, at least to each other, quite gentle. But if you buy Bob Kenney's argument that predators of large and wily prey are more intelligent, then right whales are probably not all that clever. Outsmarting a copepod does not require much brain power, though finding a large concentration of copepods may be a bit more challenging. Right whales are grazers, and their particular form of grazing requires an enormous amount of brute strength and stamina. If you make a cup with your hand and sweep it through a tub of water, the water presents significant resistance to your hand. A right whale needs to overcome this resistance as it feeds, but its "cup," or mouth, is the size of a car, and the whale may push it through the water for hours on end. This kind of brute strength and stamina come in handy in other ways too.

Like most large whales, right whales avoid predators primarily by being big. Add to that the enormous brawn of a right whale, and you have a pretty good defense mechanism without needing to invest a lot of brain power. The predators that do threaten right whales—sharks and killer whales—target mostly the calves and the subadults. Mothers and juveniles fight back with incredible feats of might and precision. Roger Payne writes:

> A friend of mine once saw a large adult male killer whale about thirty feet long attacking a subadult right whale in shallow water.

The subadult was lying at the surface in a submissive posture, its body motionless. The killer whale swam over its flipper, whereupon with a single stroke of that flipper the subadult lofted the male cleanly into the air. The entire body, even though it was being pushed broadside through the water, cleared the surface. If this was the blow from a subadult right whale using the flat of its flipper, imagine what the blow from an adult using a lateral slash from its tail might do. (106)

Though right whales' feeding behavior might tend to get them into trouble, their enormous strength and their pugnaciousness help them survive their initial encounters with fishing gear. They are often (though not always) able to simply carry the gear away. This is a great advantage if you are concerned with your next breath, but imagine the force required to part a three-quarter-inch three-stranded nylon rope. Once the animal has wrenched itself loose, it may have pulled loops of line dangerously tight around its rostrum, flipper, tail, or body. And finally, in the rare case when an entangled right whale is found and reported, they are extremely difficult, even dangerous, to disentangle. As a result, the record for disentangling right whales is dismal.

It seems that no matter which of the baleen whales we're concerned with—the pugnacious right whale, the curious humpback, or the wimpy minke—we may never know how intelligent they are, and we cannot rely on their help in our efforts to help them.

Falling into romantic notions about whales is dangerous for the whales and for the people who would help them, even if those romantic notions were the basis for whale protection in the first place. We will not be able to do the Vulcan mind-meld with a humpback (as Mr. Spock did in the 1986 movie *Star Trek: The Voyage Home*) and tell it to open wide so we can please remove the gill net from its mouth like a stray piece of dental floss. So if the whales won't cooperate, no wonder disentangling them is so rarely successful.

*   *   *

One more question about the minds of whales has haunted me since I first endeavored to learn about whale entanglement: How much should we worry about their pain and suffering? I was appalled the first time I

Figure 6.1. Humpback whale with severe tail entanglement. The flukes are twisted, indicating that the animal may have dislocated its spine near the tail during its initial struggle to shake the gear. The rope has cut deeply into the leading edge of the left fluke. This animal was successfully disentangled but was unlikely to recover from these wounds. Photo courtesy of the Center for Coastal Studies and taken under the authority of Scientific Research and Enhancement Permit No. 932–1489–04/PRT009526, issued by the National Marine Fisheries Service and U.S. Fish and Wildlife Service.

heard the bellows of an entangled whale, not only because the whale is monstrous and panicked and unpredictable. Those bellows are also an expression of terror and pain, unmistakable and haunting. I may not have had a yardstick for measuring a whale's intelligence, but I am equipped with mammalian instincts that told me the creature was in agony.

I have combed through hundreds of ghastly images and videos of entangled whales that were maimed and sickened, and I could not help being affected. Oozing wounds infested with sea lice, where rope had sawed through skin, blubber, and into bone, causing a gangrenous infection in a living leviathan. A dead baby right whale on a beach with gashes sliced into its flanks when a ship ran it down. A doomed and emaciated humpback with a dislocated tail and deep gashes carved into its flesh, waving its flukes gingerly, listlessly. Whether whales are intelligent or not, I cannot deny that they suffer when they are entangled, and instinctively, I do not want them to suffer needlessly.

Here I should admit to a modicum of hypocrisy; as a fisherman and a scientist, I have injured and killed more than my share of animals. I eat meat, fish, and fowl, generally without giving it a second thought. And though I say I respect all life, the fact that whales are mammals—not qualitatively very different from my cat, for instance—weighs in their favor. As pragmatic and evenhanded as I like to believe I am, I must admit that I care more for the suffering and dying of an individual whale than I do for, say, an individual fish.

"What, in your instinctive assessment, would constitute needless suffering?" you might ask. That's a good question, and I can only say that it's like pornography: I know it when I see it. That's not useful if we're trying to agree on what is best for both whales and fishermen, but often it is just this kind of inexpressible emotion that drives public policy debates, especially those concerning "charismatic megafauna" such as whales. Yet in the halls of justice or the boardrooms at the NMFS offices or in meetings with fishermen, the suffering of the whales almost never comes up. Instead, our concern for the whale's suffering is a personal thing: we wince looking at a grisly photo or read with grim fascination a newspaper article about an entangled whale.

In sorting through endless hours of interview tapes and reams of notes, I have come to understand that the suffering of the whale flows as an undercurrent beneath every dialogue about entangled whales. Even those with a strong stomach and the analytical view of a scientist, or those accustomed to death, those who kill for a living like fishermen, are not immune—even if they try to deny it.

I asked people who deal most closely with the pain and terror of the whales—whale rescuers—whether the suffering of the whales bothers them. Nearly every one said that it didn't. But the way they spoke about their work betrayed a concern for the suffering of the animals that they did not admit, even to themselves.

Jon Lien shrugged and said, a little gruffly, "It doesn't bother me at all."

But remember, in recounting the story of the whale with the line embedded in its blowhole, Jon flinched just thinking about the pain.

"God! That musta hurt something awful," he said.

Among the whale rescuers, Stormy Mayo, the dahlia-growing philosopher, was among the few who would unabashedly admit to being moved by a whale's pain. Remember his words about Ibis?

"I reached into that wound, which must have been six inches deep, ostensibly to feel how deep her blubber was. It was an open wound. And the seminal moment was when I reached in, and she started bleeding. You know, it was almost a bonding experience. Suddenly, just the blood said, 'I'm a feeling, sensitive creature.' I will never forget that moment when that blood came out. I'd obviously, probably hurt her. . . . Wow."

Bob Bowman, the Maine disentanglement coordinator for CCS, once told me, "I see the whales as statistics. I'm in it for the fishermen."

But in almost the same breath he said, with ill-concealed regret, "I killed a whale once." A minke whale had gotten into a herring weir on Grand Manan, a Canadian island off the down east coast of Maine. "We killed it because we didn't get it out correctly."

As they tried to free the whale, loops of net draped over its back, and it wouldn't surface. The minke stayed submerged until it suffocated. In recounting this story, Bob knitted his brow and looked out his kitchen window as if he could see the incident played out on his front lawn.

Bob went on to say, "I think if one guy, one fisherman catches a minke whale"—remember that many, if not most, entangled minkes are found dead—"they feel horrible. Horrible! It sticks with people. They don't forget it."

And I hear similar sentiments from fishermen themselves. Several fishermen have told me privately that they have disentangled whales, even though it is illegal to do so. They tell me they want to help the whale get out of its jam but also to avoid the regulations they believe will result if they report the tangled whale to authorities. So they "take care of it" themselves.

"I don't like to see the old fella sufferin,'" Newfoundland fishermen often tell Wayne Ledwell, Jon Lien's successor.

So everyone seems to be concerned for the suffering of whales, whether they will admit it or not, but why is that relevant to the debate over how and whether to protect them? Because different people have different values about whales, different kinds and degrees of sympathy, and they bring these to the table when they talk about whales and fishing gear.

Part of my research for this book was a survey that asked 186 people involved with whale or fishing issues about their values and attitudes toward whales, fishermen, and fisheries. The sample included fishermen, environmentalists, animal rights activists, government officials, many members of the Atlantic Large Whale Take Reduction Team, as well as members of the general public. Lots of subtle and interesting things emerged from the responses to the survey that speak to important differences of sentiment and values.

One question asked, "When making regulations to protect whales from entanglement, federal officials should consider:" In answering this question, most respondents—three-quarters of the fishermen included—agreed that saving an endangered species should be the first or second priority for federal officials. And not surprisingly, animal rights activists typically placed "minimizing the whales' suffering" as the number one or number two priority.

But the respondents disagreed on what came next. More than half of the commercial fishermen believed that impacts on fishing communities were at least as important as the suffering of whales. Note that fishermen placed a high priority on *communities,* not on maximizing fishing opportunities per se. By contrast, environmentalists and animal rights activists often placed the well-being of the whale above the well-being of fishing communities. What's more, many animal rights activists believed that when a disentanglement team is working to remove fishing gear from a whale, preventing the whale's death and relieving the whale's suffering should be their *top* priority, *even above the safety of the disentanglement team.*

Of course we all knew that animal rights activists and fishermen usually do not see eye to eye. But the survey gives us some insight into why and how they disagree: they have something very important in common. They both have deeply held convictions that guide their actions and their decisions.

Many animal rights activists believe so strongly in protecting the welfare of whales that they will place themselves between a whale and a harpoon. They intend to protect whales at all cost. And they believe, rightly, that whales are in trouble.

By the same token, fishermen are often deeply committed to their communities, many of which have relied on fishing for centuries. And they believe, rightly, that their communities are in trouble. Each group reckons it is under attack from the other—and to some degree they are. The whale-huggers versus the fish-killers.

It's hard to imagine that the two sides could find some common ground, but there are inklings of hope. For instance, the vast majority of fishermen who responded to the survey believe that endangering whale species was not an acceptable consequence of fishing. For their part, a majority of environmentalists and animal rights activists believe that the fishing industry is an important part of their nation's culture and economy.

Even now, there are a few people willing to walk across the lines of battle.

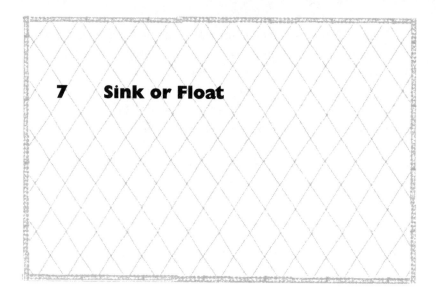

7 Sink or Float

Fishing Gear for the Future

Remember: one dead right whale could shut down the whole fishery.
Scott Kraus, whale biologist for the New England Aquarium,
speaking at the Maine Fishermen's Forum, February 2002

Whales and fish make for strange bedfellows. If you don't believe this, attend any event that draws together people with some interest in the problem of whale entanglement and see for yourself. The annual meeting of the North Atlantic Right Whale Consortium is one such forum.

According to its mission statement, the North Atlantic Right Whale Consortium is a "group of researchers, conservationists, representatives from the shipping and fishing industries, technical experts, representatives of U.S. and Canadian government agencies, and state and provincial authorities dedicated to the conservation and recovery of the North Atlantic right whale, the rarest large whale in the world." In other words, the consortium is a group of people with a common interest in the fate of the right whale, but with very different reasons for their interest. This variegated group keeps in touch mainly through photocopied newsletters and e-mail, but once a year they meet to share information about right whales gathered in the previous year.

In October 2002, some 166 of these folks attend the annual meeting of the Right Whale Consortium—that's approximately one attendee for every two right whales in the North Atlantic. The setting for this meeting is, with intended irony, the New Bedford Whaling Museum.

Over the great hall of the museum hang two whale skeletons, one a humpback and the other a mammoth blue whale with great curving jaw bones. Because even the bones of whales are soaked with fat, the skeletons exude a faint but discernable scent that is familiar to anyone who has been within a mile of a dead beached whale—rancid whale oil. The odor adds to the historical ambiance of the museum—the whalers lived with it day and night during their multiyear voyages. Under the skeletons on this fall day, the gathered crowd gobbles catered sandwiches and sips coffee from paper cups. And the air about them is redolent with more than whale oil.

I attend several similar events each year in my work in academia, writing and map making. Typically, the mood of such a crowd is almost festive. A conference or large meeting is usually a little vacation—a guilt-free, sanctioned, and often paid-for time away from work and family in which to reunite with friends and colleagues. The mood at the 2002 Right Whale Consortium meeting is hardly festive, however, and the reason is plain. The scientists and regulators who have spent the year chasing the world's most endangered large whale have mostly bad news to report, in spite of the positive spin the feds try to put on the situation.

Though some people attending the meeting have made important strides in preventing ship strikes, and the calving season produced a promising number of calves, the news on right whale entanglements is nothing short of grim. So far in 2002, at least eight right whales have been reported entangled in rope and fishing net off the Atlantic coast. While rescue teams spent the season attempting to relocate and disentangle the endangered animals, they succeeded in clearing the gear from just one—and this young whale later washed up on a Nantucket beach dead of its injuries. Another entangled right whale shed its wraps of net and rope, apparently without help, but six remain with potentially lethal entanglements. Clearly, the federal plan to protect right whales from entanglement in fishing gear is not working.

Everyone attending the meeting knows about the studies by the New England Aquarium: the entangled right whales that are reported account for only a small percentage of all those that collide with fishing gear. If the aquarium's estimates are accurate, then between 10 and 20 percent of the right whale population—between thirty and sixty whales—collided with fishing gear in 2002. This is bad news for nearly everyone attending the meeting. Fishermen worry about new regulations; conservationists fear for the future of the species; scientists scratch their heads wondering what they can recommend to protect the animals; and the regulators are getting ulcers under the watchful eyes of agitated fishermen, litigious environmental groups, and appearance-conscious congressmen. The only people at the conference who take heart are those intrepid folks hoping to sell the government on their patented new "whale-safe" fishing gear.

Under the skeletons, people mill from table to table. Some smile, shake hands, or hug someone they haven't seen since last year. But many engage in a vigorous, urgent sort of networking. A few pull reports and proposals from briefcases and push them at someone across the table. Groups huddle together listening to someone speaking and gesticulating earnestly. Three heads lean over a laptop computer looking at graphs. A man waves a lobster buoy attached to a piece of rope by a specially designed weak-link. Once in a while I see someone rise and take a circuitous path from his or her table to the coffee urn, apparently avoiding someone in the crowd. Tension mingles with the smell of dead whales.

At my table, Scott Kraus, the director of the New England Aquarium's research team and a leading right whale expert, plots with Sean Todd, professor of marine mammal studies at College of the Atlantic in Maine. Sean got his Ph.D. at Memorial University in St. John's, Newfoundland. During Sean's tenure in Jon Lien's lab, graduate students were required to help with whale rescue. Drawing on that experience, Sean has been consulting with the state of Maine, training fishermen to disentangle minke whales. Scott Kraus has asked Sean to chair an open forum to brainstorm ideas for solving the entanglement problem.

"Eleven right whale deaths this year," Scott says, hunching his tall frame over the table. He nods and waves his hands to emphasize the point.

Scott explains that if you count the four known deaths—one from entanglement, one from a ship strike, and three from unknown causes—plus the six entangled whales that the CCS team couldn't get free and were likely to die, you have eleven deaths in the population of about three hundred just this year—at least eight caused by humans. I jot a quick math problem on my notepad and find that this makes for a death rate of 3.7 percent this year—and that's just the dead whales we know about.

Scott usually has a wry, easy manner, but now his voice betrays a sharp edge of frustration. He speaks too long, and his deep voice booms, drawing attention from the half dozen of us sitting at the round table.

The numbers he is worrying over are indeed reason for concern. The federal government, based on the "best available science," has decreed that the PBR, or potential biological removal, for the right whale is zero. In other words, even one right whale dead of human causes is more than the species can bear. Moreover, with a PBR of zero, killing any right whales, by mistake or on purpose, violates the U.S. Marine Mammal Protection Act, the Endangered Species Act, and possibly one or two international treaties.

"We gotta start thinking out of the box," Scott says. Amy Knowlton, one of the New England Aquarium scientists, sits down at the table. She offers Sean a list she hopes will serve as a starting point for discussion at the brainstorming session the following morning. Amy is one of the chairs of a committee charged with addressing the problem of ship strikes, or ships colliding with and killing whales. The ship strike committee has accomplished a lot under her direction in the past couple of years, and she hopes that a little leadership and organization would move the entanglement issue ahead. Clearly Amy and Scott have desperate hopes for the forum.

Sean suggests that Scott might be a more apt moderator.

"I'm not in a position right now to be an unbiased participant," Scott replies, waving a hand and slouching over the table further. "I'm . . . I'm just too close to it."

* * *

After lunch, the crowd piles into the auditorium of the museum where scientists and government officials make short presentations, with graphs and bulleted lists projected on a huge screen.

Dave Morin, a member of the Center for Coastal Studies' disentanglement team, briefly tells the story of each of the eight right whales the team has tried to rescue in 2002. His tone is that of a doctor telling a patient the prognosis is bleak.

"Overall this year has been pretty dismal," Dave tells the group. "We're not too optimistic on the outcome on most of these cases, unless someone does something soon. And as you know, we're probably not going to sight some of these animals over the next couple months. So it's definitely been a dismal year.

"Our big message is that disentanglement is not a solution to the entanglement problem. We're still looking for good ways to disentangle right whales. We're not that great at it."

Population experts, including Hal Caswell from Woods Hole Oceanographic Institution and Richard Pace from the Northeast Fisheries Science Center, show graphs of population and survivorship with jagged lines tending unmistakably (and statistically) downward.

Next, Scott Kraus reviews his recent survey of entanglement mortality in the right whale population. He has gathered data from the federal government, from Amy Knowlton's work on the photos in the catalog, and from the records of the CCS whale rescue team.

"This is the bad news," he says, showing a graph with two jagged lines trending upward. Scott has analyzed the photos in the catalog using two different statistical tools, and the two lines represent the results of each analysis. "Both the entanglements versus identification and the entanglement scarring rate versus appropriately photographed animals showed significant increases in entanglement. So whatever is happening out there, it's happening with increasing frequency and doesn't bode well for the future."

Scott pauses, leans his tall frame pointedly on the podium, and speaks more slowly.

"Now, this is the part where, even though I took the data from everyone else and they can all take credit for that . . . I have to take responsibility for this. My general feeling is that we had a lot of management efforts this year. And the National Marine Fisheries Service rightfully took a lot of responsibility for trying to deal with this problem, including SAMs, DAMs, breakaways, weak-links." (SAM and DAM are acronyms for different types of fisheries closures under the federal Whale Take Reduction Plan: Seasonal Area Management and Dynamic Area Management.)

"A lot of things went on," Scott continued. "In spite of that, we had the *worst year of entanglement we've ever had in the twenty-two years we've been studying right whales.* The sum total of deaths in right whales this year is probably going to be eleven animals. That would be considered in other years a biological catastrophe for this population, and it certainly matches the curves that you see from Hal Caswell and Richard Pace showing declines in recent years."

*   *   *

Later that day, John Higgins stands at the front of the auditorium and addresses the audience as though a drill sergeant has just ordered him to stand and deliver. Having stepped away from the microphone, he stands at ease, hands behind his back, and shouts with a marching cadence. About his feet lay samples of fishing gear he has brought for demonstration.

"The National Marine Fisheries Service . . . Protected Resource Division . . . continues in their efforts . . . to reduce the threat . . . of serious injury and death . . . to our Atlantic . . . Large . . . Whales!"

A gear expert for the Fisheries Service, John Higgins's job is to come up with and test fishing gear that entangles fewer whales or helps the whales get out of the gear unharmed. He is a big man. In his denim shirt, black jeans, and leather boots, John looks like he would be more at home standing around a bait barrel on a Maine fish pier. John's stand-and-deliver manner seems incongruous in this group of mostly academics, a couple of dozen government regulators, a few conservationists, and a handful of fishermen. Most everyone in this crowd tends to hedge and equivocate when talking about right whales—but not John Higgins. He speaks with the certainty of a soldier marching to war.

"I've brought along with me today a sample of some of the gear modifications that are used in the commercial fishing industry, directed to the strategies recommended by the Atlantic Large Whale Take Reduction Team. Those strategies are": (he holds up one thick finger) "reduce the vertical lines in the water column. Number two" (another finger) "provide a weak-link in the surface section of the water column, and third, provide a weak-link in the bottom section of the water column."

These three recommendations refer primarily to the buoy lines that mark traps and gill nets—two types of fixed fishing gear. The idea is to minimize the number of buoy lines in the way of the whales. The fisheries regulators can do this by requiring long strings of traps or nets that are marked on both ends, rather than marking each trap with a single buoy, or they can simply reduce the amount of fishing gear allowed in the water. Where fishermen have to have buoy lines, the regulators can require them to place weak-links at the surface near the buoy and at the bottom near the trap or net. Lines connecting traps or nets on the bottom can also float up into the water column.

It was odd to hear John list these recommendations in this way. The Take Reduction Team, composed of scientists, fishermen, environmentalists, and government regulators, rarely agrees to anything. Most of the "recommendations" that NMFS attributes to the team are actually produced by coaxing the surly group to offer some bit of guidance in the last hour of a two-day meeting or by combing the meeting minutes for some nugget of consensus after the dust settles. Hard science and certainty are rarely part of the mix. But the way John lays them out, the recommendations seem like firm and certain courses of action chosen by a group of informed and judicious people.

I don't believe John intends to deceive anyone at the meeting into believing that broad consensus exists on the Take Reduction Team. That would be particularly difficult, since most of the members of the team are in the audience. John is simply doing his job: he was charged with making the plan work with weak-links and specialized rope, and this collection of gear is what he and his colleagues are testing.

John bends down and picks up two pieces of rope; one has a bullet-shaped lobster buoy attached. "I'll start by talking about the lines used in the fixed-gear fisheries," he says. "Lines can be characterized under two categories: groundlines and buoy lines."

Groundlines connect strings of traps. Lobster fishermen usually use floating line—as opposed to sinking line—to connect their traps because it floats free of the bottom and won't chafe or become tangled on rocks.

John holds up the two kinds of line in turn. "Groundline and buoy line," he says, then tosses the buoy line aside.

Figure 7.1. Single-pot gear with right whale. Single lobster traps (left) and crab traps (right) are marked by individual buoys. Drawing by T. Johnson.

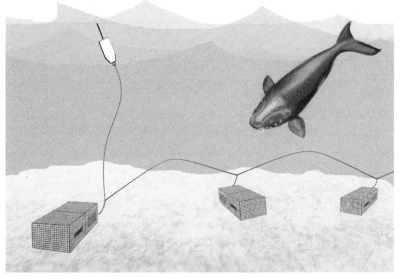

Figure 7.2. Lobster trawl using floating ground line, with right whale above. Underwater video footage has documented buoyant loops of ground line rising an average of sixteen feet into the water column between traps. Drawing by T. Johnson.

"Floating groundline can create an entanglement threat," John says unequivocally. "Floating groundline can create buoyant arcs, floating up." He lifts the loop of line above his head and declares: "Vertical lines in the water column!"

"Neutrally buoyant line—which this is an example of—neutrally buoyant line sinks." He drops the line to demonstrate how neutrally buoyant line sinks. This elicits a few chuckles from the crowd.

"Big deal, traditional sinking line sinks! What's the big deal about neutrally buoyant line?" John asks rhetorically. "Neutrally buoyant line sinks *soft*. Traditional sink line sinks *hard;* it abrades, chafes, with the possibility of loss of gear, which nobody wants. Whales can get entangled in lost gear just as easy as they can in gear that gets hauled regularly, maybe easier. So traditional sink line chafes, abrades, parts. That's why fishermen use floating line. Neutrally buoyant line sinks *gentle, soft*.

"The National Marine Fisheries Service has over sixty-five miles of neutrally buoyant line now in the commercial fishing industry. When we started this project a couple years ago, there wasn't a single manufacturer of neutrally buoyant line. There're now nine manufacturers of neutrally buoyant line competitively making this product."

Many scientists in the audience believe neutrally buoyant or sinking line, which does not loop up into the water column, offers the best hope for preventing entanglement. Now the trick is to sell the idea to fishermen. Many lobstermen in Maine—a vocal and politically organized force—are skeptical that the new groundline will work in Maine because of the rocky bottom along their coast.

The fact that nine manufacturers are producing neutrally buoyant line is good news. In later field tests, however, neutrally buoyant line is found to move around and therefore chafe more than sinking line, which lies more firmly against the bottom. So the promise of neutrally buoyant line may fade.

Next John moves on to demonstrate weak-links. He holds up a buoy attached to a line with a weak-link, a gray plastic figure eight.

"Weak-links at the surface are intended to allow the buoy to break free—to break the buoy free from the buoy line—once the load on the line exceeds the compromise strength of that weak-link." With a flourish, John gives the rope a yank and pulls the buoy off the line; the weak-link has been cut in advance.

He goes on: "The traditional swivel typically has a strength of some-wheres around fifteen, sixteen hundred pounds. A weak-link, this weak-link, has six hundred. It's designed so that when line gets caught in the whale's mouth, as we know sometimes it does, and the whale's swim-ming along, once that load is put onto the line it breaks off. These weak-links go for about a buck-fifty at any commercial fishery supply store. Another type of weak-link that a commercial fisherman can rig up if he doesn't want to spend the buck-fifty and he doesn't particularly want a swivel, you can simply take the buoy line, crimp it back to itself with up to seven three-quarter-inch hog rings, like a stainless steel staple."

Weak-links seem sensible enough, and the way John presents the con-cept, most anyone would be convinced. In fact, no one knows whether weak-links help whales free themselves of gear or whether they help the whales carry off gear that will eventually kill them. Weak-links are in the federal plan because they are cheap and easy for fishermen to use, and from the federal court's perspective, it seems like a good idea. The plan that requires the weak-links was devised and implemented after environ-mental groups sued the Fisheries Service because they were not protect-ing whales from entanglement, so looking good for the courts is impor-tant to NMFS.

Finally, John goes on to outline the federal regulations on fishing gear that are to take effect in the coming months.

"Starting January 1, 2003, it will be required in the commercial fish-ing industry in the lobster and the sink gill-net fishery to have a weak-link at the surface, *or* no floating line in the buoy line, *or* no floating line in the ground line. That will be in all state waters virtually from Rhode Island, Mass., New Hampshire, to Maine."

After his talk, John has time for a few questions.

"It sounds like the breakaway would reduce entanglements," one man says, when in fact for weak-links to work, the animal has to be tangled in the gear.

"I would say that they reduce serious entanglements," John nods.

"How do you know?" the man asks.

"I would say that that's what we're shooting for. Once it's entangled, this reduces more serious entanglements. It reduces serious threat."

This federal plan as it stands in 2002 relies on weak-links as the pri-mary gear modification to protect large whales. This choice has enraged many people close to the issue because they believe that floating groundline poses a greater threat than buoy lines. Requiring sinking or neutrally buoyant groundline is sure to save whales, they say, while weak-links are still an unknown.

Another man asks if John has received any complaints about the new gear regulations coming in January.

"I get complaints all the time," he replies. "If I couldn't handle that I wouldn't be good at this job."

*　　*　　*

In all fairness, I should point out that some other Take Reduction Teams convened by NMFS have been somewhat less controversial and more productive than the Atlantic Large Whale TRT. Most of these other TRTs, however, dealt with threats that were less grave and left some wiggle room for enforcement. And often real solutions were at hand, needing only to be implemented. A case in point is the Harbor Porpoise Take Reduction Team.

A great many of the smallest whales—dolphins and porpoises—have perished in fishing gear. But it also turns out that these quick, agile, and apparently quite perceptive animals are pretty easy to warn away from nets.

Beginning in the 1960s, gill nets became the preferred method for catching groundfish in the Bay of Fundy and the Gulf of Maine. Unfortunately, monofilament gill nets are also very good at catching harbor porpoises. The fine nylon netting is difficult to detect, even with a porpoise's echolocation; as the number of gill nets rose, harbor porpoises were drowning in nets in increasing numbers.

A harbor porpoise is essentially a toothed whale small enough to carry in your arms. They aren't particularly gregarious, friendly, or exciting to watch; they don't even make a visible spout when they rise to the surface for air, and their dark gray backs blend in with the steely-colored surface, so it can be tough to catch a glimpse of them. No one really paid attention to the problem of harbor porpoise by-catch until it became an extreme annoyance to fishermen, and scientists discovered the porpoise population was in a nosedive. Environmental groups proposed the harbor porpoise for listing under the Endangered Species Act in the early 1990s.

Under the Marine Mammal Protection Act reauthorized in 1994, the U.S. federal government convened a Take Reduction Team very much like the one convened for large whales, to address the harbor porpoise problem. The scientists, fishermen, and conservationists on the team recommended that the National Marine Fisheries Service close certain areas to fishing when the porpoises were typically most concentrated and require pingers (little noisemakers) on nets to warn away the porpoises. The Fisheries Service implemented the plan, and new regulations after the collapse of the groundfish stocks drastically reduced the number of nets in the water. The by-catch of harbor porpoises dropped dramatically.

Scott Kraus's experiments on pingers in New England suggested that they reduced the average harbor porpoise by-catch per net by as much as 90 percent. Apparently their excellent hearing and their agility allowed the harbor porpoises to avoid the source of the annoying sound. Though some porpoises still drown in gill nets and the population is still in some danger, most are able to avoid the net. The Gulf of Maine/Bay of Fundy harbor porpoise was removed from the list of candidates for protected status under the U.S. Endangered Species Act in September 2001.

If only it were that simple to significantly reduce the number of large whales entangled in fishing gear. Large baleen whales do not have such acute hearing, and they can't maneuver as well as their smaller toothed cousins. And some scientists argue that baleen whales are simply less intelligent.

*   *   *

In the late 1980s and early 1990s, Jon Lien and his graduate students had begun to test pingers to see if they could be used to warn away humpback whales from cod traps and gill nets. Their first experiment involved placing the noisemaker in the water where humpbacks were feeding, then observing the whales' reactions to the noise. Unfortunately, many of them, rather than avoiding the area, swam over to investigate. Humpbacks are nothing if not curious.

Next, Jon wanted to see if the nosy whales could be deterred by some negative stimulus—in other words, if humpbacks could be trained. He and his students drove around with the noisemaker in a boat, and whenever a whale came around to check out the source of the noise, the researchers used a crossbow to shoot it with a special arrow with a hollow point. This biopsy dart is usually used to collect small plugs of whale skin for analysis, and Jon and his students knew from experience that the whales didn't like the dart. The results of the training experiment were inconclusive; some whales avoided the noise after the dart treatment and others seemed to forget about the dart. Undaunted, Jon tweaked the design of his homemade pingers made of PVC pipe and Radio Shack electronics and began handing them out to gill-netters and cod trap fishermen in Newfoundland. And they seemed to help, cutting the number of entrapments and entanglements by about half, not quite as dramatic as the results for harbor porpoise, but not bad. Fishermen requested more pingers. Apparently at least some humpbacks could be taught.

In 1992, however, Jon's pinger experiment was cut short by the cod moratorium. Only a handful of sentinel fishery traps and nets carried pingers in the following few years. Surprisingly, as gill-netting slowly began again in the late 1990s, pingers were out of vogue. The Gulf of Maine and Bay of Fundy gill-netters in Canada and the United States used pingers, and still do, because they are required under the porpoise Take Reduction Plan. But Newfoundland gill-netters are not required to use pingers, nor are lobster or crab fishermen anywhere.

The idea of using pingers to deter large whales has been raised more than once at the Atlantic Large Whale Take Reduction Team meetings, but it has never gained much support. One important reason is that it is tough to make pingers work in a pot fishery. Imagine the cacophony a million pingers would produce if they were deployed on every buoy! It would probably drive all of the whales out of the North Atlantic forever.

*   *   *

On the second day of the Right Whale Consortium meeting, Sean Todd chairs the much-anticipated brainstorming session. The discussion raises very few new ideas and is surprisingly polite. Several people who in private interviews have consumed hours of my microcassette tape ranting about the failure of the Take Reduction Plan only hint at their criticisms in the forum. Some who have engaged in heated politicking in the lobby under the skeletons now speak their minds using pointed omission. So the trick to understanding much of the conversation is in reading between the lines. Without understanding the underlying agendas and intentions, many of the statements would seem like a series of bizarre non sequiturs.

As the discussion proceeds, a handful of federal officials sits in a cluster of seats on one side of the auditorium, taking vigorous notes. I wonder if they are reading between the lines too.

The group begins by posing several questions of principle.

"There's a dichotomy here: preventing entanglement versus preventing serious entanglement," Amy Knowlton, says, proffering a starting point.

In other words, which set of solutions should we focus on? Should we continue to rely on weak-links and disentanglement teams, which are meant to mitigate entanglements, not prevent them? Or should we focus our attention on preventative strategies like sinking groundline or fisheries closures, clearly not the solution that fishermen prefer?

Stormy Mayo raises his hand. "Whatever record finally goes out of this forum should include a statement," he says, "maybe in a preamble, that disentanglement is not the solution."

This is the primary message the CCS team intends to bring to the meeting. Decades of experience has led them to the conclusion that disentanglement is an expensive last resort that fails far more often than it succeeds, especially with those big ornery right whales. A few of the CCS whale rescue people want the feds to remove disentanglement from the Take Reduction Plan entirely, but arguing that case would put them in a very awkward position: for several years now, a large portion of the CCS budget, including a few full-time salaries, has come from the Fisheries Service for the disentanglement program. The CCS team would much rather spend the money and effort on work that would save more whales and get the fishermen out of hot water, but the feds are apparently bent on pouring money into disentanglement. Everybody can agree that saving entangled whales is a good thing, but it's much harder to get consensus on prevention measures.

"Is it the view of this group that gear modification is the only way to resolve this issue?" asks Phil Clapham, a NMFS scientist and one of the leading experts on right whales. Phil is in an awkward position too. As a NMFS employee, he is not in a position to take sides, but he needs the support of other scientists to argue for change within the agency.

Sean Todd asks Phil, "Does gear modification include the SAMs and the DAMs?"

"No," Phil responds flatly.

Phil Clapham and a colleague wrote the scientific paper that the NMFS regulators say they used as the basis for the wildly unpopular and ineffective Dynamic Area Management (DAM) plan. NMFS scientists ignored the most crucial parts of this paper—those that showed the plan could not work.

"How about instead of 'gear modification,' we say 'fishing practices'?" offers Sharon Young, a whale advocate for the Humane Society of the United States.

Sharon Young is a veteran marine mammal advocate who sits on several government advisory committees and Take Reduction Teams. Hairsplitting on questions of language is a very important part of HSUS's role in the process of protecting whales—lawsuits are the only power the whale advocates can wield when NMFS fails to comply with the law or enforce its own regulations. And often the outcome of a lawsuit hangs on subtle interpretations of language.

"I want to lower the standards a little bit," Scott Kraus puts in. "Over time, the rate of entanglement is about the same—60 percent—but now we're getting more mortality. I don't mind if they get entangled, but they need to get out."

In a practical sense, it seems like the main priority in the Take Reduction Plan should be to save whales' lives, as Scott proposes. But technically, under the U.S. Marine Mammal Protection Act, virtually any human interference with the right whale is considered a "take," even if the whale escapes with its life. For most other marine mammals, there is some wiggle room allowed under the law, permitting some "take" as long as it doesn't put the species as a whole in jeopardy.

For right whales, however, there is very little wiggle room left, either biologically or legally, because the species is in such grave peril. For instance, even if weak-links do help the animals escape tangling gear (which is very questionable), the whale must become entangled before they can work—thus constituting a take. So environmental groups could argue in court that if the plan places too much stock in reactive strategies, it is inherently illegal. What's more, no gear technology or rescue team could be 100 percent effective; even with the most effective reactive measures some whales would die. So practical or not, Scott's idea that the plan should focus on reactive strategies is legally and politically dangerous.

Bob Bowman, CCS's Maine disentanglement coordinator and a consummate devil's advocate, raises his hand and speaks from the back of the room. He wonders if the studies on entanglement scars are giving an accurate picture of the problem. "Scars are an indication only of the survivors," he says. "They don't count mortality rates and serious injuries."

Next the group focuses on fishing-gear technology. A guy with a patented "whale-safe" flexible weak-link stands up to tout his invention. He uses the term "whale-safe" several times in his pitch to the crowd. Nobody in the room—with the possible exception of the guy with the fancy new weak-link—believes for a moment that any fishing gear could be "whale-safe." "Whale-friendly" is the politically correct term most people have begun to use, even if it is only slightly less misleading.

"One question is which part of the gear is causing entanglement," says Dan McKiernan, a Massachusetts state fisheries manager. "We need to look at probability. We continue to see a lot of floating line with wraps around the rostrum." Dan tells the group about his studies that show that floating groundlines in lobster gear make loops up to sixteen feet above the bottom. "To me, this is an extra-risky piece of gear."

"You very rarely see a whale come ashore with gear," says whale veterinarian Michael Moore. "This suggests fishermen are cutting gear away [from dead whales]."

Someone suggests placing ID tags on trap and gill-net gear to help scientists identify which part of the gear is most likely to catch whales.

"You're not likely to get fishermen to go along with that," counters NMFS scientist Phil Clapham.

The line-marking idea has been raised countless times. Fishermen have mostly successfully fought any regulations that would require them to put identifying tags on their gear, not wanting any particular fishery to be implicated as the whale-killers. As for cutting away gear, many fishermen, especially in Maine, have told me that they do indeed cut gear away from whales, sometimes alive, sometimes dead.

The state of Maine has begun teaching fishermen the basics of disentangling minke whales and has provided some of them with the specialized tools for the job. The folks at Maine's Department of Marine Resources say, aptly, that if fishermen are going to disentangle whales, then they should be taught to do it right. Even so, some people at CCS and in the federal government worry that Maine's training is not rigorous enough and could endanger both whales and fishermen if they feel overly confident when they approach the animals. Many people in the room worry that if fishermen disentangle whales without the proper experience and training, they will leave gear on the whale that will later prove fatal. So this little secret of the fishing industry has caused quite a lot of debate.

Bonnie Spinazzola, the executive director of the Offshore Lobstermen's Association, stands up in the back of the auditorium. "I understand the problems with ID-ing gear or part of the gear," she says; fishermen do worry that it could lead to additional regulations. For any plan to be successful, "you need to support the industry."

"What we're looking at is lengths of rope that are cutting into whales lethally," Scott Kraus puts in, bringing the discussion back to the question of mortality. "Work on line itself has not really been done, and that's what's killing whales. We don't really know if weak-links work. I think there's a need for hypothetical testing for all models of gear modification."

Bruce Mate, a scientist from Oregon State University, brings up federal marine pollution laws that prohibit disposal of plastics in the water. "There's the question of positive control of the gear," he says. "How do we maintain positive control of the gear? The onus is on the fishermen."

Translation: the fishermen are litterbugs.

"I guess that's why fishermen cut gear off dead whales," someone puts in.

Bonnie Spinazzola, in representing offshore lobster fishermen, seems uncomfortable with the direction the discussion is taking. "We're looking at putting a person on sinking ground line," she says. "So if the fishermen are working on line and the scientists are working on line, doesn't it make sense that we should at some time start working together?"

Michael Moore, the vet, suggests that engineers from Woods Hole Oceanographic Institution could help with designing alternatives to floating groundlines.

"You could add conservationists to that," Sharon Young of the Humane Society puts in.

"Isn't that supposed to be what the Take Reduction Team does?" someone asks.

This falls flat. Getting multiple stakeholders together to solve the problem is exactly what the Take Reduction Team is supposed to do but clearly hasn't. A few people in the room have in the past gone so far as to recommend disbanding the team, believing that the team meetings actually feed conflicts between conservationists and fishermen rather than allowing them to work together. My own research on the matter corroborates this claim, showing the fishermen and whale advocates on the Take Reduction Team are far more polarized than their counterparts in the general public.

Dan McKiernan, the Massachusetts fisheries regulator, has recommended disbanding the team and starting over. He stands up at the back and tells the group that in 2003 and 2004, all of Cape Cod Bay will have sinking groundline as part of the settlement of a court case brought against the state of Massachusetts over right whale protection.

"And *certain states* north of Massachusetts will need to address this," he says.

Dan is saying that Massachusetts fishermen are making sacrifices for whale protection, while fishermen and regulators in other states—most notably Maine—have dragged their feet in addressing the problem presented by miles of floating groundline looping into the water column along the rocky shores of Maine.

"Previous recommendations by this group went over like a lead balloon with the fishermen in Maine," Bob Bowman says, "I think because they weren't involved."

Laura Ludwig, a former lobster fisherman and now the coordinator of Maine's Whale Take Reduction Program, responds in her characteristically upbeat way. "I think it's great to tap into the fishermen and what they have to offer. I do think there might be a lot of information that doesn't get to the table because of the threat of restrictions."

Many in the room believe that the Maine program is an elaborate stalling tactic funded by a big federal grant. Maine's plan has three primary components: teaching fishermen to disentangle minke whales; encouraging fishermen to report entangled whales; and posting on a web site a map showing where some whales have been reported in Maine waters. In other words, the plan is entirely reactive, including almost nothing meant to prevent entanglement and requiring no concessions of the Maine fishermen beyond a few gear changes required by the feds.

Someone proposes the idea of an ombudsman to link scientists with fishermen, an idea that actually gains some sway.

Bonnie Spinazzola raises her hand again. "I think you're assuming that fishermen and scientists can't sit down and talk. We want to solve this problem as much as you do. I believe that most of us think disentanglement is not a solution. We want to keep fishing and we want to sit down with scientists and entertain ideas. Now is the time to sit down and talk."

"There is no shortage of ideas, and there's lots of information that's not available," says Scott Kraus. "It seems to me that we've let down the fishing industry. We need a standing research committee. I think the fishermen are frustrated with this willy nilly regulation. I *really* think this is the way to go."

"I think that's a great idea," says Bob Bowman. "Fishermen interpret as retribution the regulations that are actually in place to protect them."

Michael Moore suggests an industry-science liaison.

"I agree with Bob on the need for real science to support these measures." Bonnie Spinazzola puts in. "That's the problem, we need to work together."

Sharon Young from the Humane Society generally agrees with the idea of such a committee but worries that it could turn into another incarnation of the Take Reduction Team.

"The Take Reduction Team mandate is to bring together stakeholders, but the process is bogged down by what can't happen," Sharon says. "What we need is an out-of-the-box group. We've done the stakeholder thing a lot."

Finally, Mary Colligan, one of the federal regulators who has been quietly listening and taking notes, raises her hand.

"The Take Reduction Team *is* our stakeholder group," Mary says. "And lately we've had some success, but we need other stakeholders." She speaks about bringing other trap fishermen onto the team who are targeting crab and slime eels.

I wrack my brain trying to think of what Mary means by "some success" in reference to the TRT. A separate committee charged with addressing the ship strike problem has indeed had some successes, but in the context of right whale entanglement, the subject of this discussion, success is hard to come by. The TRT has not met in a year and a half, and after the last meeting, several members of the team, mostly fishermen, vowed never to attend another. In terms of preventing entanglements, the numbers speak for themselves: eight reported entangled right whales, including one dead and six others likely to die, not to mention humpbacks, minkes, and sundry other whales.

As the discussion wraps up, Mary Colligan offers to convene a science/fisheries liaison group, and Amy Knowlton says she will assemble an e-mail list.

The group files out of the auditorium to mill and politic under the skeletons.

8 The Damn DAMs

A Box Big Enough for the Leviathan

For a successful technology, reality must take precedence
over public relations, for Nature cannot be fooled.
Richard P. Feynman, physicist

The Maine Fishermen's Forum is held in February each year on the weekend most likely to have rotten weather. In the lobby of the Samoset Resort in Rockland, the fishermen look a bit hemmed in and out of place. In between sessions, they mill on the carpet among booths where they examine the latest gear and stock up on freebies from vendors. They laugh and catch up with friends. One booth in a prime location on the way to the lobby is manned by a team of NMFS officials. Their table is littered with piles of bulletins explaining what the fishermen will need to do to comply with the new whale Take Reduction Plan, now in force.

A man in an insulated plaid shirt and jeans walks almost hesitantly up to the NMFS table and picks up the flyer about the lobster-gear requirements. As he reads, Glenn Salvador, a soft-spoken colleague of John

Higgins, sidles up in his characteristically unassuming way. Glenn begins to explain the different gear choices to the fisherman, pointing to the page. The fisherman nods impassively, still looking at the paper. Glenn picks up a weak-link from the table to show him how to attach his buoy and pot warp. Slowly, while Glenn is speaking, the fisherman knits his brow and his jaw drops just a little.

I know exactly what the fisherman is thinking. I'm sure I wore the same expression when I first tried to comprehend the information on that sheet. After a minute of staring at it, all I could discern was that fishermen had a lot of choices for modifying their gear to conform to the plan, but I would need a quiet room and a few cups of coffee to figure out where and when they could use which gear.

The fisherman politely thanks Glenn, having uttered barely a word, then walks away, brow still furrowed. This was the moment I realized I was not the only one confused by NMFS's elaborate plan to protect large whales in the Atlantic.

*   *   *

I have since spent many hours teasing apart the plan. In addition to the hodgepodge of gear choices John Higgins spoke about, fishermen must also figure out where they can fish. The Take Reduction Plan includes a dizzying array of polygons drawn on charts that shift and change with the season and the movements of whales.

These polygons are areas where certain restrictions apply certain times of the year, and NMFS has no fewer than five different types of polygons, many of them overlapping, within which they impose restrictions—either gear modifications like those John Higgins described or closures. NMFS establishes the boundaries of the polygons by analyzing where and when spotter planes and research vessels see right whales. Essentially, they make a map with a spattering of dots, each dot representing a right whale someone saw once, and they try to draw a box that would enclose as many dots as possible. The idea is that if lots of whales were there in the past, they are likely to be there in the future. But it turns out that even the lumbering right whale is too fast for the feds.

The Endangered Species Act calls for NMFS to establish critical habitat areas, places that are important to endangered species where restrictions on human activities may apply to protect the creature of concern.

For the right whale, that was pretty simple. Everyone knew by the early 1990s that some right whales spend lots of time feeding in and around the Great South Channel east of Cape Cod in the spring and summer. And a few right whales like to hang out in Cape Cod Bay in the late winter and early spring. So the first lines NMFS drew with the first incarnation of the TRP in 1997 were the critical habitat areas (CHAs) where fishing is prohibited for part of the year (see map 8.1).

The Seasonal Area Management (SAM) polygons were added in 2002 to cover more whale-dots to the east of Cape Cod. Fishermen can set their gear within the SAM areas, but they have fewer gear-modification choices, depending on the season. Map 8.2 shows that the SAMs are

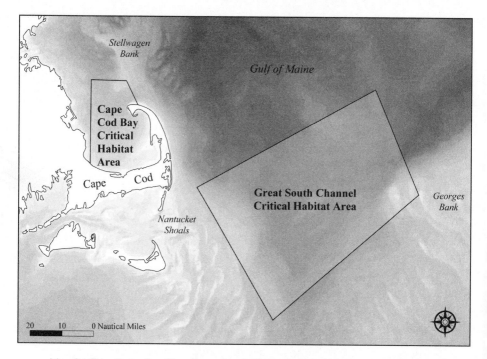

Map 8.1. Take Reduction Plan: Great South Channel Critical Habitat Area and Cape Cod Bay Critical Habitat Area (CHAs). The Great South Channel CHA is closed to all lobster and gill-net fishing from April 1 through June 30; weak-links and special gear marking are required for the remainder of the year. The Cape Cod Bay CHA is closed to gill-netting from January 1 through May 15, while additional restrictions apply to the lobster fishery; for the remainder of the year, requirements vary for state and federal waters. Drawing by T. Johnson; data provided by Commonwealth of Massachusetts and GIS Data Depot.

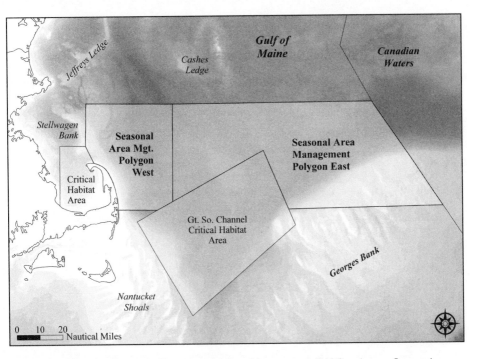

Map 8.2. Take Reduction Plan: Seasonal Area Management (SAM) polygons. Seasonal Area Management West is in effect from March 1 through April 30, Seasonal Area Management East from May 1 through July 31. SAM rules require stringent modifications of both gill-net and lobster gear. Drawing by T. Johnson; data provided by Commonwealth of Massachusetts and GIS Data Depot.

pretty large; SAM Polygon East alone covers about 3,600 square nautical miles. The combination of the CHAs and the SAMs cover much of the fishing grounds used by fishermen from Chatham on Cape Cod.

Several zones cover the lobster fishery as a whole (see map 8.3). The states have jurisdiction over the inshore lobster fishery up to three miles offshore, though the feds can enforce some restrictions right to the beach. NMFS manages the Northern and Southern Nearshore waters, as well as the Offshore Lobster waters. The requirements under the whale TRP are in addition to other requirements the fishermen must follow to keep the lobster stocks healthy and avoid running afoul of other species at risk.

And there's more! With the 2002 version of the TRP, the feds added additional gear-modification requirements for fixed-gear fisheries in certain federal waters in Cape Cod Bay and the Gulf of Maine, except in the

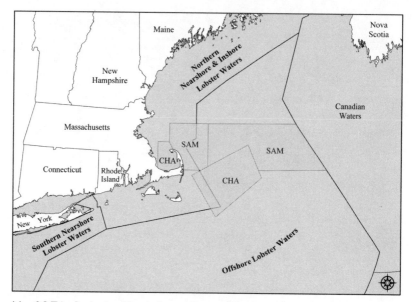

Map 8.3. Take Reduction Plan: Lobster Management Areas. Gear modifications for lobster-trap fishing vary among the lobster areas. Additional modifications are required where the lobster areas overlap critical habitat areas, Seasonal Area Management polygons, and other regulated zones. Drawing by T. Johnson; data provided by Commonwealth of Massachusetts and GIS Data Depot.

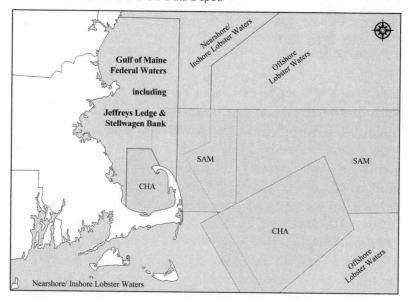

Map 8.4. Take Reduction Plan: Gulf of Maine Waters, including Jeffreys Ledge and Stellwagen Bank. The federal waters of the Gulf of Maine bounded by this polygon are subject to additional gear modification, except where those waters are designated as Cape Cod Bay Critical Habitat Area. Drawing by T. Johnson; data provided by Commonwealth of Massachusetts and GIS Data Depot.

Cape Cod Bay CHA or the SAM West Polygon, where other restrictions apply (see map 8.4).

*   *   *

And then we come to the polygon scheme that is the least loved of all.

"We call 'em the damn DAMs," says Gary Ostrom, a Cape Cod lobsterman.

No one can remember who first raised the idea of Dynamic Area Management, but most everyone agrees it emerged at a Take Reduction Team meeting. Stormy Mayo cringes when he says he's pretty sure he first uttered the word *dynamic* in a TRT meeting but insists that the current form of DAM is not really what he had in mind.

Dynamic Area Management is another one of those federal plans that makes a lot of sense on paper. The idea is simple: if you see a few whales in an area, tell the fishermen to take their gear out of the water until the whales leave. So if right whales show up in a place where there isn't a polygon, you make an instant polygon to accommodate them.

Certain questions immediately arise: How many whales are enough to justify telling fishermen to get their gear out of the water? And how big an area should be closed? And for how long? To answer these questions, the NMFS folks asked their whale scientists to get out their maps with the whale-dots again and see what they could call a feeding aggregation (right whales are probably at most risk of colliding with fishing gear when they are swimming around with their mouths open).

Phil Clapham and Richard Pace at NMFS's Northeast Fisheries Science Center, two of the best whales-and-numbers guys in the business, took on the task. Looking back at right whale sighting data from 1980 to 1996, Clapham and Pace identified clusters of whales sighted on a particular day and checked to see if whales were sighted in the same general area within the next ten days.

They found that if you saw at least *three* right whales in the same general area on a given day, you were likely to see right whales in the same place over the next couple of weeks. They called these clustered sightings "events."

In their April 2001 report on the study, Clapham and Pace wrote that the "average duration of an event is about two weeks."

Clapham and Pace went on to caution that even traveling whales or whales in lower densities can hit fishing gear:

No amount of analysis of existing survey data will produce a result separating whales at risk from whales that are not. For example, while one might define a trigger as, (say) "four right whales observed in a 100 [square nautical mile] area," it would be incorrect to assume that three right whales seen in the same area would be at zero risk of entanglement. Scientifically, there is no doubt that a single right whale feeding in an area with fishing gear present would be at a distinctly non-zero risk of entanglement (and thus potentially of death). Given this, the fundamental question is how much risk of entanglement is acceptable? This issue is ultimately one of policy rather than science.

In other words, there may be four whales in one area where the DAM is triggered, but there are 296 somewhere else. Just because you don't see one of those other 296 feeding with a bunch of its buddies doesn't mean it can't collide with fishing gear.

But in January 2002, the DAM rule was published in the *Federal Register* in spite of outcry from all camps, especially the lobstermen. The new rule required NMFS to close or require gear modifications in an area when three or more right whales are seen within a seventy-five-square-mile radius.

*   *   *

"What you're expecting is dangerous at best, and it's not enforceable."

This is Leroy Bridges' comment on the DAM plan when I meet him at the Maine Fishermen's Forum. Leroy represents the Downeast Lobstermen's Association on the TRT. When he isn't at meetings, he runs his thirty-eight-foot lobsterboat out of Sunshine, Maine, fishing eight hundred traps, the maximum allowed under his permit. Leroy's detractors call him a loose cannon, while his friends say, "Leroy tells it like it is." Once, when a TRT meeting had become particularly rancorous, Leroy said of the whales, "I'd just as soon shoot 'em!" The room fell silent and jaws dropped when he uttered these heretical words.

I ask Leroy about this incident when we meet at the Fishermen's Forum. "Did you actually *say* that at the TRT meeting?"

A self-satisfied grin spreads over his face under his engineer's cap. "A technique that I use is one of shock," he says.

While NMFS trots out the new regulations in the hotel hallway, Leroy reclines on wicker furniture and shakes his head, gazing out the window over the moored lobsterboats in wind-tossed Rockland Harbor. He explains that the DAM rule can't work.

"If DAM is imposed and you have to take your traps out of the water," he says, "where are you gonna go with those traps? You're gonna go *outside*, you're gonna create a *wall!*" He explains that if lobstermen are ordered to take their traps out of a DAM area, they will simply move them to edge of the closure, building a fence around the whales.

Leroy goes on tell me that he can pick up and move seventy traps a day in flat, calm weather. In rough weather, he can move sixty. So for a fisherman with the maximum eight hundred traps, it would take a minimum of twelve days to comply with a DAM closure. And according to Clapham and Pace's report, an event lasts an average of two weeks.

"It's ridiculous!" says Leroy.

*   *   *

The first test of the DAM rule came on April 14, two months later. On a routine whale search mission, a NMFS spotter plane counted eight right whales in a small area about twenty-five miles east of Cape Ann, Massachusetts, triggering a DAM closure for the first time. NMFS ordered gillnetters and lobstermen to remove their gear from a 1,700 square mile area off of Cape Ann in late April and early May. Map 8.5 shows the first two DAM closures, the first comprising a corner of SAM West and a larger L-shaped area to the north and west.

On April 19, *five days* after the whales were sighted, David Gouveia, marine mammal coordinator for the Northeast Region, sent an e-mail to "interested parties" with advance notice of the DAM closure, but most fishermen learned about it when they received a letter dated April 25. The order was published in the *Federal Register* on April 26, and the closure took effect on April 28—*fourteen days* after the whales were sighted.

Now recall the Clapham and Pace report: "The average duration of an event is about two weeks." But it took NMFS two weeks to begin the DAM closure. The instant polygon was apparently not so ready at hand that it could be conjured at a moment's notice.

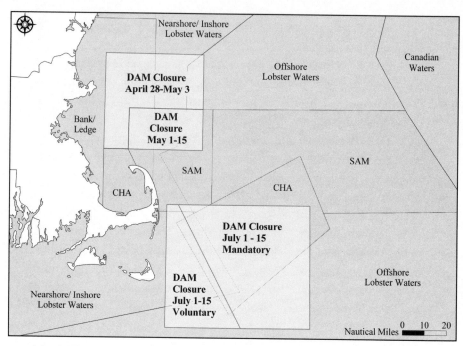

Map 8.5. Take Reduction Plan: First two Dynamic Area Management (DAM) closures, 2002. Dynamic Area Management imposes closures or gear modifications when three or more right whales are seen in a 75-square-mile radius. The first two DAM closures were in April–May, when eight right whales were sighted on April 14, and in July, following the June 18 sighting of a concentration of seventy-five right whales in the Great South Channel CHA. The National Marine Fisheries Service asked fishermen to refrain from setting gear in the region to the west of the mandatory closure. Drawing by T. Johnson; data provided by Commonwealth of Massachusetts and GIS Data Depot.

Mary Colligan is the assistant regional administrator for protected species in NMFS's Northeast Regional Office. She is a calm, no-nonsense sort of person, which must be a great boon to her in her work at NMFS. Before taking on whales, Mary worked on Atlantic salmon, an issue that is just about as frustrating and embattled as the whale issue. In spite of this, she is quietly and unflaggingly optimistic.

I visited Mary at the NMFS office in Gloucester during that first DAM closure. She told me at the time that there were right whales in the area when the DAM closure went into effect on April 28. She also told me that the U.S. Coast Guard was moving more resources to the area, educating fishermen and planning on enforcement actions if they weren't complying with the DAM closure, but that's not quite what I heard from fishermen.

Ron Hemeon, an Essex, Massachusetts, lobsterman, had eight hundred traps set in the DAM polygon. He received official notice of the closure just two days before he was to have his traps out. To understand the spot Ron was in at the time, picture a lobsterboat, a big offshore lobsterboat about forty feet long. The back deck of the boat, called the platform, is where Ron must stack his traps if he ever needs to move them. In heavy weather, he can move about thirty, stacked up and tied down. He can fit about fifty if he has great weather. At the time of the closure, all eight hundred of Ron's traps were in the DAM area, most more than thirty miles offshore, so to haul the traps out of the water and bring them ashore, he could make just one round trip a day. Even if he worked around the clock, it would take him at least two weeks to clear his gear from the polygon. And then where would he put them?

"I didn't really do much about it because there wasn't too much I could do," Ron told me. "It took a month to get the gear set up out there in the winter."

He moved a handful of traps to the outer edge of the closed area—just as Leroy Bridges had predicted—but could do little more to comply with the order.

According to Ron, other fishermen were also in the same predicament. "I had to travel through the area almost every day during those two weeks," he said, "and I didn't see a lot of gear being moved."

The Coast Guard was charged with enforcing the DAM, but Ron says when he saw Coast Guard officials in the area during the closure, he was not approached. In the end, the Coast Guard reported that they spoke to several fishermen and gave a few warnings.

"It's just impossible in so many ways to expect people to move in two days," Ron says. "And they're not even giving the other rules a chance to work." He has complied with the new whale-friendly gear requirements by investing in sinking groundline, weak-links, and lighter buoy lines. In addition, he is using longer strings of traps to minimize the number of vertical lines in the water.

When I called Bill Adler, executive director of the Massachusetts Lobstermen's Association, to ask how Massachusetts lobstermen were handling the DAM, I got an earful; he was hopping mad. I had already heard this from Mary Colligan and her colleagues at NMFS who had been field-ing phone calls from Bill's irate constituents.

Bill told me that because the order came early in the season, only a couple dozen lobstermen had gear in the area when the DAM closure was announced, and most of these were only fishing four or five hundred traps, but even so, few fishermen could comply with the closure.

"The fishermen don't like to be illegal," Bill said, "but nobody could get all their gear out in time!"

Still, Mary Colligan insisted that although the DAM model is not per-fect, it is an effective management strategy.

"I do think it's effective," Mary told me. "The limitations are in that it's a reactive process. We understood the limitations, but it's just one tool in the toolbox."

Like fishermen, many scientists criticize the plan, saying right whales can swim more than fifty miles in a day as they wander in search of plankton patches to feed on. So the whales that trigger a DAM closure could be hundreds of miles away by the time the closure goes into effect two weeks later. And if the average event lasts two weeks, the whales are most likely to have left the area while NMFS was sending letters to fisher-men.

In addition, the most efficient way for fishermen to comply with the DAM rule is to move their gear just outside the closed area—as Ron did, leaving a "fence" of vertical lines for animals moving out of the area. This fence of gear may be more dangerous than anyone previously thought, especially given the new information about how, where, and when right whales move from place to place.

*   *   *

In recent years, researchers have begun to track the movements of whales using advances in satellite and computer technologies. And it turns out that whales move quite a bit more than anyone had ever ex-pected. Bruce Mate at Oregon State University has tagged dozens of whales—sperm, fin, humpback, and gray—with small radio transmit-ters that can be tracked by satellite. In 2000, Bruce turned his attention to right whales feeding in summer in the Bay of Fundy. To almost everyone's surprise, the Bay of Fundy whales, which researchers com-monly called "summer residents," often left the Bay of Fundy to make a

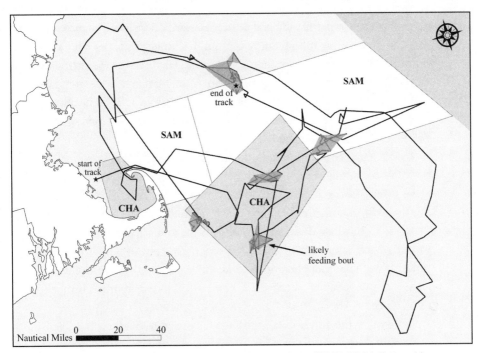

Map 8.6. Satellite telemetry track of entangled right whale #2223, "Calvin," tagged by the Center for Coastal Studies and tracked for thirty-six days in March and April 2001, before shedding the gear with the buoy attached. Notice that Calvin crossed boundaries to critical habitat areas at least a dozen times and fed at the edge of the Great South Channel CHA on at least two occasions. Drawing by T. Johnson; data provided by Commonwealth of Massachusetts, GIS Data Depot, and Center for Coastal Studies; analysis by Santiago Salinas and Diana Choksey.

lap around the Gulf of Maine or explore the continental slope before returning to the bay.

Not everyone was surprised, however. The CCS team has been tagging entangled right whales since 1999. They attach a hard plastic and metal telemetry buoy to the entangling gear and use it to help disentanglement teams relocate the whales. These tags have yielded some very interesting data too. My students and I have begun mapping and analyzing the tracks of these animals and find that, indeed, they rarely stay in one place for very long. Remember that Churchill, fatally entangled, towed his telemetry buoy for a thousand-mile round trip from the Great South Channel to the Gulf of St. Lawrence in less than a month.

Map 8.6 shows the telemetry track of another entangled right whale tagged by the Center for Coastal Studies in 2001. This nine-year-old female, in spite of the rope twining around her flipper with the telemetry buoy attached, swam more than 1,600 nautical miles in the thirty-six days CCS tracked her. That's an average of more than forty miles per day. Note that she crossed boundaries of critical habitat areas at least a dozen times in that period, apparently feeding on at least two occasions right at the edge of the CHA polygon.

In looking at Bruce Mate's whales and additional right whales tracked by CCS, this same pattern often emerges. They commonly, though not always, feed in small confined areas, then travel before feeding again, often making a circuit back to where they started. So if a researcher sees the same right whale in the Bay of Fundy twice in the space of a couple of weeks, in the interim it might have gone on a jaunt of a few hundred miles. It will take more testing to tease out the details of why and when whales move, but even these preliminary results have important implications for the DAM rule.

Remember the whale-dots, sightings data used to calculate the likelihood of finding a right whale in a given box at any given time? It seems that many of the whale-dots are on the move, crisscrossing the boundaries of all the polygons all the time. If you see three whales in a small area at one time, you are in fact likely to see whales there again within the following couple of weeks. But they are not necessarily going to be the *same* whales, and if they are the same whales, they may have left the area and returned in the two weeks it took you to implement a DAM closure.

If in that two weeks you have ordered all the fishermen to move their lobster and gill-net gear out of the area and they have placed a forest of traps around the closed area, instead of protecting whales from entanglement, you may have made it far more likely.

*   *   *

After sorting out the details of the Take Reduction Plan, I am left with a patchwork quilt of overlapping management regimes (map 8.7). I wonder how a fisherman could possibly have sorted out the boundaries and the gear requirements while keeping food on the table, the boat afloat, a crewman paid, and the gear repaired.

And this is the fourth iteration of the plan. NMFS implemented the first Interim Final Rule in 1997. In 1999, they implemented the Final

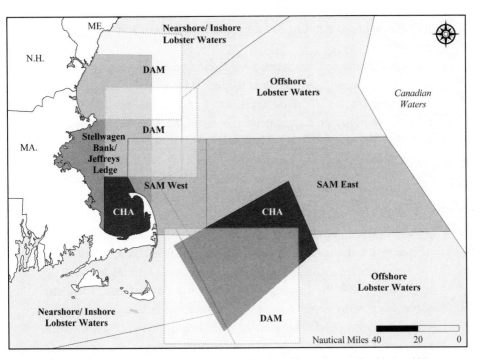

Map 8.7. Take Reduction Plan: A patchwork of overlapping polygons. The National Marine Fisheries Service implemented an Interim Take Reduction Plan (TRP) for North Atlantic large whales early in 2002. The plan imposes at least five separate management regimes for New England and Mid-Atlantic fixed-gear fisheries. New England lobster fishermen and gill-netters may be subject to as many as three overlapping whale protection regimes in the same area, in addition to regulations for individual fisheries. Drawing by T. Johnson; data provided by Commonwealth of Massachusetts and GIS Data Depot.

Rule, then modified the Final Rule in 2000. The current TRP, which NMFS calls an Interim Final Rule, was implemented in 2002. Another "Final Rule" is due in the next year or so.

* * *

Lobstermen and gill-netters all over New England have told me that unenforceable rules like DAM destroy trust and leave the fisheries open to additional regulations or closures if whales continue to die from entanglement. Many, Ron Hemeon and Bill Adler included, would rather see coastwide, year-round gear modifications to protect whales wherever they are, so they can put an end to complex regulations and dynamic area closures.

Gary Ostrom is a lobsterman on Cape Cod who spends almost as much time in meetings as he does fishing. He represents Massachusetts lobstermen on the TRT. One winter day in 2002, we sat at his kitchen table in his house on Cape Cod to talk about the Take Reduction Team and NMFS's current Interim Final Rule.

Gary told me that the team had agreed on several recommendations that NMFS ignored in making the latest rule. The fishermen on the team insisted that the DAM rule could not be enforced, but NMFS went ahead with the plan anyway.

"The real problem is that the Endangered Species Act puts people out of business without making a difference in the species," Gary boomed. "Right whales are worth saving, but the Endangered Species Act won't do it. We don't need the Endangered Species Act, we just need common sense. My son, he's twelve years old, he wants to be a marine biologist when he grows up. I don't want my son to grow up and ask me why there are no right whales left."

If the U.S. Endangered Species Act and the Marine Mammal Protection Act don't lead to commonsense measures to protect whales and fishermen, how do the whales and fishermen fare in neighboring Canada, which until recently had no analogous legislation?

9   Sparring with the Leviathan

Canst thou draw out leviathan with an hook? or his tongue with a
cord which thou lettest down?
Canst thou put an hook into his nose? or bore his jaw through with
a thorn?
Will he make many supplications unto thee? will he speak soft words
unto thee?
Will he make a covenant with thee? wilt thou take him for a servant
for ever?
Wilt thou play with him as with a bird? or wilt thou bind him for
thy maidens?
Shall the companions make a banquet of him? shall they part him
among the merchants?
Canst thou fill his skin with barbed irons? or his head with fish spears?
Lay thine hand upon him, remember the battle, do no more.

Job 41:1-8

"He's a saucy fella, i'n't he?" Wayne said of the whale. Wayne's brogue
and his knack for understatement came from his childhood in a Newfoundland fishing community. My hair dripped ice-cold water down the
back of my Mustang suit as I knelt in the bow of the Zodiac. Wayne
made small talk with a fisherman. The whale flailed and bellowed
nearby. This was whale disentanglement, Newfoundland style.

*   *   *

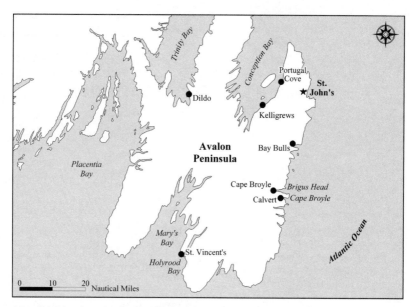

Map 9.1. Newfoundland's Avalon Peninsula. Drawing by T. Johnson; data provided by GIS Data Depot.

The previous afternoon, on August 8, 2001, a fishing boat had left the pier in a tiny village on the southeastern coast of Newfoundland's Avalon Peninsula. The stout, high-sided boat took advantage of a break in the weather, rumbling its way between the cliffs that enclosed the bay, and headed for the Grand Banks. When they had cleared the bay, the skipper pushed the throttle forward another notch.

Not long after, someone aboard spied a disturbance on the water, a whale caught in fishing gear, splashing and bellowing. The captain of the fishing boat picked up the mike on his VHF and called his fish buyer to report an entangled whale two miles off Cape Broyle, thirty miles south of St. John's. The fishing boat continued on to the fishing grounds while the fish buyer called a toll-free number, the Entrapment Assistance Program hotline, to pass on the message.

That afternoon, I was sitting at a picnic table tapping at my laptop. The stiff wind had finally relented, so the door to the cabin sat ajar to let in the sunlight and warm summer air. A gentle breeze carried bird songs and sounds of the farm—Jon and Judy Lien's farm in Portugal Cove. I heard footsteps and unfamiliar voices on the porch, then two boys, both about ten years old, rushed in through the open door, out of breath.

"Are you Tora?" one of them asked.

"Uh, yeah," I nodded.

"You should call Julie right away."

Together Wayne Ledwell and Julie Huntington were Newfoundland's Marine Animal Entrapment Assistance team, a program with a very long name and a very small budget. For the most part, Julie handled logistics and communication while herding their three boisterous kids. Wayne roamed the island towing a Zodiac on a trailer behind the family's minivan and coaxing local fishermen to help him wrestle whales, turtles, sharks, and other large creatures out of fishing gear.

"Wayne's got another whale," Julie told me over the phone. "He's leaving at about six in the morning if you want to go with him."

I rose to the alarm in the predawn dark and gathered my sea boots, a little lunch, and an extra set of clothes, remembering what Wayne had told me two days before: When the weather cleared, the fishermen would go out to check their gear and then someone would find a tangled whale.

Just as the sun rose, I arrived at Wayne and Julie's home in a subdivision out of town just a few miles from the Liens' farm and helped Wayne carry gear out of his garage and into his van. We loaded two coolers full of equipment, two orange exposure suits, and coils of line into the back, then slid the door shut. After hooking the trailer up to the hitch on the minivan, we set off along Route 10, which winds through the villages of the southeastern shore of the Avalon Peninsula.

While we drove and drank coffee, Wayne told me in his Newfoundland brogue what he knew about the whale. It was most likely a humpback—nearly all the entangled whales he rescued were humpbacks. This one had been reported about two miles off Cape Broyle. Wayne knew the area well; he had grown up in Calvert, just south of Cape Broyle. We would put in at the slipway in Calvert, he told me, then drive the Zodiac around the cape to look for the whale.

In his late forties, Wayne had graying hair and a wit that bespoke his Irish heritage. He had a master's degree in biology and had worked for Jon Lien releasing whales at the height of the entrapment program in the late 1980s and early 1990s. His training in disentanglement had been very perfunctory. Soon after he arrived to work for the Whale Research Group, he and Jon had released a whale while a CBC television crew filmed them.

After one whale, Jon said, "Okay, you do it now."

Wayne and Julie had met when he was working as Jon's assistant and she was a student in Jon's lab. When Jon began to ease himself out of the disentanglement business, the Department of Fisheries and Oceans (DFO) asked Wayne and Julie to take on the task. They run the program for all of Newfoundland's 15,000-mile coast. They also handle any marine mammal strandings and visit schools to do education programs about whales. Their annual budget from DFO in 2001 was just $47,000 (Canadian).

*   *   *

The program was typical of Canada's ad hoc approach to endangered species protection. The Canadian wildlife service maintains the Committee on the Status of Endangered Wildlife in Canada (COSEWIC, typically pronounced "cozy-wick"), which is a group of scientists created in 1977 charged with determining which species should be included on Canada's list of species at risk. COSEWIC has no legal status, so its findings are merely recommendations. Once a species is designated by COSEWIC to require attention, it is up to Environment Canada's Species at Risk program to act on behalf of the plant or animal in question.

Unlike in the United States, there are no grand legislative mandates in Canada, and there is no special status for marine mammals. The Species at Risk program is generally guided by a hodgepodge of legislation and the principles laid down in 1996 by the Accord for the Protection of Species at Risk. This agreement among the federal, provincial, and territorial governments is simply a commitment to a national conservation strategy for species at risk, a vow to coordinate their efforts. The commitments are peppered with words like "provide," "address," "consider," "emphasize," "recognize," "monitor," and "improve." Under the accord, the Canadian Endangered Species Conservation Council was formed to provide leadership and guidance on questions involving species at risk. That's about it. As for what is done for each individual species, the Species at Risk program cobbles together recovery and habitat stewardship plans using whatever tools and money are at hand, and the various federal agencies involved have modest budgets to dedicate to species at risk.

Because of this ad hoc system, the whale disentanglement program has been juggled between agencies like a ticking time bomb. DFO, Environment Canada, Provincial Fisheries Agencies, and even the Coast Guard have each taken on part or all of the program at one time or another since Jon first began releasing whales in the 1980s.

In light of the ad hoc nature of wildlife protection in Canada, the deeds of Jon Lien, Wayne Ledwell, and a great many of their Canadian colleagues seem all the more remarkable. They have accomplished a great deal with no clear federal mandate or large-scale commitment of funds. They saw a need and acted upon it without the threat of lawsuits or legal penalties, always on a shoestring. Where the legal system left off, civil society took up the slack.

All the ad hoc cobbling may be about to change, however. The Species at Risk Act, after wending its way through the labyrinth of Canadian parliamentary process for five years, has finally become law. The intent of the act is to formalize, codify, and coordinate Canadian policy on endangered species. What this will mean for whales remains to be seen, but DFO, anticipating new mandates from Parliament, has begun to put a few more resources into whale protection in the Northwest Atlantic. So far, few of these resources have made it to Wayne and Julie's entrapment assistance program.

*   *   *

This early morning, Wayne and I drove down the Avalon Peninsula to look for an entangled humpback off Cape Broyle. We towed the Zodiac through Calvert, Wayne's hometown. A few men in caps and jeans turned from their conferences over tailgates to stare.

Wayne smiled and waved, then speculated on what the men said about us after we passed. "'Look at them university fellas lookin' for whales or some such,'" he improvised. "'You see them suits they wear? Them big orange suits?'" He flashed his Irish smile.

Calvert's slipway—or what had been a slipway—sat behind a small abandoned building, apparently an old fish plant. After the cod crash, the government had stopped maintaining a lot of the slipways in the small communities around the island, and Calvert's was no exception. I got out to direct as Wayne backed the trailer toward the water. I waved and stumbled over a slope of big cobbles that rolled under my sea boots and twisted my ankles as I walked. When the trailer was about fifty feet from the water, Wayne stopped.

"I think we'll just have to push the trailer down," he said as he opened the door and climbed out. "I don't want to get the tires stuck in the rocks here."

We pulled on our boots and Mustang suits and loaded the gear into the Zodiac. The suits certainly looked silly, but the neoprene liners would provide warmth if we got wet and floatation if we went in the drink. After unhitching the trailer, we struggled to coax it over the cobbles to the shore, leaning with all our weight onto the trailer's frame. Finally, we untied the boat and slid it into the water.

After we climbed aboard, Wayne guided the boat under a bridge and into the bay. He twisted the throttle until we hurtled toward the tip of Cape Broyle; a previous trip with Wayne aboard the Zodiac had taught me that he wasted no time with leisurely rides. Shouting over the noise of the motor, he pointed out the sloping rock face where the Calvert fishermen used to put a row of cod traps. They drew lots for the best spot along the shore at a town meeting every spring.

Kneeling in the bow, I gripped the yellow hand ropes to keep from tumbling backward toward the stern. Every wavelet tossed me in the air and lifted my knees an inch or two off the metal floorboards, making me grateful for the spongy neoprene of my Gumby suit, which absorbed the shock when I landed. My muscles still ached from the last ride I had taken with Wayne, and as we rounded the cape, I wondered if we would need to search for hours as we had a few days earlier. That search had left me so sore I could barely get out of bed the next day.

Just as this thought occurred to me, the tip of the cape hove into view. Wayne pointed to Cape Broyle, which loomed over our port side.

"It's the highest on this coast," he said over the din. Brigus Head humped up before us, enclosing the north side of Admiral's Cove, the deep harbor of the community of Cape Broyle. The earth had heaved up layered stone and tipped it on its side to form these dramatic headlands. Glaciers and relentless winds and seas had carved deep into the softer layers, leaving craggy jutting rocks topped with stunted pointing spruces. Sheer cliffs plunged into the sea, and their bases hosted a feasting hoard. Gulls and terns whirled and screeched in the air while puffins and murres bobbed on the water and dove to gorge on capelin below.

"There's a blow!" I yelled to Wayne above the engine.

"Humpbacks!" He nodded.

Among the frenzied birds, we saw spouts of mist. Just a few yards from the cliff face, two shiny black backs rolled slowly in unison to show curving fins, then two tails rose into the air and disappeared into the grey-green water. Beneath the waves, the whales and the birds chased schools of capelin toward the steep rock wall and scooped up the cornered shimmering mass as it hit the barrier.

When we rounded the cliff, we saw a few more whales just inside the arm of Cape Broyle. A high-sided blue fishing boat about forty-five feet long lolled in a gentle swell between the headlands that formed the mouth of Admiral's Cove. A gill net draped over the side as they hauled it aboard.

"There's a shoal area here." Wayne pointed to the spot where the fishing boat was hauling gear. "It's called Horse Rocks."

Wayne steered the Zodiac toward the fishing boat, and as we approached, we saw a whale blow and splash awkwardly just beyond.

"It's just like you said," I told Wayne. "They came out to haul their gear when the weather cleared, and here we are."

At first we assumed that the splashing whale was caught in the net the blue boat was hauling aboard, but as we drew closer, we saw that this net led into the water toward Cape Broyle, not toward Brigus Head and the whale. The whale had run afoul of someone else's gear. Wayne drove us around the fishing boat and toward the whale. The animal rolled and blew and splashed with its tail. Apparently this was the whale we were looking for, though there was no way to know for sure.

"Is it a minke?" I asked Wayne when we were still a hundred yards away. It seemed smaller than the other whales we had seen that morning.

"No, that's a humpback. A big one, about forty feet long."

As he spoke, the whale dove and showed a black hump with a humpback's fin.

"Oh, yeah," I said, "look at that." With the specter of the animal's back, its immensity became suddenly apparent. The leviathan.

Each time the whale's twin blowholes emerged at the surface for a breath, it emitted an appalling bellow, the voice of struggle and distress. The terrified bawling was what I imagine a great dinosaur would sound like trumpeting an alarm or struggling while under mortal attack.

"Aaaoooonh!" A prehistoric and archetypal sound of panic and pain.

"I've never heard a humpback make a sound like that," I said to Wayne.

"Yeah, that's how they sound when they're distressed, you know, when they're stressed." He seemed unfazed by the animal's flailing.

The sound and the size of the animal left my heart pounding. It suddenly occurred to me that Wayne intended to approach this whale close enough to cut away the fishing gear. I couldn't imagine how we were going to do that. The whale swept its tail flukes, nearly as broad as the Zodiac was long, in wide arcs as it tried to free itself of rope and net, sending sheets of spray into the air.

Wayne steered us past the whale and began to assess the situation while the animal twisted and splashed. A pair of orange buoys, each about a foot and a half in diameter, floated near the whale.

"There's the tail, see?" Wayne called. While we circled, the whale lifted its flukes in a low curving line out of the water, allowing us a brief glimpse of its tail and tail stock.

"No gear on that tail," I said.

I gaped in awe at the thrashing, bellowing beast, trying to reconcile this picture with all the things I had been told about humpbacks by people who had disentangled them:

"They let you work on 'em," Jon Lien had said. "Humpbacks are wimps. They get tired out easily, so you can do what you want with 'em."

"I like working with humpbacks." Wayne had told me. "The animal will let you work on 'em."

"Humpbacks are pussycats," another whale rescuer had said.

This whale didn't look like a pussycat to me, but Wayne seemed unperturbed. Maybe this was normal behavior for pussycat whales, I thought.

"What's it say on that balloon there?" Wayne pointed at the orange buoy.

"Uh," I squinted to read the magic marker lettering on the ball. "Keith something?"

"Yeah, Keit' . . . it looks like an 'H.'" Wayne brogued, circling the ball more closely. We couldn't make out the last name because the ball was tilted at an awkward angle, leaving all but an "H" submerged.

Wayne steered the Zodiac toward the fishing boat where two men were still hauling gill-net gear over the side. It was a peculiar sight to see the dainty little green net rising from the water over the seven-foot-high

Figure 9.1 Humpback whale. Note long, light-colored flippers, slender body, knobby snout, and ridged back with small dorsal fin. Drawing by T. Johnson.

sides of the boat. After the cod crash, most Newfoundland fishermen had sold their trap skiffs and gill-net boats. A few turned around and replaced the old vessels with brand-new oceangoing boats for the crab fishery, an investment of $200,000 or more. Many of these holdouts had kept their cod permits and still set their gill nets with their monstrous new vessels, in spite of small cod quotas and even smaller catches. When the cod came back, they said, they wanted to be one of the few left in the fishery. The captain of the blue fishing boat apparently planned to be among them.

A young deckhand in orange foul-weather overalls hauled the net in by hand over the side, a task made easier by the fact that the net held no fish at all. He pulled the net with gloved hands at a steady plodding pace and stacked the monofilament at his feet on the deck.

Wayne pulled alongside. "That your net?" he asked the deckhand. Apparently it is the custom for men on the water in Newfoundland to speak to one another without raising their voices, regardless of engine noise and the wind in their ears.

"Whaa?" Nearly everything must be repeated at least once.

"That your net there?" Wayne jutted his chin toward the struggling whale.

"No. Don't t'ink so." The deckhand stopped pulling and the captain, an older man of perhaps forty-five, emerged from the wheelhouse door.

"Says Keit' on it," Wayne told the men. "You know a Keit' somebody?" Wayne was hoping to find the owner of the net to ask for his help.

"Whaa?" The captain asked.

"That balloon says Keit' on it," Wayne repeated. "You know somebody from Cape Broyle named Keit'?"

Wayne, the captain, and the deckhand could think of three or four fishermen in the area named Keith.

"What about Keith so and so?"

"No, he usually sets his net further out that way." A wave of the arm.

"Whaa?"

"He usually fishes further down the shore that way."

"Down the shore that way?"

"Yiss."

Silence. Everyone nodded.

"You going to make your quota?" Wayne asked about the cod catch.

"We're hauling our gear," the deckhand shook his head. "There's nothing. We're just taking it all in."

Another silence. More nodding. The Zodiac squeaked against the high blue side of the fishing boat and the outboard idled.

"How long you going to be out here?" Wayne asked.

"Whaa?"

"You gonna be out here a while?"

"Yeah, we got another net to haul down there." The captain jutted his chin toward the cape. "We'll probably be another two hours."

"You got a cell phone on there?" Wayne asked,

"Yiss."

"We should probably have somebody out here standing by, you know."

"You want me to call Fisheries?" the captain asked.

"You have their number?" Wayne asked.

The captain returned to the wheelhouse to look for the number, and a silence ensued. Wayne and the deckhand nodded.

"I'm from Calvert," Wayne finally told the deckhand.

"Whaa?"

"I'm from Calvert there."

"Oh, are ya?" the deckhand said impassively.

Silence. Nodding. The outboard chattered while the whale splashed and grunted nearby.

Finally the captain emerged from the wheelhouse with a cell phone but no number.

It seemed to me that Wayne really had no intention of calling DFO anyway. If he had wanted DFO involved, he could have called the hotline number or Julie at home. The philosophy of the program had always been to help fishermen take responsibility for their own problem. He wanted the fishermen, not DFO officials, to stand by while we wrestled with the whale. He asked the captain to keep an eye on us while they were hauling their nets. The captain nodded, and we returned to the whale. The deckhand resumed his plodding hand-over-hand to pull the gill net aboard.

As Wayne circled, we tried to see through the foam and green water how the whale was tangled. We caught another glimpse of the tail flukes, which were free of gear but red and chafed on the forward edges. The trailing edge of the dorsal fin and the bumpy ridge on the animal's back were also scraped and raw but showed no gear. The animal must have been struggling for a long time to be so scratched up.

Finally, the whale raised the top of its head out of the water for just a second, allowing us to see its mouth. "Yup, he looks like a big old alligator," Wayne quipped. This was how a fisherman had described a humpback to him once. A humpback's head bears dozens of bumps, each with a single stiff hair and a mass of sensory nerves. The scientists call these bumps tubercles. They give the animal a keen sense of touch and the look of a knobby alligator when they rest with their narrow rostrums at the surface of the water.

The lower jaw of the animal had a nasty scrape, but we could see no gear in the mouth.

"He must have it wrapped around his flipper," Wayne decided. "That'll make it easier."

Sure enough, the animal's writhing soon allowed us a brief glimpse of some gear near the right flipper.

Wayne made passes along the side of the whale, and we tried to peer through the sloshing green soup to see the flipper more closely, but we couldn't make out any details. Another tight circle around the buoy finally showed us the name: Keith Hayden.

"Ah, I forgot the camera again." Wayne shrugged.

"Do you ever try to take fluke shots to identify them?" I asked.

"Naw, no time." Wayne was supposed to document the entangled whales whenever possible, but it's difficult to take a picture while driving a Zodiac, wielding a knife in an inflatable boat, and avoiding getting clobbered by a six-foot flipper. So the camera often didn't get used, unless Wayne could persuade a fisherman to snap a few shots.

As we circled the whale, it now seemed just a bit calmer, no longer flailing and splashing. Instead, it alternated swimming in tight circles and trying to drive ahead to the north. The snorts and bellows grew less frequent and less desperate. When the whale attempted to swim north, its progress was apparently impeded by the ground tackle of the gear it was dragging along the bottom. Though the leviathan pumped its tail hard in the water, producing curling eddies on the surface, the orange buoys moved forward just a yard or two with each attempt. The wind picked up a bit from the southeast under fair weather clouds.

Ordinarily, Wayne would wait for the animal to settle before approaching, but each time the whale surged northward, it dragged the ground tackle along the bottom toward another fleet of gill-net gear that stretched between an orange buoy near the tip of Brigus Head and a white float out toward the open ocean. We realized that we may not have the luxury of waiting if we were to save the whale or the gear. But sixty yards or so still separated the whale from the second net—we had a little time to devise a plan.

Wayne steered the Zodiac toward this second fleet of gear. We examined the orange float and found that this gill net, too, belonged to Keith Hayden. If we couldn't stop the whale from driving toward the north, it would catch this second fleet of gear, possibly drowning itself and destroying all of Keith Hayden's gill net in the process. We returned to the struggling whale.

"Grab that buoy there," Wayne instructed as he pulled near the orange floats that accompanied the whale. Still kneeling in the bow, I reached with both hands to pull the buoy aboard and then, under Wayne's guidance, started hauling in the green nylon line. I could feel the weight of ground tackle and lead line as I hauled hand-over-hand. The whale became more agitated and began to splash and bellow again; apparently the gear was tightening on its flipper and causing pain. I could feel the animal tugging the green line. Then suddenly the beast turned and came toward us.

"Drop the line," Wayne said as he reached for the throttle.

I quickly tossed the coils into the green water as Wayne backed away from the approaching whale.

Then as we circled close to the struggling animal again, Wayne told me to get a mask and snorkel out of the blue cooler full of equipment.

"Now put that on," he ordered. "Put it on."

Apparently Wayne expected me to put my head in the water to look at the thrashing humpback. Pushing aside trepidation, I fitted the mask on my face and tried to tighten the straps enough to seal the rubber against my prominent nose. The whale circled and circled, and we circled and circled the whale, but we never got close enough for me to stick my head in the water. I knelt in the bow with the mask on and the snorkel in my mouth, feeling awkward and silly as we drove around and around the whale.

Finally, Wayne noticed that the blue fishing boat had finished hauling their first net aboard. So we left the whale to chat with them. The deckhand and captain were both on deck as we pulled alongside.

"We're going to have to wait 'til he quietens down a bit before we can do anything," Wayne said.

"Whaa?"

"We're going to have to wait 'til he quietens down a bit."

"Yiss."

Nodding. Silence. All eyes looked at the snorting whale.

"Keit' Hayd'n it says on the balloon there," Wayne told them. "You know Keit' Hayd'n?"

"Whaa?"

Wayne repeated the question. The captain and deckhand looked at each other and nodded.

"He lives here in Cape Broyle," the captain offered.

"He lives here?" Wayne asked.

"Yeah."

Nodding. Silence.

"Aaaaooonh!" bellowed the whale, sending an arc of spray into the air with its flukes.

"We've got to wait 'til he quietens down a bit."

"Whaa?"

"He's got to quiet down a bit before we can do anything."

"Yeah."

Silence. This time even I found myself nodding like a Newfoundland fisherman.

"How long you out for?" Wayne asked. "You going in now?"

The captain answered, "Naw, we got one more fleet of gear to haul in that cove there." He swung an arm toward a small indentation in the sheer rock on the north side of Cape Broyle.

Wayne asked if they could call Keith Hayden to come down and help us, but there was no phone book aboard. We returned to the whale as the big blue boat rumbled off to haul their last gill net of the season.

The whale seemed to be tiring a bit. It stopped bellowing and occasionally rested for a few moments at the surface, taking calm and quiet breaths: "Pfffft-huh." So Wayne became more aggressive as we approached this time. Kneeling in the stern, he steered the outboard alongside the animal and told me to put on the mask and snorkel. I made my way to the port side of the Zodiac, then fitted the mask to my face and put the mouthpiece in my mouth.

"It's some job getting over the side," he said, "but you'll do it. Now go! I gotcha. Go!" He grabbed the back of my Mustang suit.

The whale floated before me in the green water about six feet away. I lay my belly on the port pontoon and held onto the yellow hand ropes. With Wayne shoving me, I stuck my face in. Icy salt water immediately filled my mask and my nose. I struggled to get my head out, but Wayne held me down, pinning me to the pontoon.

"Uuugff!" I grunted through my snorkel like an entangled whale. My arms and legs flailed, until Wayne finally let me up.

"You won't fall in," he said when I came up sputtering and pulling my mask off. "I got you."

"I wasn't worried about falling in. My mask was full of water." I tightened the rubber straps until they pinched the flesh of my cheeks, forming a tight seal. Wayne circled around and maneuvered the Zodiac alongside the whale again. I stuck my head in the icy water and arched my back trying to see the whale. Wayne held the back of my suit and kept the Zodiac alongside the swimming leviathan.

This time, Wayne shoved me so far over the side I thought I would go overboard "Uuugff!" I said again, flailing. Wayne let me up.

"Don't be afraid of falling overboard. I gotcha," he said, tugging at the back of my suit to reassure me of his grip.

"Okay." I took a deep breath and poked my head in the ice bucket again, clinging to the ropes.

My head was finally getting numb, so the water didn't seem quite so cold (one veteran of this business has told me that sinus headaches and congestion are a constant annoyance for disentanglers). Apparently I wasn't going to fall overboard, so I could finally try to get a look at the creature. I found this to be no easy matter. Viewing a whale from this position—leaning over the side on your stomach—is akin to hanging from your knees on the monkey bars in a playground, trying to see an angry elephant standing behind you. Even when I couldn't see the monster, its presence was palpable, close and powerful and unpredictable. This sense of vulnerability made me eager to see the animal; if it was going to take a swing at me with a long flipper or accidentally clobber me with its knobby head, I wanted to see it coming. I craned my neck and arched my back to look in the direction of the leviathan a few feet away but saw nothing more than a looming black shape in luminous emerald water. When a wave humped up under the boat, my snorkel filled with water. I came up sputtering and told Wayne we needed to get closer.

We circled closer several times, getting within a few feet of the "big ol' alligator" as it milled around the mouth of the bay. I dispensed with the snorkel and opted for holding my breath, dunking my head into the green bubbly world of the whale for a few seconds at a time. With the concentrated effort of trying to see the whale, I momentarily forgot that I was placing my head within a few feet of a monster. I slowly got the knack of the awkward task of peering at the whale, but I saw very little. The water, translucent green and cloudy with plankton, permitted a view of only a few blurry feet at a time: a section of flipper, part of a looming black head, or some black hunk of animal I couldn't identify. I could hear the motor buzzing.

"What did you see?" Wayne asked when I lifted my dripping head.

"Not much. I could see the front of the head, but no gear." I pushed my wet hair out of my face and ice-cold water ran down the back of my Mustang suit, soaking my shirt underneath.

The whale had remained surprisingly calm as we began this procedure. Whether it was curious about the buzzing creature that circled it or needed a rest, I couldn't say. But as we continued to invade the animal's personal space with our noisy motor, it began to bellow and thrash again. The inkling of trepidation returned, and I pushed it aside.

"I saw the mouth that time," I told Wayne when I emerged once. "I didn't see any rope. It has a nasty scrape on its lower jaw that looks yellow like it's infected." I would learn later that sores on whales often collect masses of yellowish whale lice, small crustaceans known as cyamids.

On another dunk I saw a long white knobby fin slashing forward and backward through the water directly under the boat but couldn't make out the place where the fin joined the body, so I couldn't tell if there was gear on it.

"How are you at steering a boat?" Wayne finally asked.

"Okay," I shrugged.

"Okay, get my goggles there. They have prescription lenses."

I dug Wayne's goggles out of a cooler and stowed his glasses carefully. Wayne and I switched places; I knelt in the stern and took over the throttle while Wayne prepared to hang over the side. The outboard was a new four-stroke that handled smoothly, so I could guide the Zodiac easily, though I was not nearly as adept as Wayne. He took the plunge three or four times but saw no more than I did. A couple of times when the humpback surfaced for a breath, we caught another glimpse of the rope near the flipper, but we couldn't make out how it was tangled.

Finally, we knelt soaked and cold in the Zodiac wondering what to do next while the creature writhed and surged toward Keith Hayden's other net. Then Wayne spotted another fishing boat hauling a gill net in a small cove just inside Cape Broyle. This was a smaller, more traditional gill-net boat made of fiberglass and only partially decked over, sporting a rough, boxy wheelhouse and big hand-painted numbers on the white side. Wayne decided to pay the boat a visit and ask them to stand by while we worked on the whale.

When the Zodiac drew closer, I could see three men in the bow of the gill-net boat hauling the gear. Two young men in their twenties in foul-weather overalls and baseball caps picked the catch and by-catch out of the net. An older man of perhaps fifty- five kept tension on the net as it came aboard the boat around the winch. Wayne told me the older man was a Calvert fisherman named Lloyd Sullivan; the other two were Lloyd's sons.

As we pulled alongside the fishing boat, Lloyd said, "Well, hello, Mr. Ledwell! You looking for a whale?" I grabbed onto the cap rail as the pontoon bounced against the hull and stood with Wayne to speak with Lloyd.

"Well, we found 'im. He's a saucy one, too."

"Just shoot 'im," one of the sons suggested. The boys had fresh freck-led faces.

Wayne smirked. "Oh, well that wouldn't do 'im any good."

"Bring back the whale hunt." Lloyd spoke with an edge in his voice. He was stout, with a round face, and he wore a long dark raincoat instead of the ubiquitous orange foul-weather pants.

"This is Tora." Wayne gestured toward me. "She's a writer. She's not much for talking, but I'll let her tell you what she's about. She's visiting from Massachusetts, doing her research."

"A writer, huh?" Lloyd said, with more than a hint of disdain.

"I'm interested in whales and fishermen," I told Lloyd, "and how fish-ermen feel about whales." I shrugged, not knowing what else to say.

Lloyd laughed with little mirth. "I'll tell you about whales." He nodded and narrowed his eyes. "Soon, there'll be a million of 'em and no fisher-men."

While we talked the winch in the bow turned, dragging the green monofilament net up from the bottom. A hydraulic motor turned the winch, which was made of two car tires stacked on their sides. Lloyd held tension on the net, hauling it hand-over-hand and keeping the float line and the lead line jammed into the groove between the two tires. The catch was mostly sculpins, all spines and fins, with their distended air bladders protruding from their mouths and threatening to burst their pink stomachs. A few puffins and murres came up in the net, too, stiff and tangled. The short, skinny cod were few and far between, and an occasional flounder added to the catch. At intervals, Lloyd pulled a lever to stop the winch and allow his sons to pick fish and birds out with gloved hands. They lobbed the birds and sculpins into the water and sorted the flounder and cod into totes.

Lloyd lifted a sculpin by the gills and shook it at me. "Do you get sculpins in Massachusetts?" Then he took the bloated fish and slammed its head on the cap rail before tossing it overboard.

"Yeah, we get 'em," I responded. "And I think the fishermen do the same thing with them."

Lloyd held up a baby cod by the gills with an angry flourish. The fish couldn't have weighed more than a pound and was quite dead. He tossed it over the side.

Wayne asked Lloyd if he would come and stand by us as we tried to disentangle the whale.

"Oh, I don't know," Lloyd responded, busy at the winch again.

"You got a cell phone on there?" Wayne asked him.

"He does." Lloyd jabbed a thumb at one of his sons working the net.

"I was thinking about calling Fisheries," Wayne told him, "maybe get 'em to send somebody out."

This caused Lloyd to laugh out loud—he wasn't about to call Fisheries for any reason.

"Oh, we'll keep an eye on ya." Lloyd nodded.

We buzzed away and returned to the whale, who now bellowed and splashed with renewed vigor, just a few yards from Keith Hayden's other gill net. While we circled, the creature made another pull toward the north, closing the distance even more.

"Well, I guess we should try to get him away from that net," Wayne sighed. He maneuvered the Zodiac between the whale and the net, where we proceeded to shout at the saucy monster as it plowed its way through the water.

"Go on!" we yelled, standing in the boat. "Git!"

"You don't want to go this way," I told the whale. "Trust me." I clapped my hands, knowing the whale could hear me.

For a moment, the whale stopped struggling and rested with its blowholes and the top of its head at the surface. It was apparently listening.

"Go on, shoo!" I clapped again, four times: clap clap clap clap.

Then the whale did a very odd thing. It gave four short grunts: "Unh! Unh! Unh! Unh!"

"What was that?" I asked Wayne. "Do . . . whales usually do that? Do they . . . respond when you shout at them?"

Wayne didn't answer; he just stood in the stern with his wet hair and his mischievous smirk. He shrugged.

This was the only sound the whale had made other than the dinosaurian bellows, and it left me wondering how much the creature understood about us and the situation it was in. The saucy whale did settle down a bit and seemed to be suddenly curious. Instead of swimming away from us and our whining outboard it came toward us. It rolled once to one side with one eye near the surface of the water to inspect us as we passed a few yards away but was apparently unable to lift the tangled right flipper out of the water as it rolled.

Realizing that we were not going to be able to drive the whale back, Wayne steered us away from Keith Hayden's net, and the whale followed. Those who think whales have some kind of mystical connection with humans might have thought this nameless whale was being friendly, following the voices that had called to it. But seeing the big ol' alligator advancing, I had the distinct feeling this was not a friendly encounter.

Wayne decided it was time to act. The wind was picking up, and if the whale continued on its northward trajectory, it would soon cross a line between the buoys marking Keith Hayden's other net. As we approached the two orange floats trailing the whale, Wayne directed me to pull them aboard. Then he hauled on the green polypropylene line while I sat on a cooler and coiled the rope on my arm as it came aboard. As we took up on the line, we were apparently cinching the rope on the humpback's flipper. It began to bellow and thrash again, swinging its flukes in wide arcs.

Wayne kept pulling, and I coiled, gathering a heavy, dripping mass of green rope until my arm ached inside my orange neoprene suit. When we could see the net coming to the surface as Wayne pulled, the whale, now just a few yards away, started circling around to its left, turning toward us. It passed very close by our port side. When its flukes were even with the boat, the creature swung its tail toward us, spraying us with sheets of water. Wayne kept hauling, and I kept coiling.

"Get that coil there!" Wayne snapped. I was too busy watching the whale and had fallen behind in my coiling, leaving dangerous loops of rope in the clutter at the bottom of the boat.

The whale circled again, and I could see eddies in the water produced by its tail pumping beneath the surface. The green sea roiled over the working flukes. As it advanced toward us again, I asked Wayne, "Do you think he's *trying* to hit us?"

"Well, I don't know." He shrugged where he knelt near the stern. "Probably," he said, shooting me a smirk.

The dark form, with its alligator head at the surface, passed close by the port side again, slowing a little as it came alongside. It seemed to be judging the distance for the next blow. When its tail was level with the boat, the leviathan lifted its flukes out of the water, swinging first left—the wind-up—then sweeping right. The wide black flukes slammed the port pontoon with such force I nearly fell off the cooler and into the water. I grabbed a yellow hand rope with my right hand and hugged the coil of line in my left arm to avoid dropping it in a mass on the bottom of the boat. There was no longer any doubt in my mind: the saucy whale was attacking us. At this realization, I was fascinated—I had no time to be frightened.

As the whale pulled away, Wayne pointed to the cooler I sat on. "There's a knife in that cooler." he said. "Get it out now."

Holding the green coil in my aching left arm, I knelt on the floorboards and dug in the cooler with my right. There was a filet knife with a white plastic handle and a razor sharp blade. To my horror, it had no sheath. Now I was frightened.

"This knife?"

He nodded. "Just give it to me when I tell you."

Now the whale was advancing again, trumpeting with each breath. We were about to get another whack, but this time I had an unsheathed knife with an eight-inch blade in my hand. I put the knife on the cooler and sat on it as quickly as I could before the monster's next blow. The whale swung left, then right again and hit the Zodiac square on the port pontoon, shoving the boat sideways through the water. I felt the hard rubbery edge of the whale's tail on the back of my hand as water sprayed over us. I was keenly aware of the knife under my butt as I struggled to keep my seat.

"I don't know about this knife here," I said to Wayne. "Can I put it away?"

"No! We're gonna need it." He looked at me and noticed the blade of the knife jutting out from under my butt. He motioned for me to move, took the knife and positioned it so I sat only on the blade, leaving the handle easily accessible.

The saucy whale delivered more blows with its tail each time it circled. Under the onslaught, we couldn't pull the net aboard or haul ourselves close enough to the animal to even attempt to free the tangled flipper. Finally, Wayne decided that if the whale kept slamming the Zodiac it might puncture the pontoon with the barnacles on its tail. So he began backing away each time the whale approached.

"Okay," Wayne told me when he was preparing to back away, "ease off on that line."

Though we had the net nearly at the surface, I let a couple of coils go as Wayne backed away and the saucy whale took a futile swing, drenching us again but missing the Zodiac.

While the creature made another pass, I glanced up to find Lloyd and his boys looking on from their boat about thirty yards away. I was certain that this saucy humpback's behavior was providing more fuel for Lloyd's already low opinion of whales. The wind was piping up near twenty knots, and clouds began to move in, covering the sun at intervals and chilling my wet head and neck.

When its next swing failed to hit the mark, the saucy whale changed its strategy. Widening its circle, it approached head-on. This time it didn't slow down. Instead it drove forward, apparently intending to ram us with its head. Wayne backed away again, and I fed the line back into the water so we had the slack to do so. We did this little dance with the whale for three or four more passes, taking up on the line each time the whale retreated and giving it a bit of slack when we needed to back away.

Finally, Wayne decided that all we could do for the whale was to cut the float line and ground tackle off one end of the net. Sometimes, he told me, if you cut away the anchoring gear, they can "wiggle out" if the net stops twisting and can unwind from the flipper. Even if the whale couldn't wiggle free of the net, at least we could save Keith Hayden's other gill net if the whale wasn't towing ground tackle across the bottom.

Although the whale's ramming strategy required more and faster maneuvering, the wider circles gave us more time between maneuvers with each go-round. As the saucy humpback moved away, frustrated and spraying us with its slashing tail, Wayne hauled in on the rope as fast as he could.

"Gimme that knife!" he commanded when the end of the net appeared at the surface.

I handed it to him and helped hold the net at the surface while he sawed frantically, keeping one eye on the circling bellowing monster. My left arm burned from holding the green coil for what now seemed like an eternity. Before Wayne could saw through the line, the whale was picking up ramming speed. We let the net go and backed away. When the saucy whale was past the Zodiac, it flicked its tail to deliver a hundred gallons of water on our heads and continued to circle. Wayne hauled the net to the surface again and sawed at the line as fast as he could.

"Okay, he's gone!" Wayne dropped the line, passed me the knife, and backed the Zodiac off just as the whale made its turn toward us again.

As we retreated, though, I could still feel the weight of the whale taking tension at the other end of the line in my hand.

"I don't think he's free," I told Wayne. "I can feel him taking up on the line."

Wayne took the rope and hauled on it for a moment. Suddenly it came loose from the net. He pulled the end aboard and presented it to me with another smirk. I took the line, wondering what exactly we had just done, exactly what part of the gear Wayne had cut.

"This whale had a bight of the gill net rolled around its pectoral fin," Wayne told me later. "The buoy rope was tangled into it. What I cut was one cabled net and the buoy rope together. This allowed the whale to free itself as the cut end pulled back through and around the flipper. This was why the whale went on a longer leash. It didn't seem to be totally untangled when we left, but the end pulled and it freed itself. Whales are very sensitive when caught around the pecs."

I am completely at a loss to explain how Wayne gathered that much information from the brief glimpses we had of whale parts and gear. Amazing.

The saucy whale, now swimming freely, moved off toward Cape Broyle to the south, away from Keith Hayden's other net. We went to talk to Lloyd and his boys.

Figure 9.2. Wayne Ledwell with the Zodiac, the rig that survived the "saucy" whale. Photo by T. Johnson.

"He's a saucy fella, i'n't he?" Wayne said as we pulled alongside Lloyd's boat.

All agreed with impassive nods. "Yiss."

I sat on the port pontoon and held onto the cap rail to keep the Zodiac alongside. The men held the customary conference of Newfoundland mariners: silence and nodding, punctuated by a few comments.

"You goin' in now?"

"Mmm." A nod.

"Well, I think we'll stay out here for a little while to keep an eye on that fella." Wayne jutted his chin toward the saucy whale.

Nods. Silence. Wayne seemed to be taking a break after our encounter with the belligerent leviathan. I finally had a moment to notice that my clothes were soaked inside my Mustang suit. Water from my wet hair flowed in rivulets down the back of my neck and soaked into my cotton shirt.

After a few minutes of nodding and taciturn comments, Lloyd turned his bow toward Calvert, and we set off to check on the saucy whale, who still thrashed and trumpeted near the cliffs of Cape Broyle, apparently unaware that it was now able to move freely. Under the towering rock face, Wayne told me to put on the mask. He maneuvered the Zodiac behind the bellowing creature.

"See if that net is trailing behind there," he told me.

I bellied up to the pontoon and put my head in the icy emerald water. Near the vague dark shadow of the whale's flukes, I saw the end of the net trailing loose, a green glowing ghost pursuing the saucy whale. Wayne moved in so I could look from other angles, but each time we approached, the animal turned on us, its knobby alligator head homing in on the Zodiac. Even with three or four more furtive dunks, I never saw the other end of the net. Clouds now dominated the sky, and the wind grew steadier so Wayne concluded we had done what we could.

We left the saucy whale in the bay and headed for Calvert under the sinking sun, making our way past the feeding humpbacks and whirling birds under the cliffs. The seething life in this cleft between the capes centered around the capelin that ran in unseen hordes beneath the waves. Although these hordes were just a vestige of the runs Wayne and Lloyd had seen when they were young, the fishermen and the voracious whales of Calvert and Cape Broyle were lucky to have had any capelin. The gaping maw of the capelin seine fishery had intercepted the bulk of the shimmering hordes, and the North Atlantic's silver riches now fertilized fields of wheat and fed farmed fish thousands of miles away from Newfoundland.

A few days earlier in a bay on Newfoundland's Northern Shore, I had ridden with Wayne in the Zodiac through a maze of inlets and harbors, looking for an entangled humpback. The capelin had barely run at all in Leading Tickles that year, leaving the surrounding sea apparently devoid of life.

10 The Killick

A Symbol of Newfoundland

On every land's-end, monstrous capes jut into the sea and soar skyward.
They loom out of the fogs like forlorn sentinels. They are watching
for God, waiting for Him to return to bless the land He has so long
deserted.

Patrick Kavanagh, *Gaff Topsails*

Late one afternoon a few days before Wayne and I encountered the saucy whale in Cape Broyle Harbor, Wayne's wife, Julie, had called me at the Liens' farm. She had told me, "Wayne has a whale" and would be leaving for Leading Tickles within the hour. I rushed to pack my rain gear and sea boots into my car and drive to their house, eager to disentangle my first whale. Leading Tickles is a tiny community at the end of a tiny outcrop of land on Notre Dame Bay, a patch of water enclosed by the Baie Verte Peninsula on the northern shore of Newfoundland. It would take about four hours to drive to Leading Tickles, and Wayne wanted to be there at sunrise, so we were to leave that afternoon and stay at a bed-and-breakfast nearby.

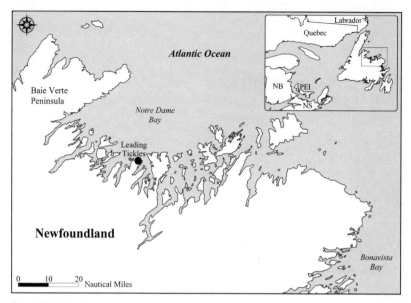

Map 10.1. Northeastern Newfoundland. Drawing by T. Johnson; data provided by GIS Data Depot.

I had only corresponded with Wayne and Julie by e-mail, so this was to be our first meeting, and I hoped to make a good impression. Instead, I got lost trying to find their house and arrived just as Wayne was about to give up on me. The van was already loaded and the trailer already hitched. When I drove up, Wayne was standing in his driveway in a T-shirt and khaki shorts with his hands on his hips. I parked my car, climbed into the passenger seat of the van, and apologized.

Wayne started the van, and we set off, chatting awkwardly. He spoke with a thick brogue, an accent shared by the scattered Newfoundland communities populated by Irish descendents. Apparently a recent stint living in Wisconsin had left Wayne's accent undiminished. I struggled to understand him, asking him to repeat himself nearly every time he spoke.

"How many kids do you have?" I asked.

"T'ree."

"How many?"

"T'ree." He held up his pinky, ring, and middle fingers.

When I took out my steno pad to take notes of our conversation, Wayne smirked. He glanced around as if looking for a fellow Newfoundlander to share in his amusement.

On the highway, we passed an aging Oldsmobile parked askew in the grass off the breakdown lane. Arrayed on the wide hood of the car was a row of mason jars filled with yellow-orange fruits floating in murky liquid. Wayne gestured toward the jars as we passed and asked, "Have you had any bee kepples yet?"

"Bee kepples? I don't know what bee kepples are."

"They're burries."

"I . . . I don't . . . burries?"

"Oh, you probably call them 'beeries,'" Wayne offered.

"Beeries?"

"You know, blackbeeries, strawbeeries . . ."

"Oh, berries! I get it. No, I haven't had any berries," I said. "Bee kepples? Hm, why do they call them bee kepples?"

"Not *bee* kepples," he said, "*bay* kepples."

This was the nature of our conversation for four hours as we wound our way along Route 1. Slowly I began gleaning more and more of what Wayne said, but it would take a few more tries to figure out what "bay kepples" actually were.

After several calls from pay phones looking for a place to stay, we finally pulled into the Blue Jay Bed and Breakfast in Northern Arm, a few miles away from Leading Tickles. As we climbed out of the van, one of the proprietors greeted us in the parking lot, hoping to keep us from disturbing her guests. It was nearly eleven, and they had already turned in. She told us her name was Georgette.

"Do you have a room?" Wayne asked, telling her we would need to leave early in the morning to look for a whale tangled in fishing gear off of Leading Tickles.

"Oh, you must be that whale man," Georgette said.

Wayne explained that he was not Jon Lien but had worked with Jon.

"Well, we're full tonight," Georgette told us. "But I'll tell you what, you two can have our bed. We'll sleep downstairs."

"Well . . . uh . . . there's a little problem with that," Wayne said, rubbing the back of his neck. "Uh, we're not married."

"Well, we're married," I offered, "just not to each other."

"Oh," Georgette waved a hand. "Do you think we care about that?"

"Uh, no," Wayne stammered, "see, we don't . . . uh . . ."

"Oh! You don't sleep together." Georgette put her hand to her mouth, embarrassed. "Well, why don't you come on in? We'll figure something out for you."

Before turning in, we chatted with Georgette and her husband, Reg. They told us about their new enterprise, a tour service called Mussel Bound, which they operated with a local man who raised mussels. They took tourists out on the bay aboard a boat, showing them the mussel aquaculture operation, then feeding them a mussel dinner. Tourism and aquaculture were just two of the industries that people had pursued after the groundfish crash. Because of his work on the tour boat, Reg knew a Leading Tickles lobsterman who could help us find the whale in the morning. In spite of the late hour, Wayne called the lobsterman, Jeffrey Noseworthy, who agreed to help and gave Wayne directions to the slip-way in Leading Tickles where we were to meet him at six in the morning.

Reg set up a cot in the living room for Wayne, and I slept in Reg and Georgette's prim and ruffled bedroom. We rose at five and met Jeffery Noseworthy a bit late after losing our way on the rutted roads that wind down each finger of land jutting out from the island.

"Are you Jeffrey Noseworthy?" Wayne asked through the window of the van of a man waiting by a pick-up near the slipway.

"Yiss." Jeffrey was a stiff and quiet man of about thirty. He wore a cap pulled down low, leaving his face in shadow.

After we launched the Zodiac on the slipway and donned our bright orange suits, Jeffrey, stone-faced and shy, led us out onto the bay in his stout fiberglass open boat. He kept one hand in the pocket of his jeans while holding the throttle on the outboard with the other. When we got out into the bay, the two boats separated to search for the whale. I kneeled in the bow of the Zodiac and scanned the horizon for spouts, clinging to the hand ropes while Wayne raced around the labyrinth between cliffs and rocks. The Zodiac pounded over the busy chop, tossing me and the gear into the air with every wave.

The bay looked like a steely gray desert, cold and strikingly—eerily—free of life. The Zodiac and Jeffrey's lobsterboat were the only vessels in view. No buoys bobbed in the water to tell of nets below. A lone gull or two sluggishly spiraled over the surface, scanning for morsels, finding none. A cluster of five or six black birds sat on the water, not bothering to dive. Clouds grayed and lowered the skies, lending the sea a slate color that seemed to emphasize the tragedy that had befallen the bay. Dark green hills covered with stunted late- summer trees humped up at the sides of deep inlets carved intricately into the margins of the island.

We rendezvoused with Jeffrey after a half hour of futile searching. While I hung onto the rail of Jeffrey's boat, he and Wayne partook of the customary Newfoundland exchange.

"Did you see him?" Wayne asked.

"Huh?"

"No whales?"

"No."

Silence stretched shapeless and indistinct like the gray horizon, like the future. We nodded. We watched the slate gray water.

"Anybody fishing here?"

"No." Jeffery explained in a barely audible voice that Leading Tickles fishermen had taken their gear out of the water and given up on the idea of catching their quota of codfish this year. There was no hint of emotion in his voice as he spoke of the waning fishery.

Nodding and silence. My arm began to throb from holding the Zodiac to the white side of Jeffrey's boat.

"I can pay you for your time and your gas," Wayne offered.

More nods. Blank horizon.

Finally, we separated for another search, which involved more racing around looking for blows.

"There!" I called and pointed when I caught a brief glimpse of a fast-moving black back and a scythe-shaped fin. "It looked like a minke whale, or maybe a pilot whale, but not a humpback," I told Wayne. "No gear."

We waited but never saw the animal again. After a couple of hours of searching, we gave up. What was left of the capelin run had already passed, so what was left of the cod, birds, fishermen, and whales had fled the area too. Even the entangled humpback was long gone. Back at the slipway, Wayne paid Jeffrey, thanked him for his trouble, and gave him a sticker and a pamphlet about the Entrapment Assistance Program. Then we hauled out the Zodiac and set off on the four-hour drive back to Wayne's house.

On Route 1 near Gander, Wayne said, "Now we're gonna get you some bee kepples." He swerved into an Irving gas station parking lot where a small stand displayed quarts of strawberries and rows of mason jars like the ones we had seen on the Oldsmobile. We climbed out of the van.

As we crossed the lot to the berry stand, I asked, "Okay, Wayne, I have to figure this out. How do you spell bee kepple?"

"B-A-K-E-A-P-P-L-E," Wayne said. "Bee kepple. See?" He pointed to a piece of cardboard near a row of jars at the stand.

"Oh! Bakeapples! I get it!" Bakeapple is the Newfoundland name for cloudberries—large, orange raspberry relatives. I had never tried them.

Wayne sidled up to the stand and asked the young girl in a conspiratorial voice, "How much for the bee kepples?"

"Seven dollars."

"Seven dollars!?" Wayne clasped his hand to his heart and staggered backward, gasping in feigned shock.

The girl smiled.

"What about the strawberries?" Wayne asked, pointing to the quart baskets.

"T'ree-fifty."

We bought the strawberries, which were small and sweet and tender. They were gone by the time we pulled into Wayne's driveway two hours later.

*   *   *

A few days after our futile visit to Leading Tickles, Wayne and I drove to his hometown and found that saucy whale off Cape Broyle. After we had survived the animal's attack and cut away the anchor and buoy line from one end of the gear that wrapped its flipper, the whale had swum away from Keith Hayden's second net. I stuck my head into the water and saw the net untwisting, green and ghostly, as it trailed behind the whale. When Wayne determined that we had done what we could to help the whale, we headed for Calvert's snug harbor in a rising breeze.

As we motored around the cape ringed with birds and whales, Wayne spotted Lloyd's boat up ahead and gunned the throttle to catch up. "We're gonna get a tow in," Wayne said. He handed me a coil of line. "Here, tie that onto the D-rings there on the bow for a tow line. Now you'll get an interview with a *real* fisherman."

Lloyd's eyebrows shot up when we pulled alongside and Wayne told me to hand off the tow line. I did as I was told, and one of Lloyd's sons took the line.

"Tow us in?" Wayne asked.

Lloyd was steering the boat from the wheel at the back of the wheelhouse and didn't answer. His son already had the tow line in his hand.

"Climb on," Wayne told me.

I did so, nervously, remembering Lloyd's cold greeting from earlier in the day when he had flourished the pathetic little fish like an indictment. Wayne went forward to chat with the boys while I stayed in the stern near the wheel with Lloyd. The deck behind us, formed of boards over an unused fish well, was strewn with rain gear, extra sweaters, rope, plastic bags, and empty soda cans.

"We're not very tidy here," Lloyd said, keeping one eye on steering between the cliffs as he tried to shove the clutter into a neater pile. He found a plastic bag among the items in the pile and fished out a couple of chocolate chip cookies.

"Cookie?" He held one out to me.

I smiled and accepted the offering.

Lloyd drove the boat near an outcrop of rock at the mouth of Calvert's harbor to set his gill net. He put a piece of broomstick into a hole on the starboard rail, then picked up a coil of rope with an orange float on it and tossed it over the side, leading the line around the broomstick to keep it clear of the propeller and the Zodiac trailing behind. When the float trailed astern, Lloyd threw the anchor over and allowed the net to snake from the bow where it was piled, around the broomstick, and over the side. The men in the bow just stood clear as the net set itself. When the other anchor and float were away, Lloyd turned the bow toward the harbor. We talked while he steered.

"Have you lived in Calvert all your life?" I asked.

"All my life," he said. "My family came to Calvert in the early 1800s."

"How long have you been fishing?"

"Uh . . . since 1960." Until the moratorium in 1992, Lloyd had fished cod traps, drawing lots from a hat at the annual town meeting to determine the site he would fish. "All along here," he waved a hand with thick fingers to indicate the shoreline of the harbor, "used to be every family had a place to land their fish, and stages and flakes where they split and dried the cod." He paused, looking ahead. "I used to fish traps in the summer, and in August and September I'd go handlining offshore," he said with a distant gaze, seeming to peer into the past. "Yeah, in the morning you'd go out and fish for cod and come in and get your bait for the next day. In the evening, you'd jig for squid in the harbor."

Nearly everyone in town helped to jig for squid to bait the men's hooks. Wayne remembered being goaded by adults to get jigging—jerking the line—when they found him daydreaming in the dory with his line in the water.

"Are your kids staying in Calvert?" I asked, referring to the baseball-capped boys in the bow. "Are they going to be fishermen?"

"Oh, there's nothing left." Lloyd said bitterly. "Too much greed." He set his jaw. "Too much greed."

Lloyd told me that he had never sold his permits and was determined to continue fishing for cod in any way he could. He still had a permit to fish salmon, which used to grow to enormous sizes in the ocean and return to Newfoundland's many rivers every summer. But eventually the fisherman's gill net had interrupted too many homeward journeys. Now the once-great runs of salmon consisted of only a few stragglers. Lloyd had not fished for salmon for several years but was determined that he would when the stocks recovered. Unlike Lloyd, most Newfoundland fishermen weren't holding their breath for the salmon to return. They had moved on to fishing for crab, turbot, or capelin.

While he waited, Lloyd gill-netted for the few cod he could catch, went crabbing on his larger boat, and did odd jobs in Calvert.

"In New England, the government has been buying back boats and permits," I told Lloyd. "And the only people who can afford not to take the offers are the people with big boats that can roam around to different fishing grounds. They're consolidating the fishery into a few big boats and the little guys have to sell. In my home on Cape Cod, hardly anybody fishes any more. I think the government is taking the heart and soul out of the small fishery."

At this, Lloyd turned to me with genuine surprise. He seemed shocked to find someone from away who understood the problem of small fishing enterprises giving way to large ones.

"That's exactly the way it is here," he said intently. "Big boats. Sixty-five footers. Now they're giving permits for eighty-five, one hundred footers. I never sold my permits."

"For us, the biggest problem with the big boats is that they concentrate the wealth," I nodded. "They could employ more people in the fishery, even with tighter quotas, if they kept the size of the boats down."

Lloyd nodded. "My enterprise used to support my family and my brother's family. Well, he's dead now." He glanced at his boots, then pointed along the southern shore of the harbor. "Over on that side of the harbor, those houses up there, not one fisherman in any of them." Lloyd estimated that half of these folks were summer people. The rest commuted to work in St. John's. "There used to be thirty, forty fishing enterprises. Now there's six. Pretty soon, there'll be no fishermen here. Too much greed."

As we talked, some of the bitterness seemed to fade from Lloyd's round face. His gruff countenance gave way to sadness.

"When you fished cod traps here, did you take out the young ones and set them loose?" I asked.

"No," he said. "No time. We knew we probably should, but no one else did it." He paused, thinking, gazing forward as he steered. "I guess if we trap again we probably will have to do that."

Lloyd pulled the boat up to the pier in Calvert, and he and his sons lifted four totes of fish, two of flounder and two of cod, out of a hold built to contain more than a thousand pounds of fish. The total catch for the day was fewer than four hundred pounds.

Wayne and I said goodbye to Lloyd and his sons, got into the Zodiac, and made our way under the bridge to the slipway, where the bow nudged the strand of round cobble. We climbed out of the boat. The empty trailer rolled down the beach easily enough, but once we had pulled the Zodiac onto the trailer and lashed it down, the two of us couldn't pull the trailer up the beach. Our feet slipped on the wet cobbles. So Wayne hatched a plan. We tied one end of a rope to the trailer and the other to the hitch on the van, which sat about fifty feet away. Then Wayne drove the van forward while I tried to give the trailer a boost out of the cobble. Soon the trailer sat on high ground. Wayne grinned as he emerged from the van to untie the tow line and hitch up the trailer.

When we had stowed our gear, including Keith Hayden's float and line, we changed out of our wet clothes. I climbed in the passenger side, and Wayne sat in the driver's seat. He paused before he turned the key. It suddenly occurred to us both that we had just spent the better part of the day being attacked by a whale.

"Well, that was . . . interesting," I said.

Wayne turned to me with a look of disbelief, shook his head and laughed.

*　*　*

As he drove through his hometown, Wayne seemed to be in a wistful mood. Calvert itself seemed in a wistful mood, quiet and uncertain. Several men stood on the fish pier, hands in pockets, chatting as though they were waiting for a boat to arrive loaded with fish to be toted out. Lloyd's catch had required just two men to unload, but a half dozen had been on hand to help.

"These places are only fifty minutes from St. John's," Wayne said, "and there's still not enough happening for them. It's criminal what's happening to them. DFO's accumulating quota, concentrating it, all because some economist in Ottawa thinks it's best. I don't know, maybe that's it. Maybe Newfoundland has had its day."

"Yeah, I've been worried about that in New England too," I nodded. His mood was catching. "Probably the fishing is all over. We're just watching it die."

"I think they know. I think they know it's all over." He steered around a corner and thought a moment. "So the whale problem will resolve itself with no fishing. They can't even catch fifty-seven hundred pounds of fish." This was the season quota for gill-netters on the Avalon's southern shore and roughly the average quota throughout Newfoundland. By August, many gill-netters had given up, despairing of ever making the quota.

Wayne went on. "We as a people, you know, Newfoundlanders, we kind of failed. We should have known. I mean I was fishing too. I'm as much to blame as anybody. There was more at stake than fellas out in the boats."

We drove to Wayne's father's home, a modest ranch house overlooking the harbor. His father was away, but Wayne let himself in, and we sat in his father's kitchen eating bakeapple jam on bread his father had baked. Wayne talked about his childhood, a typical Newfoundland one. For Wayne's generation, growing up in Calvert, or in nearly any small Newfoundland community, was all about cod.

"Summer was just fish fish fish," he said. "Fish for supper."

The community of just a few hundred was populated almost entirely by fishing families. Fishermen worked cod traps in thirty-foot trap skiffs, which they filled to the gunwales with cod. Kids spent their summers jigging for squid, spreading salt fish on the drying racks called flakes, and cutting out the tongues of discarded cod carcasses. They sold the tongues to the fish buyers to make pocket money.

Once Wayne and a friend baited fishing hooks with liver and caught a dozen seagulls, which they stuffed into the lobster traps stacked near the fish flakes. The gulls squawked and clucked in their makeshift wooden cages as the boys tried for more birds. Finally an aunt put a stop to the game. "What you are doing is very bad," she told the boys.

Wayne fished with his father when he was old enough, pulling up the web to concentrate the fish on one side of the trap, then scooping thousands of cod into the trap skiff until it was "flat full of fish."

"When people got old, their hobby wasn't to go watch TV, it was to go down to the wharf and see who caught how much . . . how big. When that died, those fellas had nothing to live for. The cod fishery offered a very marginal existence," Wayne said, "but it was enough. When the cod went . . ." His voice trailed off, and he shook his head. "You could live on fifteen to twenty thousand a year.

"It was pretty rare to see a whale in those days. When we'd see a whale, we'd get scared, bang a can against the boat. My father was totally terrified of whales. Once a whale was breaching and came toward the boat. We just dropped the gear and went home."

*   *   *

After our snack at Wayne's father's house, we drove through Cape Broyle looking for Keith Hayden. Wayne rolled his window down as we wound our way along the main road and waved at a pick-up heading the other way. The men spoke through the windows.

"I'm looking for a fisherman named Keit' Hayden," Wayne said to the two men in the pick-up.

They looked at each other and nodded. "Yeah," the driver said, "Keit' Hayden lives up there, up the hill at the end on the left." He pointed to a road just ahead.

At the top of the hill, Wayne asked a little girl on a bicycle, "Is this Keit' Hayden's house?" New vinyl-sided houses lined the street and sported curly door knobs and front doors made of aluminum with little etched glass windows.

"No, he lives there," she pointed, "but he's not home."

Wayne left the floats and the coil of rope on Keith Hayden's back steps with a note saying, "I took this off a whale." He included his phone number in case the fisherman had any questions.

As we drove off, Wayne said, "Usually, you know, when the whale's quiet and you can get all the gear back . . ." He shook his head. "You know, today we lost Buddy's gear. When you can get it back, it's really satisfying."

(Buddy is a moniker Newfoundlanders give to any person they don't know well, the equivalent of "that guy" or "so and so." If someone speaks of a person who lives in the next town, they say, "Buddy down the shore" with a jab of a thumb over the shoulder. A St. John's band calls itself "Buddy and the Other Fellas.")

Next Wayne drove the van to the end of Cape Broyle, where we could get a look at the harbor, hoping to see if the saucy whale was still in the vicinity. A steep and rutted road of red dirt wound toward the point. Wayne parked on the side and set the brake. We hiked a short way down the road to the edge of the cliff and gazed down upon a dizzying vista that took in the harbor mouth and the distant horizon. Whales swam and blew, but the water was so far below that we couldn't make out any details of their movements. We had forgotten the binoculars in the van.

"That one's acting kind of funny." Wayne pointed to a whale that splashed a bit when it surfaced.

We shrugged, gave up, and retreated down the road. As we approached the van, Wayne motioned for me to follow him toward a divot in the cliff. "Tora, come on, I want to show you something."

He led me down a little path into a cleft in the cliff that enclosed a small cove. Waves sloshed in the shadows cast by the steep rock walls of the inlet. When we came to a flat spot on the cliff, Wayne pointed toward the reddish dirt to a wood and stone contraption tied together with rope. "What is that?" he quizzed me, crossing his arms to wait for my answer.

I squatted down to examine the object. Two boards, each about a foot and a half long, crossed at the bottom and were nailed and notched together. Each arm of the cross was carved to a point. Halfway along each arm of the cross, a hole accepted a tenon at the end of a vertical piece of wood a couple feet tall. The four vertical pieces were tied together with rope, caging in a large egg-shaped stone.

"I don't know," I said.

"Well, what would you use something like this for?"

"Is it some kind of anchor?"

"Yes," he said, delighted that I had hit the mark. "It's a killick, a symbol of Newfoundland." Wayne explained that when he was growing up, most Newfoundland fishermen had used these homemade anchors to moor their boats and nets.

"Every spring, my father used to send me out to find killick stones," Wayne told me. "Because every year you'd lose some of them, you know. My father used to curse them things, they were so hard to deal with. They're a symbol, you know."

I reflected on the killick and the day's events as we stepped up the stony path to the van and climbed in for the drive toward St. John's.

On the way up the coast, Wayne pulled the van over to the side of the road in Bay Bulls, a town not far from St. John's that had turned to tourism since the groundfish crash. The government had recently built a new pier in Bay Bulls, and the slipway was in good repair. Whale-watch boats and kayak- and canoe-rental businesses lined the waterfront. Restaurants sold fish and chips. While Wayne went to get coffee, I eavesdropped on a cluster of British tourists who ate fried food at a picnic table in the courtyard of a restaurant.

"I wonder why they called it Bay Bulls," a woman said.

"I think they thought the bay was shaped like a bull," a man answered.

In the mouth of the bay, perhaps half a mile away, a pair of feeding humpbacks threw their flukes in the air and dove into the depths. The tourists, intent on their fish and chips, never noticed.

*　*　*

Two days after Wayne and I wrestled with the saucy whale off Cape Broyle, Keith Hayden called Wayne to thank him. When he had returned to check his gear, he had found both fleets of gill net intact. Apparently Wayne had been right: by cutting away the anchor from one end of the net, we allowed the whale to shake off the rest of the gear. The saucy whale had gotten away clean, and Buddy got his net back.

*　　*　　*

Wayne had said twice that the killick was a symbol for Newfoundland, apparently eager for me to understand. But he didn't elaborate, and I gave up puzzling about the killick until a week later when I spied a basket of trinkets in a St. John's gift shop. Surrounded by sweaters knitted by women in remote outports and jams made of bakeapples and partridge berries was a basket of miniature killicks. I picked one up and examined it. Tiny spruce sticks formed a cage for a smooth little egg-shaped stone. The top, where the anchor line would have been tied on a real killick, held a loop of twine for hanging or holding keys. The little killick was sweet and ingenious, but it gave me an uneasy feeling—the same itchy, unnerving feeling I have when I see tourist shops on Cape Cod selling miniature wooden lobster traps or toy animals with googly eyes made from quahog shells.

The killick and the quahog and the lobster trap are symbols of the past, but not a past that the fish-and-chips and trinket-buying tourists could ever envision. It's not a quaint romantic past when life was simple and easy and good, when mothers wiped their hands on their aprons and smiled as their children played carefree on the shore and their husbands landed their ample catch at the town wharf, joking and laughing among friends and relatives.

Wayne had said, "Every spring, my father used to send me out to find killick stones. My father used to curse them things, they were so hard to deal with."

Until a generation ago, life in a small Atlantic coast town was like a killick, a thing you made with ingenuity, a few sticks, and a well-chosen stone. Working on the water, living on an isolated windswept rock, scraping a garden out of the sandy soil, making things out of the materials at hand, living at the whim of tide and weather. It was not a beautiful life because it was simple or easy. It was beautiful because it was so hard, because you and your family and your community had to scrape a living out of sea and sand and stone, and you lived, maybe not well, but well enough. Life is beautiful if you have used your tenacity and ingenuity to bring home a tote of fish or a bucket of clams at the end of the day. Every day you survived was, in some small measure, a beautiful day. And many days were not beautiful.

Of course these are things that kids rarely understand. When you're a teenager, life in a small town seems anything but beautiful. It is backward and trivial, filled with dirty little secrets and small minds, the whispering dead and desperate inconsequential lives. The "close-knit" community is stifling and seems ready to swallow you up. A future of hard work and unrequited desire looms large in a small town. You promise yourself that, if you can escape the vortex, you will never look back.

Some of us do look back, though, especially if we came from a place where life was beautiful for some of the right reasons. But the cod and the whales were no match for human tenacity and ingenuity, so in our generation, many of us looked back to find the places of our youth changed, irrevocably disassembled.

Some returnees have come back to find their hometowns turned into movie sets with clean one-dimensional facades and gift shops hawking symbols of the old life, as though a lobster buoy key chain and a McDonald's filet-o-fish sandwich could impart the health and virtue of hard work on the sea. I returned to Cape Cod to find that the backwater of my youth had been engulfed by sprawl. It felt—and still feels—like strangers are tromping through my living room, gawking at my things as though they are in a museum.

The communities in New England and the Canadian Maritimes that still rely on fisheries have moved on to other species. Many prodigal sons and daughters who return home to go fishing are targeting species their parents regarded as "trash fish." In Maine, it was the sea urchins the locals called "witch's tits" and "whore's eggs." On Cape Cod, it was the dogfish, the small sharks we had always thought of as pests that ate our bait and wrecked our lines. In Newfoundland, fishermen turned to snow and queen crab. Capelin, lobsters, bony little scup, and flatfish like fluke and turbot got scooped up in efficient newfangled gear. Now the urchins, dogfish, capelin, turbot, and crab are getting scarcer. Fishermen are wrangling over scup quotas. If we continue to fish down the food chain, maybe next we'll be arguing over copepod quotas.

Other wayward children have wandered back home to find ghost towns populated by a few hold-outs. Jon Lien told me this story in August 2001:

"A couple weeks ago I went out to dissect a beached whale in a place called Port Albert. In the eighties they had two hundred people there, and now they have seventy. But there was hope," Jon raised a finger. "They had one child. They had one five-year-old child still at home. They were so proud of that child. They brought the child up and introduced him to me, so we took his picture sitting on the whale, and they got it in the local paper: 'Port Albert has a child.' And it was very important for people to know because it meant they weren't gonna die.

"What's happened is that anybody that's got half a chance, that's young and has a work history, they come onto the Avalon Peninsula. We've led the economy of Canada in growth—unfortunately. I can say that, I have a job, but it comes at great cost. It's brought about the shift from the rural outports onto the Avalon and areas like this."

As the past dissolves before our eyes, some people mourn the tragic loss, beg for the vestiges to be preserved, yearn for the old days. But when we are alone at night staring at the ceiling, we can't escape the fact that the ways of the past have led us here. Some fishermen like to insist that there are many more fish out there—groundfish, swordfish, tuna, dogfish, crab—than fisheries officials in Canada and the United States believe. Tight quotas, they say, are an injustice visited upon them by wealthy, litigious environmentalists in collusion with skittish government officials. Some of the depleted stocks are beginning to recover, but anyone who has spent a long lifetime fishing the waters of the North Atlantic cannot deny that many are still just a vestige of what they once were.

In the words of oceanographer Jeremy Jackson, "To pretend that we can understand the loss of all these fisheries by blaming it on things like climate change is to ignore the obvious fact that we ate these creatures and they're not there anymore."

If we were to return to the ways of our parents, we would seal the fate of the fisheries, but if we abandoned what they taught us about beauty and ingenuity and tenacity, we would give up our capacity to mend the world they left behind.

So I stand in a St. John's gift shop holding a miniature killick like a fulcrum between the past and the future. This object is the symbol of a past only half longed-for and a future only half welcome. I place the killick back in the basket and move on.

*　*　*

"Soon there will be a million whales and no fishermen," Lloyd Sullivan had said.

Lloyd and many like him have not found a way to leave the past and look to the future, even as they move on to new fisheries like crab or turbot. Beginning with the moratorium in 1992, the Canadian government spent more than $8 billion in the Atlantic provinces to offer fishermen free retraining programs and unemployment benefits, a program that came to be known as the "Package." The purpose of the Package was to help fishermen make the transition out of the fishing industry. Most took the money, but few of the older fishermen took the retraining, arguing that they were too old to move into another industry. They preferred to wait for the fish to come back. In the meantime, if they were stubborn and had the money to refit, they went crabbing or fishing for capelin or turbot. But ultimately, they saw these new fisheries as temporary. The cod would surely return, as long as they left them alone for a few years. The older fishermen became what fisheries officials call "latent effort," people waiting to return to catching fish.

If Lloyd Sullivan represents the older Newfoundland fisherman bitterly clinging to the past and waiting for the cod to return, then thirty-three-year-old Robin Butler of Kelligrews represents the new generation of Newfoundland fishermen, a leaner and savvier bunch who rely on several enterprises to stay afloat rather than staking all their hopes for the future on just one or two species of fish. When Robin Butler caught a humpback in his net in July 2001, he was delighted to call Fisheries about the whale and eager to help Wayne free the tangled animal.

"He's a natural at it," Wayne told me of Robin. "You should phone him."

When I called, Robin said he would be willing to take me out on his gill-netter to show me his fishing operation and to tell me the story of his entangled whale.

So, one sunny morning I meet Robin Butler at the dock in Foxtrap near Kelligrews on the southeastern shore of Conception Bay.

"Hi," I say as I climb out of my car. "You must be Robin."

"You're Tora?" He offers a big hand. With an easy smile he welcomes me aboard and sets me immediately at ease, telling me where I can stow my camera and my backpack near the back of the wheelhouse. A bit stout with a clean-shaven round face, Robin wears a pair of green foul-weather pants. I look over the neat deck while Robin's cousin and father help to bring ice and fuel aboard.

When all the ice and fuel is stowed, Robin enters the wheelhouse and starts the motor. As he pulls away from the dock, he switches on, one after another, the GPS, depth sounder, VHF, and an FM radio tuned to a local country station. We motor out onto Conception Bay to haul Robin's gill net under a low gray sky.

Robin Butler has been his own boss for much of his adult life. He is a professional scuba diver and has been all over the world diving for work and pleasure. Before getting his own fishing boat, Robin ran a business that supplied groceries and other provisions to offshore fishing boats.

When he started fishing for himself, Robin chose to buy a small versatile outboard boat rather than to risk a huge investment in a large diesel crab boat like so many others had done. Now he fishes in the sturdy twenty-five-foot fiberglass vessel for crab and cod. With a large outboard motor and a wheelhouse full of electronics, Robin and his mate, cousin Chris Butler, can range up to twenty miles from their berth at Foxtrap. The boards enclosing the fish holds in Robin's boat can be moved and reconfigured to contain a couple of tons of crab or a couple totes of cod. He supplements his fishing income with scuba diving.

Chris, twenty-six, attends college during the school year where he is studying to enter the petroleum industry. He spends his summers working for Robin—for now.

The day I join them on Conception Bay, Robin and Chris seem like they have been working together long enough to have a quiet understanding. While Robin drives and chats with me, Chris fires up the motor that turns the winch for hauling the gill net. He has it ready when

Figure 10.1. Chris Butler (left) and Robin Butler standing next to Robin's multipurpose fishing boat. The spoked winch visible on deck is used for hauling gear aboard. Photo by T. Johnson.

Robin pulls up to an orange float. Chris gaffs the float aboard and begins to haul the net to the surface with a wrap around the turning winch. The contraption looks like a wheel hub made of steel rod turning on its side on a box mounted at the back of the wheelhouse. The rope, monofilament netting, and floats jam in the "V" where the spokes of the two sides of the winch meet to impart the hauling force of the hydraulic motor.

Robin loans me a pair of white nylon knit gloves so I can help pick the fish out of the net. Then he shows me how to use the lever to operate the winch while he holds tension on the net to keep it jammed in the spokes without tangling. The motor turns and a few small brown spotted cod and big red crabs with long spindly legs emerge from the deep thirty fathoms below.

"That's good there," Robin prompts, and I pull the lever to stop the winch. Robin and Chris deftly pick the fish and crustaceans out of the net, while I fumble to extract a single crab, all bumps and tangles, from my portion of the web. The monofilament twists around the crab's long legs in an incomprehensible mass, and I have barely made any progress

Figure 10.2. Robin Butler grins over a thirty-pound codfish.
Photo by T. Johnson.

when Robin says patiently, "Go ahead and turn it on. It's easier to get 'em out of the net when you have more room."

I relinquish the crab to the experts and turn on the winch. It drags up more crabs and a few fish. I stop the winch, and Chris and Robin pick them out. And so it goes for hundreds of feet of net. We chat and warm up to one another.

A sharp filet knife rests in a groove at the starboard rail, and as each cod comes aboard, Chris takes the knife in his right hand and holds the fish by the gill plates in his left; then, in one swift motion, he slices open the neck and cuts the gills away from the body, releasing a gush of crimson. The dead fish flops into a tote.

"So are these fish about the average size?" I ask, pointing with my gloved hand to indicate a skinny specimen about a foot and a half long.

"Yiss," both men answer." Robin goes on, "They used to be much bigger, twenty, thirty pounds about. But now, five, ten pounds is the average."

When a big cod, weighing perhaps thirty pounds, appears at the rail, we all exclaim over it. I pull my camera out and snap a couple of shots of Robin struggling to pull the fish out of the tangled web. This fish is by far the largest cod I have seen since the stocks collapsed.

Chris has a nifty trick for picking the crabs out of the net. Since their long knobby legs are typically wadded up with the web, Chris shakes and turns the net until he can get a hold of the crab's body. Then, holding the carapace, he peels the net off of the legs like he is removing a pair of pants.

"We want to catch these fellas later," he says once as he tosses a crab over the side.

Most of the crabs make it back into the brine unharmed, but a few are smashed and crunched to a pulp when they are caught under a line against the spokes of the winch. Robin sets aside a few crabs for me to take home to the Liens.

As we work, my net picking improves little, but I become more or less competent at operating the winch. After an hour of work, the net rests in a pile on the deck and two totes are filled with cod. Robin ducks into the wheelhouse and steers the boat around to a new spot where he hopes there will be fewer crabs and more cod. Then he signals to Chris, and the net snakes over the stern, diving for the bottom. When the net is away, Robin shuts down the motor and lets the boat drift on the blue gray water of the bay.

"There," he says, sitting down on the starboard rail and crossing his arms. "Now we can tell you the story of the whale."

*   *   *

Robin had fished for a few years with his father, then on his own for several years without ever catching a whale. Then one July day when the capelin were running, Robin and Chris went out onto Conception Bay to haul Robin's gill nets. As they were bringing in the first fleet of gear, another fisherman motored over to say that a whale was caught in a gill net nearby.

"Not sure whose net it is," the fisherman told them.

"We went to go haul our next fleet," says Robin, "and when we did that, there it was."

"The whale was lucky enough that he was able to haul the whole net to the surface." Chris adds from his seat on the stern rail.

Robin went on, "The head rope, the green one, the one that had the floats on it, that's what he had in his mouth." Robin showed me with his hand how the whale had been caught. "'Course he was in after the capelin and that's how he picked it up. We were probably in twelve or fifteen fathom of water, eh?" He glances at Chris for confirmation, "which is pretty shallow."

"So," I ask, "you came up to the net and what was the whale doing?"

"He was just, uh, just sitting on the surface. We thought he was dead at first, but then every three or four minutes he was breathing. It was at least that long, if not longer."

"He was relaxed." Chris says.

Robin nods. "He was pretty relaxed. He wasn't thrashing or nothing like that."

"So what did you do? Did you try to haul the gear?"

"No, we came up on him and looked for a time and talked about it, wondering what to do. Finally we phoned the Department of Fisheries."

After four or five calls on the cell phone, Robin finally reached Julie Huntington, who told him that Wayne was on his way. It was a busy summer day on Conception Bay: the capelin were running. As Robin and Chris waited for Wayne, thirteen stout capelin seiners milled around the bay, setting nets one after another. They encircled the shimmering schools with a fine-mesh net, then cinched the bottom tight and scooped them aboard. Minke and humpback whales chased the capelin too, while the meager run of cod swam after the silver fish beneath the waves.

"Did the other whales notice the one in the net?" I ask.

"Well," Robin offers, "I think they were fishing themselves, just doing their thing. I thought we seen another humpback outside there. It could have been waiting for that one or . . . I don't know."

"So you spent this time standing by the whale with your cell phone?"

"Yiss," Robin nods. "He was just floating at the surface; he wasn't moving at all."

"What did the whale look like? How much of its body was out of the water?"

"Just his back," says Robin, motioning with his hand to indicate the curving posture of the creature in the water. "His blowhole wasn't in the water, so he only had that little curve up out of the water, that's it. So that's why we didn't know how big he was 'til we actually got up close and looked down and seen it was a forty-foot humpbacked whale."

With logistics arranged by cell phone, it took a couple more hours before Robin, Chris, Chris's friend Steve, Wayne, and Wayne's friend Jim Miller were all finally on the scene with Robin's whale. When they arrived in the Zodiac, Wayne and Jim circled the tangled creature to assess the situation. They each donned masks and snorkels and ducked their heads beneath the swell to have a look. Then Robin climbed in the Zodiac and took a turn with the snorkel. They circled and dunked for nearly an hour.

"I seen these two flippers, I guess, on the side. They was white," Robin says recalling the glimpses he had of the whale in his gill net. "I seen the tail. I don't think I got a good look at him right up close."

"So you didn't see the gear in his mouth?"

"I did see the long gear hanging out a bit." Another motion of the hand.

As the whale sat mostly quiet at the surface, they were able to ascertain that the float line was in the whale's mouth, jammed between plates of baleen. The massive creature had already parted the lead line and torn the net away from the float line, so only the green nylon line with little floats remained in its mouth. Wayne, with Jim and Robin in the Zodiac, decided it was time to cut the line on one side of the mouth. Chris and his friend Steve took video footage from Robin's boat nearby.

"We went out and got the grappelin' ready," Robin recalls, "and Wayne was telling us to make sure we didn't get all tangled up, just in case the whale decides to take off. So we managed to hook the rope and we got up close to him, close enough that we were on his flank and slowed him down a little bit. We cut one side of the net."

"How close to its mouth?"

"We were only a couple, two, three feet away," he says. "Then he took us for a little ride around. He was moving a bit, blowing, getting nervous, I guess. When we cut the one side, he took a little stroll with us."

"Did he make any sounds?"

"He never made nothing of a sound. He was blowing pretty good. We were working on him for about five or ten minutes. Wayne finally said, 'We got to cut 'em and that's it.'"

Wayne told Robin that if they could cut the rope on the other side of the mouth, the whale might be able to shake out the remaining bit of line. They made a decisive move.

Robin remembers: "So then, we hauled up. We made one dash for him and hauled up on his back, close as we could get up to him, and we worked on him for about five minutes. He never dove."

They finally cut the line on the other side of the whale's mouth, and the whale was free.

"Swam away?" I ask.

"Yiss, swam away."

"And you could see the other end of your net was still hanging there, right?"

"Oh, yiss, yeah. It was the very end of the net. It was only fifteen fathom of net spoiled. It wasn't very much at all."

"We were very fortunate," Chris agrees.

"A right whale would have taken the gear with him," Robin speculates.

"You say this was your first whale?" I ask.

"First whale that we encountered," Robin nods.

"Have you heard about other people getting whales in their nets around here?"

"Oh, yiss, yiss."

"Traps," Chris offers.

Robin nods, "Especially traps, right, years ago."

"So how have people reacted before who have had whales in their gear? Did they shoot them? What did they do?"

Robin pauses, thinking back. "I think the fishermen didn't know what to do until they saw what Jon and all them are doin.' I guess somebody had to take the initiative and say 'let's start saving them and raise money.'"

"Do you think people are scared of the whales?"

"Sure," Robin laughs.

"They're twice the size again of your boat, right?" says Chris. "It wouldn't take much to capsize your boat."

"But I, myself," Robin says, "I don't think I'm brave, but I . . . I wanted to be there. That's for sure, I wanted to be there."

"Why did you want to be there?"

He ponders the question for a moment. "Well, it was the first time seeing a whale that I was that close. I dive, myself, so I like to see them right up close.

I ask Robin if people here feel differently about the whales than they did years ago.

"Yiss, yiss," he answers.

"How so?"

"I think that now many would save them, no matter what," Robin says, seriously. "The net's not worth much anyway, you know, not *really*, compared to the life of a whale."

As we sit on the rails of Robin's boat on the lumpy bay, gulls gather and form a raucous band around us, anticipating a handout. Our conversation turns to the future of the fishing industry.

I tell Chris and Robin about Lloyd Sullivan and his reluctance to give up his salmon and cod permits. He is waiting for the fish to return.

"Yiss, that's it: old school," Robin says. "Around here a lot of people are selling their permits back to the government. They're getting out of it all together, because younger people don't want to be at it anyway. Because, looking at it, they say 'I could make more money at something else.'"

"At oil, for instance." I laugh and gesture toward Chris.

"At oil," Robin nods. "Which is true, you know, that's going to be a big business around here. That's the way you've got to look at it. Do you want to be out here making twenty or thirty thousand dollars when you could be make eighty or ninety somewhere else?"

"So why are you doing it? Why are you fishing?" I press him. "I mean I know you've got other things going, right? Do you think most guys your age are doing the same thing? Do you think they're diversifying and working in some other field as well as fishing?"

"Yes, I think so. Now the fishermen here . . . well, I guess most of them are working at something else, especially younger guys. The crabbing is the only fishing that's worthwhile around here. For me, going out fishing is . . . well, I have problems working for somebody else."

"Uh-huh," I nod. "My husband says the same thing. He doesn't ever want to work for someone else."

"I don't really mind working for anybody, but I guess I need some authority or something. Is that it, Chris?"

"And I'm following orders." Chris salutes, and we all laugh.

"I've been working for myself for the last five, six years," Robin goes on, "not only doing this. I had a small business supplying some of the fishing vessels with groceries. And scuba diving was another business. And certainly, if you love the water, why not stay there, right? If the opportunity arises, you know?"

"So, Robin, do you think you're going to keep doing it?"

"Sure, yeah, just as long as it's viable. But I'll be working at some other job too."

"Do you know anybody who's making their whole living from fishing?"

Chris and Robin put their heads together and can think of one member of their community who makes his living entirely from fishing.

"Well, he goes to Nova Scotia to fish lobster," Robin tells me. "He has another crew."

"He's also got a bigger boat, that gray one," Chris chimes in. "He's going after turbot now. He already got his cod quota; he was fishing over to Cape Race."

"Huh," I say. "So he's fishing for cod, turbot, lobster?"

"He's thinking about going after hake," Chris tells me. "He's thinking about it and talking about it. He's looking for a crew. He's trying to recruit me, but I told him I'm going back to school this year."

"Is he doing crab?" I ask.

"Crab," Robin nods, "he's got the crab.

"So that's how he's doing it, he's fishing five or six species," I say. "He's not just putting all his money into one cod trap and that's the end of it."

While we speak about the future, the gulls surround, cackling and boisterous. Robin and Chris will spend the afternoon hauling their crab gear, so it's time to take me back to the wharf. But first they clean the catch of two totes of cod, slitting the bellies open and hurling the guts into the sea, finally satisfying the vociferous demands of the birds. Robin packs a plastic bag for me full of cod tongues, cheeks, roes, and a couple of filets. Then he snaps the legs off the crabs he had saved and puts these in another plastic bag.

When the blood is washed from the deck and the knives are stowed, Robin fires up the motor and drives me into the dock, where I step ashore with my arms full with the generous makings of a rare evening feast.

*   *   *

The saucy whale's attack off Cape Broyle had left me unscathed and surprisingly unruffled. After my initial alarm at seeing the flailing animal for the first time, I had simply gotten down to the business of trying to help Wayne get the gear off. When the whale took willful and calculated swipes at us with its tail, I had been more worried about the unsheathed knife than the whale's aggression. But upon reflection as I sat in the cabin on Jon Lien's farm writing about the experience, it suddenly occurred to me that I might have been in some danger if the whale had capsized the boat, putting me in ice-cold water with ropes and gear tangled around me. I might have drowned like an entangled whale. So, wanting to calm my nerves and connect with my family, I went to a quiet room in Jon's house and called my husband in Massachusetts.

After I had told him the story of the saucy whale taking swipes at the Zodiac, my husband paused, thinking. "Wow, that is so funny," he said. "A woman at work was just asking about you today, and I told her you were in Newfoundland doing research for a book about whales and fishermen. And she said, 'Oh, I *love* whales. They're so gentle and spiritual.'"

11 Pissing on Trees

Fishermen and Conservationists Lock Horns

I think she's lying, and she thinks I'm lying.
Jon Our, Cape Cod gill-netter, speaking about
whale advocate Sharon Young

I sit in a darkened classroom in the Mount Desert Island High School in Maine. Even though it's June, a bitter cold rain spits at the window, and I can see grim gray clouds hugging the mountains. Seated around me, looking exceedingly uncomfortable in the hard metal and plastic chairs, are several local fishermen. These guys, mostly lobstermen, have come to learn how to disentangle minke whales. Most are in flannel shirts and jeans, a few wear caps, and nearly all sit slouched in their chairs with their arms crossed, wearing inscrutable expressions. Fishermen adopt this posture so commonly in settings like this that I have come to call it the "fishermen's meeting pose."

It's not just the chairs making them uncomfortable; the tense political context surrounding New England's whales and fishermen pervades the room. Many of the fishermen worry that participating in this program to disentangle minkes would be tantamount to admitting that Maine's fixed-gear fisheries are killing whales.

Laura Ludwig, who coordinates Maine's Large Whale Take Reduction Program, has asked these Mount Desert Island fishermen to come. Laura is a former lobsterman and has also worked in Canada assisting research on blue whales. Today she is dressed in jeans and a button-down shirt and seems a little nervous.

The state has hired Sean Todd to work with Laura in offering a series of workshops for local fishermen on getting whales out of fishing gear. Sean, a marine mammal scientist at College of the Atlantic in Bar Harbor, paid his dues disentangling whales for several years with Jon Lien in Newfoundland. The idea behind the Maine program is to build a network of trained fishermen along the Maine coast who can respond to minke entanglements. Sean is showing the group a PowerPoint slide presentation, going through the basics of disentangling whales. On the screen is a photo of a minke whale, the smallest of New England's baleen whales.

"With a phone call to Laura, that's the whale that you can approach," Sean tells the fishermen. He gestures toward Laura, who sits in front of me, nodding. "Under Section 18 of the Marine Mammal Protection Act, the state has a permit to release minke whales. You will be deputies of the state—that's why the call is necessary."

Bob Bowman, the Center for Coastal Studies' Maine disentanglement coordinator (and my brother-in-law), is standing behind me. He also has his arms crossed and may be the cause of Laura's apparent nervousness. "Hm," he says quietly. There is some debate about whether the state has the authority to deputize fishermen to disentangle whales, and Bob believes they do not. For now, however, Bob says nothing more.

"You are not greenhorns," Sean tells the fishermen. "You know what lines are on this whale. You know what to expect. Given the area where you find the animal, you know what lines are going to be there. Remember: safety at all times. It's only a minke whale—there's no reason for anyone to be a hero."

The faces in Sean's audience are still stony. I wonder if the fishermen are put off by Sean's British accent, his academic background, or perhaps the PowerPoint.

"What we're describing here is not the solution, it's a Band-Aid," says Sean. "What we really need to come up with is a solution that is reasonable to the industry and to the policymakers and prevents entanglements."

He goes on to list myths about minkes. The first myth appears on the screen and he reads, "'Minke whales are small.' I don't know how close some of you have gotten to whales before, but they get bigger and bigger the closer you get. When you are actually up against them, they are *huge*. So you might think, 'He's big, but he knows what I'm doing.' This is, in fact, not true. It is very easy to spook whales, very easy indeed. They are incredibly scared of us. Bear in mind whatever you do, it's likely the animal is going to react to you."

Next Sean dispels the myth that "whales are so big you can't hurt them," advising the fishermen not to pull on the tail or the flippers.

"Next myth: 'Whales are gentle giants.' It's the old story that evolution put a smile on the dolphins' face. Whales are *not* gentle giants; they can be extremely aggressive creatures. They are wild creatures, plus they're scared out of their wits. They don't know what's happened. They have lived their entire lives never restrained by anything in the open ocean, and all of a sudden this strange green claw stops them dead in their tracks. They are scared; they are panicked. And there's a boat coming closer to them, and they can't get out of way. So expect them to try and defend themselves initially."

Sean moves on to the steps the fishermen should take when clearing rope or net from a whale. First, move onlookers away, he tells them, then use a mask and snorkel to get a look at the whale and determine what and where to cut. To remove the gear, work from the head back to the tail.

"*Never ever enter the water*," Sean says, wagging his finger. He reminds the fishermen how aggressive whales can be, then launches into an impression of Jacques Cousteau. "And we entered ze watair and we warned ze whale. Ze whale had ze sense zat we were trying to help heem. And slowly we stroked ze whale to calm heem down and zen we could make ze cut necessary to free heem. As he swam away, he breached into ze distance as eef to say thank you."

This elicits chuckles from the group, and the tension in the room thins a bit. Sean goes on to discuss the danger areas to watch out for, the most important being the tail. Then he shows the fishermen the special-ized tools the state will be giving trained fishermen, including hooked knives and grapple hooks designed to grab onto rope. Much of this equipment was designed and built by Bob Bowman.

When Sean is finished with the slide show, Laura scurries to the back of the room to turn the lights on.

"Bob, do you have anything to add?" Sean asks.

"Just that I'm on call seven days a week, twenty-four hours a day for disentanglement. You can just call the Center for Coastal Studies' 800 number or call the Coast Guard if you have an entangled whale that you don't want to deal with. *I would recommend that you don't deal with it for the simple reason that if you screw it up you could get in a lot of trouble.* If somebody finds out that you didn't do it right, then you are negligent if you didn't call in the right resources to help you. But it's up to you I suppose . . ."

Bob lets the words trail off, and the tension in the room thickens again. His main concern is that the fishermen will either hurt them-selves or botch the job by cutting the animal loose but leaving deadly gear attached with no trailing ropes with which to catch the animal again. The minimal training these fishermen are receiving at the workshop doesn't increase his confidence in the program.

In fact, Bob has been training fishermen to help with disentangle-ment for several years. Most of the fishermen in the room have been to at least one of his workshops. Bob told them not to try to disentangle whales on their own until they had some experience working alongside professionals. The intent of Bob's program was to give a few Maine fish-ermen enough experience to eventually allow them to release whales on their own. But when fishermen stopped reporting entangled whales for fear of more regulation, Bob no longer had a way to get the fishermen involved.

Also, CCS has a contract with the feds to disentangle whales along the entire east coast, and the feds have not told CCS to leave the minke en-tanglements to the state. Bob chooses this moment to bring these issues up again.

Laura Ludwig, who coordinated this event, counters, "In theory that's the protocol we're trying to establish, that the first call is made and the communications happen from my office really fast." She invited Bob to the workshop to be polite; he lives only a couple of miles down the road. I suspect she is now regretting the invitation.

Bob says that if fishermen call the Coast Guard to report an entangled whale, "the Coast Guard will immediately call their headquarters in Boston, and they will immediately call the Center for Coastal Studies. It happens in about fifteen minutes. It's only about fifteen minutes before I'm on the road."

Sean cuts in, addressing the fishermen a little nervously. "Perhaps it's really important to mention that you shouldn't try to deal with a complicated entanglement by yourself."

"It's always complicated," Bob says tersely. "The theory isn't that complicated, but doing it is always complicated."

"So you would recommend for minke whales that people should call the Coast Guard?" Laura asks Bob.

He nods. "People should call the Coast Guard. It should be reported to the National Marine Fisheries Service and the Center for Coastal Studies."

At the mention of the Fisheries Service, several of the fishermen shift in their chairs. The tension thickens yet more.

"For minkes?" Laura repeats.

"Absolutely," says Bob. "We've been doing it that way for eight years, and nothing has changed as far as the Center for Coastal Studies is concerned."

"Well it's just a different style," Laura says, visibly ruffled by this wrench in the works. "Now that we have the Maine State Whale Plan, we want to try and keep it domestic, instead of international with the Center for Coastal Studies. I'm just thinking in terms of having the network *here*." Clearly, she would rather be having this conversation anywhere but in front of a bunch of fishermen.

"I'm right here on Mount Desert Island," Bob laughs.

Laura's reference to the Massachusetts-based Center for Coastal Studies as "international" reminds me of the words of one observer: "Maine looks upon the federal government as a foreign power."

"But statewide," Laura says, "when a minke whale is the whale in question, we're going to be trying to approach that much more locally, instead of making the Center for Coastal Studies folks come all the way up for that."

"Truth be known," interjects a fisherman from the group, "we have been threatened with our livelihood. I think we all probably consider ourselves friends of whales. We've been doing this, most of us, for generations."

By "doing this," I'm not sure whether he means fishing or disentangling whales. It could be either, and no one asks.

The fisherman goes on. "But now we're faced with a situation where we are being penalized for things, whether they're our fault or not. We are trying to get on board with this program, but I'm sitting here listening to this last exchange, and I'm wondering whether I wouldn't be a hell of a lot better off to just wash my hands of it and say to hell with the whole works."

"You're saying we're not supposed to touch them," adds a second fisherman, addressing Bob.

"I'm not saying you're not supposed to touch them."

"Well, you are," counters the fisherman. "So if you're going to get in trouble, why would you even want to do it?"

"That's exactly what I'd like to settle as well," Laura jumps in. She goes on to describe a situation that happened a month ago, in which Maine fishermen had disentangled three humpbacks without a permit or any training. "One humpback was entangled and was approached under cover of darkness. They were very quiet and hush hush about it. The fishermen even consulted Marine Patrol that very first occasion. They called their local officer and said, 'Theoretically, hypothetically, what would happen if a humpback whale got caught up in our fishing gear? Would it close the fishery down?'"

"Of course it's not going to close the fishery down if it's a humpback," Laura assures the fishermen, "but if it were a right whale, you would want to be little more sensitive about it. That's the answer they got. So when the entanglement happened, the fishermen—even knowing that it wouldn't close the fishery down—decided they didn't want to tell anyone about it. Therefore there were three disentanglements, done to the best of their ability, including wrapping the buoys up in the hauler and just holding on to that whale so they could do the cutting."

This surreptitious disentanglement was unquestionably illegal and dangerous. Lashing the entangling gear to the boat can be risky for both the whale and the would-be rescuers. That kind of force can wrench or break a tail or a flipper, and if the whale panics and attempts to flee it could pull the boat over or cause lines or gear to break under enormous tension. All of this can happen before the crew has a chance to cast off the line.

"When I talked to the National Marine Fisheries Service about that at a later date," Laura continues, "I said, 'Well, what's the recourse for that? I know these guys were fearing for their livelihoods, they were fearing for their jobs, their lifestyles, etc. . . . They don't want to get punished for doing the right thing.'

"And she said, 'In fact, there are guidelines where we are not supposed to approach these animals, but in the end result the animal was helped.' There was not a punishment that happened after that situation. There was no recourse for the National Marine Fisheries Service, the Center for Coastal Studies, or other agencies like Marine Patrol, Coast Guard."

"The Center for Coastal Studies would never do that!" Bob's frustration is evident in his voice. "We are not an enforcement agency. The Center for Coastal Studies' role has always been as a service to aid fisherman. You've got a problem out there: you've got an entangled whale, you want help getting it out. That's what we do. We've got expertise, we've got equipment, and that's all we do. If you're going to get it out anyway, you might as well call somebody that knows how to do it and has some experience. And that's what our role has always been. We take notes, but there's no penalty for that. Anybody who's ever done that, who has been through this knows that if anything you get praised for doing this, even if it's unsuccessful. The whole idea of a network is that fishermen are an integral part, that's what makes this thing work."

Another man in the group says fishermen don't feel comfortable reporting entangled whales. "Most people think we're going to get punished for doing that. And what I mean by punished is more restrictions put on us."

"I can't guarantee that that won't be so," Bob admits. "But it doesn't come from us. This is a frustration that we have as well."

"Every time one of these entanglements happens," says an older fisherman who has been quiet until now, "then all of a sudden . . . the data that comes at us, we have no way of fighting it. If these guys actually keep working against us, why would we want to even get on the cell phone to tell the Coast Guard? God knows."

Now Sean speaks. "Like Bob said, I can't guarantee that there won't be more stringent guidelines coming down the road, but the best strategy against that is the involvement of the fisherman."

"That's right," Bob agrees.

A younger fisherman, still in the fishermen's meeting pose, pipes up. "The thing is, though—and I may be going out on a limb to say this—but this is the truth: There's probably more disentanglements sitting around these tables, minke whale disentanglements . . ." He doesn't finish the sentence. This is indeed a bold step, admitting that fishermen in the room had disentangled whales themselves, illegally and with no training. Before Maine fishermen became concerned about regulations, Bob was disentangling at least a few minkes every year in the state of Maine.

"I was getting a dozen calls a year," Bob has told me, "then everybody got scared and those calls dropped right off."

Bob has no reason to believe that minkes have left the Maine coast, and one glance from the nearest ocean lookout could tell him that the gear is still proliferating out there. It's also unlikely that the minkes have figured out how to avoid collisions with gear. The fishermen are maintaining a code of silence, and some are disentangling the whales themselves. They are doing this for two reasons: First, they want to take care of the situation and get back to work as soon as possible. Second, they want to avoid the regulations they feel would inevitably follow if they reported an entangled whale of any species. Lack of trust is killing whales and driving a stake between two entities that have always sought to help fishermen: Maine's Department of Marine Resources and the Center for Coastal Studies.

The candid fisherman went on. "But we never got blamed for those entanglements because nobody knew about them but us. If every time we get an entanglement it becomes a statistic, you see why we'd feel like we're going out on a limb even getting involved."

"The entanglement statistics don't come from the reported entanglements," Bob says, "because they're unreliable. We don't know how many animals are entangled based on the number of reports. In fact, we believe only about 3 percent of entangled humpback whales are reported. It's a very low number. So disentanglement is, like Sean said, it's just a Band-Aid. This isn't going to fix this thing, but it shows the efforts of the fishing industry here."

The fishermen do not seem convinced, and I doubt this little chat will cause many of them to break the code of silence. They know that in a way entanglement reports do lead to additional regulations. Scientists estimate the rates of entanglement from scars on the animals, not from reported animals. But injured and dying entangled whales—especially right whales—tell us not only that whales are becoming entangled but also that, in at least some cases, those entanglements are endangering the future of the species. They also influence public opinion on the issue. And with the DAM rule in effect, if fishermen report a right whale, entangled or not, they could be setting themselves up for a closure.

Laura reminds the group that minkes are not endangered and the stakes are not so high. The effort is more valuable as a data gathering tool, she says, and to show the feds that the industry is stepping up to the plate and doing something about the entanglement problem.

Finally, the group files out to the parking lot, where Laura has a seventeen-foot fiberglass model of a whale, which looks more like a giant corpulent porpoise with a couple of brooms in its mouth. In the spitting rain, Laura and Sean wrap the whale model with rope. The fishermen seem much more comfortable out in the rain, taking turns cutting the rope with the hooked knife on the end of an aluminum pole.

*   *   *

The groundfish crash of the early 1990s dealt a devastating blow to the trust New England's fishermen once had in fisheries managers. Environmentalists who pressured fisheries regulators to protect fish stocks were the first to lock horns with the fishermen. By the time right whale protection appeared on their radar screens, the fishermen who were still in the industry were embittered and mistrustful. They poised for their next big fight.

When Max Strahan sued the state of Massachusetts and the U.S. National Marine Fisheries Service (NMFS) in the mid-1990s, he forced both to put protection for the critically endangered right whale on the front burner. Timelines ordered by the courts in these cases set the pace for developing plans for reducing serious injury and mortality of large whales in the Atlantic. Under the Marine Mammal Protection Act (MMPA), the feds were required to convene the Atlantic Large Whale Take Reduction Team (TRT).

NMFS first gathered fishermen, conservationists, scientists, and state officials in 1996 to begin the process of developing a plan. They met several times in the first year of the Take Reduction Team because the courts had given the Fisheries Service just six months to develop an interim plan. The team's mandate was to agree on and suggest to NMFS regulations and actions that would diminish the number of whales injured or killed by fishing gear. The Fisheries Service was not required to act on the team's suggestions, but the point of having the teams was to make the stakeholders—the people who were invested in the outcome of the process—feel like they had a say. Presumably this would minimize litigation and build trust and understanding between opposing factions.

Most of the key members of the team, especially fishermen and conservationists, came to TRT meetings with a political agenda, expecting to negotiate. They played their cards close to their chests and gave as little ground as possible. One observer compared this posturing and staking out of positions as "pissing on trees," likening it to dogs marking their territory. Not surprisingly, most fishermen didn't like giving up two or three days' fishing to attend meetings and were disgruntled about being dragged into this process for a problem that many believed did not exist.

"I had no idea of the authority and the power that the green groups had in pushing for this proposal," says Cape Cod fisherman John Our, remembering the first TRT meeting he attended in 1996. "I didn't know anything about the MMPA or the ESA then. What the hell, I was a fisherman and I was fishing. And whales to me didn't mean anything; I had never caught one. All the years I had been fishing with my father and on my own, I had never caught one. You know, you see them every day. But I never had any inkling that the whales were going to be a problem for us. I went into the meeting with Bob MacKinnon. I knew of Bob, and he seemed like a guy who was pretty on top of the environmental stuff. When we had the first TRT meeting in Boston, he said, 'You've got to remember one thing: We've been convicted of murder, and now we've got to plea bargain for our sentence.'"

So TRT meetings were often contentious and frustrating for all concerned. Even so, ideas and occasionally agreements began to emerge from the process. The team rarely reached consensus but got pretty close on some points. NMFS did make a plan—actually several iterations of a plan. However, NMFS officials seemed to be the only ones pleased with plan in its various forms, and as the twentieth century waned, fishermen began to complain more loudly about constantly changing regulations. Environmentalists on the team became increasingly alarmed as whales—especially right whales like Churchill—continued to die in spite of the regulations in place.

By the time I came along hoping to learn more about the federal government's efforts to address whale entanglements, the process seemed to be in a shambles. Two environmental groups, the Humane Society of the United States (HSUS) and the Conservation Law Foundation (CLF) were suing the Fisheries Service for continuing to drag their feet and failing to adequately address the problem. Scientists on the team were discouraged and cynical, and NMFS officials felt frustrated and misunderstood. Fishermen on the team felt betrayed by the lawsuits, especially by HSUS, which has a representative on the team. Some fishermen said they would never attend another meeting. All over the coast fishermen maintained a code of silence; few would report entangled whales, fearing more regulations. And then came the "damn DAMs," in which the Fisheries Service asked fishermen to report right whales when they saw them, reports that could lead to a closure with which lobstermen could never comply.

"If I go back and tell the guys we don't see any whales, then we don't see any whales." says a representative of a fishermen's association, cagily referring to the DAM rule.

The various factions trusted each other less in 2001, if possible, than they had in 1996. It seemed that the only thing holding the group together was that the entanglement problem still existed. At least half a dozen right whales were moseying around the North Atlantic, each with rope wrapped around some part of its body. It was in this environment that I began visiting people who were on the team or close to the issue and asking what they thought about the plan, the TRT, and the Fisheries Service.

Nearly all the people I approached were willing to speak to me, and they often seemed grateful for the opportunity to expound on their viewpoint and vent their frustrations. They invited me to their homes and offices and took a great deal of time to tell me their stories, candidly and honestly. Many told me earnestly how important it was to tell the story of whales and fishermen from a broad perspective.

I found this motley assemblage of people to be deeply and bitterly divided, but I also found that they all had a great deal in common. In every case, I was impressed with how thoughtful and avid these folks were about their convictions. Each was passionately devoted to their chosen line of work. Every one of them had invested energy, time, hope, and perhaps most important, trust in their effort to solve this problem. Everyone seemed to see the conflict over whales and fisheries as a small part of a larger set of issues. If we can make this work here, they thought, maybe things could turn out okay for fisheries and whales everywhere. But every one of them felt disheartened, frustrated, and angry. The chasm separating fishermen and whale advocates was especially wide and deep, a rift between entirely different universes. And officials in NMFS's Protected Species Division were mired in red tape and pinched by the letter of the law, while everyone outside NMFS had lost faith in their ability to create a fair and effective plan to address the problem.

*　　*　　*

It was late June 2001, and the world's attention was focused on Churchill, who was still swimming around the Great South Channel with rope embedded in his rostrum. As the Take Reduction Team met in Portland, Maine, NMFS was under mounting pressure to make the whale problem go away. The Fisheries Service had recently released a Biological Opinion that predicted the right whale's demise if humans couldn't stop killing them by mistake. Because of these findings, the agency was legally bound under the Endangered Species Act (ESA) to step up the pace for implementing a more effective plan.

The agenda of the TRT meeting was largely governed by the Biological Opinion and two lawsuits before a federal judge. To make matters worse, the first expensive, high-profile attempt to rescue Churchill had failed the day before the TRT meeting began, and newspapers were emblazoned with the news.

The judge presiding over the two lawsuits suits filed by HSUS and CLF against the Fisheries Service was hearing the two cases together. Under a settlement agreement, the feds promised to step up their timetable in implementing a new plan to reduce entanglements and to pay the environmental groups more than $73,000 to cover their legal costs ($42,556 to CLF and $30,720 to HSUS).

At the TRT meeting, Roger Eckert, a Fisheries Service lawyer, explained that the judge would conduct a hearing in late August to see if NMFS was actually making headway on a new and more effective plan, and he hoped the team would help guide the Fisheries Service in formulating such a plan. The fishermen sitting at the table were furious about the suits, and their vitriol was largely directed at Sharon Young of HSUS.

When Eckert was done explaining the suit, Gary Ostrom, a Cape Cod lobsterman, was one of the fishermen who had angry words for Sharon.

"My first order of business was that I asked for Humane Society to be removed from the room," Gary says of the meeting, "I think the Humane Society [meaning Sharon] was rather surprised when they went around the room and saw how many people were not happy with their lawsuit. And I told NMFS, 'you've got two choices, you either remove her or I'll sue you.'"

"There was a call for me to step down," Sharon relates. "My response for that was, 'I will gladly step down having gone outside this process, but only if everybody else on this team who's gone to Congress, gotten on the Congressional Record, everybody who has done any lobbying outside of this team to a congressional representative gets off this team, I will gladly go. But I will not be singled out for going outside this process. We all know that the plan we got in '97 was because you guys went outside the process.'"

Sharon compares her lawsuit to a political move by an official at Maine's Department of Marine Resources. "Terry Stockwell, in particular, went to Congress without ever consulting the team and took $3 million out of the right whale budget for state purposes. Did they ever ask Massachusetts if they even wanted it? No. Was the team ever asked if that was the best use of the right whale funds? No. But he got $3 million. And I'm going outside of the process and potentially undermining right whale protection? That was $3 million dollars going to a state that claims it doesn't have any right whales. Hello?" She can't hold back a bit of sarcasm.

Sharon places the blame for the lawsuit squarely on NMFS, saying, "We would never take them to court if they weren't breaking the law. The Take Reduction Team met in '99, reached several consensus recommendations, and the agency did nothing with them. Finally we [HSUS] said 'screw that, you're breaking the law, you've been breaking the law, theoretically, since '97.'" HSUS filed a suit claiming the Fisheries Service was required by law to revisit and revise their plan because it was failing to eliminate entanglements.

"Nobody in their right mind could possibly think that plan would work. You've got at least thirteen animals that are potentially seriously injured, and you never reopened it. The Take Reduction Team keeps meeting, for what? For what, if you never listen to anything anybody says seriously? Now I take those sorts of positions very reluctantly because I know what happens. The fishermen all go nuts because I've gone outside the process."

Abby Arnold, the professional moderator hired by NMFS to guide the TRT's discussion, cut short the argument between Sharon and the fishermen, reminding the group that they had lots of work to do in a short space of time. This tactic worked to prevent anyone from walking out on the meeting, but the hard feelings remained long after.

Fishermen have a lot to say about environmentalists, referring to them as the "green groups." Many fishermen firmly believe that litigious green groups like CLF and HSUS are creating and dragging out the whale entanglement problem to make money from court settlements, grants, and donations. They don't really care about the whales, the fishermen say; they are simply exploiting prowhale/antifishermen public sentiment. These latest lawsuits are only the most recent cases in point.

"I think it's overexaggerated by far, I really do," says John Our, a Cape Cod gill-netter. "I think the green groups are using it as a fund-raiser."

"What people really need to understand is that money is fueling this," charges Gary Ostrom, another Cape Codder, talking about an earlier court settlement. "At the end of the negotiations, CLF submitted a bill for $140,000. They were working at four hundred bucks an hour! None of that money goes back to save whales, none of it. That is how they make their living. It says, 'Conservation Law Foundation,' but they're a law firm. And if we solve all the problems, we put lawyers out of business. If we took the money away, we'd see who really cared about the whales."

Gary goes on: "On the bottom of each one of these lawsuits—and this is how you tell where the enemy is—it says, 'Upon a settlement,' not upon winning, upon a *settlement*, 'you will pay all our court costs.' *That* is the enemy. Those are the people who are not out there to solve the problem. They're out to keep this thing going. Nothing is ever quite enough."

Leroy Bridges, a Maine lobsterman, is a little more cryptic. "There's too much money being made by entities," he says.

These accusations drive Sharon Young nuts. When I visit her modest southeastern Massachusetts home, Sharon tells me that "hired guns"— people hired to advocate for fishermen on committees like the TRT—are less apt to compromise in negotiations. It strikes me that I have heard the same term, "hired gun," applied to Sharon.

"Are you a hired gun?" I ask her.

"No, I don't think so," she responds thoughtfully, "because whales can't talk. Fishermen can talk."

"But conservationists can talk," I counter.

"Am I hired? Am I making a living? Are the fishermen hired? They're making a living. They're protecting their bottom line, which is making a living. I'm protecting my bottom line, which is protecting whales. So I don't see myself as a hired gun any more than a fisherman is a hired gun. I think that if I hired a professional lobbyist to represent conservation interests, knowing that that person has greater access to congressional representatives, that would be a hired gun.

"I will put my income up against most fishermen's any day. I'd trade most of them in a heartbeat. I'm not getting rich off of this. They're defending fishing because they love it. Because they believe in it, they think it deserves to go on. I believe that I care about these animals; I think they have a right to exist, as a species as well as individuals. And I want to see them go on. The whale can't say, 'This is what I need from the fishermen.' Somebody's got to be assertive because they can't. Fishermen can have a voice. They don't have to hire somebody to represent them; they have a choice."

"Do you think that others see you as a hired gun?" I wonder.

"Absolutely. You mean fishermen? Yes. One of the common plaints is, 'You get paid to be here, I have to lose money.' I should be so lucky as to lose the five thousand bucks you're going to lose today, though I know they don't make that kind of money every day."

Sharon sits on every Atlantic marine mammal Take Reduction Team, and she goes on to relate an incident at a meeting involving offshore swordfish and tuna fisheries.

"I actually lost it on one of these guys. This was a guy who owns three longline boats. We were in a bar, and he was doing the old, 'I'm losing money because I can't be on the water today.' He points at me and he says, 'Do you lose anything from your income being here?'

"I said, 'Stop right there. I can sit with a pen and a piece of paper and I can add up—because the government reports how much swordfish and tuna you get and I know what it goes for—I know what you make. You own houses on three continents and five states. You talk about disrupting the gross national product by disrupting your fishery. You want me to feel sorry for you? Do you know how many hours I work? Do you know what my hourly rate is if you add up the number of hours I put in versus the forty hours I'm paid to do? Do you have any idea what that costs me? And you want me to bleed for you because you're losing a day's pay sitting here? Give me a fucking break!' I said, 'Look I'm really sorry, and I don't want to disrupt this process, but I am sick and tired of people telling me that I'm paid to be here. Put your income against my income any day of the week and tell me I'm getting rich off of this. Put your house against my house. Put your daughter's brand-name clothes against my daughter's thrift-shop clothes, and you tell me that I'm getting paid to be here. No, I'm here because I believe in what I'm doing.'"

Of course, there is both truth and untruth in the accusations whale advocates and fishermen hurl at one another. In fact, when environmental groups sue the government for failing to abide by the law, they are entitled to recover their legal costs if they prevail, even if they simply settle. An environmentalist would argue that this is the price the taxpayers must pay to have watchdog groups who ensure that the public's resources, namely whales, are adequately protected. It is no secret that the salaries for lawyers and advocates sometimes—not always—come from money from settlements. But the salaries of environmental advocates are typically anything but extravagant. If you wanted to get rich or even live a comfortable distance above the poverty line, then environmental advocacy is not for you. Also, lawsuits are one of the few ways watchdog groups can exert influence on the actions of the agency. If they feel they have a valid case, they may avail themselves of that influence, just as fishermen may avail themselves of the influence their congressional delegations can exert.

For their part, very few fishermen are as well-off as the owner of the three longline boats who found himself at the receiving end of Sharon's tirade. Most make only moderate livings. The homes of Gary Ostrom, John Our, and Leroy Bridges are also relatively modest. These men live comfortable middle-class lives because they have been able to stay the in the business while depleted stocks and changing regulations have driven many others out.

Also, people with salaried jobs may not relate to the importance of each fishing day for a fisherman. Seasons are short, and the weather is fickle, so a meeting that takes you away from fishing for two days may cause you to miss the peak of the season or the weather window between two fronts. My husband is a commercial fisherman, and he often refers to a missed day of fishing in terms of a bill we could have paid if he had only gone fishing. Fishermen are generally self-employed; they have no sick days or benefits, and their income often fluctuates widely with each season so the whims of weather and fate can mean the difference between staying in the fishery and following the droves into other lines of work.

On the other hand, there is some truth to Sharon's claim that fishermen cry poverty to justify their opposition to new regulations. The parking lot outside a fishermen's meeting is generally packed with brand-new three-quarter-ton pick-up trucks. Remember that the value of the fishing industry in New England and the Maritime Provinces actually *increased* between 1990 and 2001. The value of the lobster industry in Maine, Massachusetts, and New Hampshire alone more than doubled in that time, and so has Atlantic Canada's crab industry. Despite their protestations to the contrary, many fishermen in these areas are not as bad off as they would like the environmentalists to believe. Most of those who have stayed the course are doing rather well, but they also know their current success rests on the edge of a knife. The fortunes of tens of thousands of fishermen now depend on lobster and crab, fixed-gear pot fisheries that entangle whales.

"One thing you have to understand about fishing is that it is a community of liars," says a whale scientist and former commercial fisherman, explaining this trend of disingenuousness among fishermen. "It's not a bad thing. It's just that no fisherman is going to tell another fisherman that he's doing well. It's just bad business to do that because the next day that guy's going to be on your tail setting lines right behind you. So it is a culture and an industry that requires for your own survival that you lie about how well you're doing. That's just the nature of the game. Now what has happened is that, because they have learned to deal with government regulators, the lies will take the form of: 'Fishing's not very good this year. I'm over-regulated. I can't catch enough fish to make a living. Blah blah blah.' That culture has now extended right into the regulatory process and throughout the entire industry. And it's perfectly normal—you just have to understand that's the way it is.

"For example, when I was scalloping, we hit a really good bed of scallops one day," the scientist-cum-fisherman goes on. "We were in an area where no one else had fished, and we came in with buckets of scallop meats; it was really a haul. When you come into the dock and you sell that stuff, the whole waterfront knows it immediately. The next day there were two boats out there. The day after that, there were four. The day after that, there were twelve. And three days after that, that bed was gone. So if you had the ability to keep it quiet, you would do so. It's in their best interest to not tell the truth about how well they're doing. The whole structure of that culture is based on an ambient level of untruth. It's not that they're liars, it's just not in their best interest to be truthful about the quality of their catch, the amount, and the quality of their lives."

An environmental lawyer who has come up against fishermen in the courts and in policy negotiations has another view of that strategy. "It may be because of a history of bad interactions, but as an environmentalist it's really hard to trust a group of people who would just blatantly lie and promote the form of policy negotiations where you take the extreme and hope that something works out toward the middle, which encourages the other side to take the extreme as well."

Despite their major differences, all of the factions agree on one thing: the Fisheries Service is a major barrier to solving the problem of whale entanglement. Many accuse NMFS of ignoring or altering recommendations from the TRT. "The government has never taken the recommendations of the Take Reduction Team and done anything with them," says a conservationist. "And they force us into the very role that the TRT process is supposed to try to obviate. They don't do anything and they force us, the conservation community, to file lawsuits."

"There's a commitment and that was shattered by this joke of a plan, a plan made in a backroom," charges a fisherman. "They just blew this on us. There's nothing they could have done to make it worse."

From scientists:

"Fishermen don't trust anything a bureaucrat says."

"I think nobody on either side trusts the National Marine Fisheries Service. After a while, you feel like you're beating your head against a wall because no matter what happens, they're going to do what they planned to do in the beginning, or what they're backed into a corner to do."

"There's the trust issue: The government has confidence in its own analysts. The fishermen know that the government is full of shit. And they're both really right."

Many feel that litigation, not common sense, drives the Fisheries Service, which is currently defending itself against approximately one hundred lawsuits.

"The problem is that the lead agency is more concerned with pleasing everyone and avoiding lawsuits. There is no strategic thinking."

"NMFS always starts behind the eight ball, because Congress gives them two dollars worth of work to do for every dollar worth of funding, so they're always behind. And then the people who really make the decisions are spineless politicians who are afraid to make decisions. So it takes forever. You've got to have every lawyer review it."

"I think the threat of legal action keeps NMFS talking," says one scientist, putting a more positive spin on the concept.

Many also accuse NMFS of being out of touch with the needs and concerns of fishermen.

"NMFS isn't a rule-making body, it's really made up of lawyers and cubicle dwellers, and it's really gotten away from a close association with the fishermen," says one state regulator.

"Typical for NMFS," says a fisherman, "they held the meeting in June—and this is our season!"

"Who are the feds?" asks a state official. "They are very conservation-minded individuals at the Science Center, who are scientists, who don't have much sympathy for the industry, but have a lot of sympathy for this endangered whale. Then you've got the folks at the regional office, some of whom know something about fishing, most of whom do not."

In reference to the DAM rule, a lobsterman simply exclaims, "NMFS has left the building!"

A gill-netter who is fed up with the Fisheries Service's constantly changing whale regulations says, "The fishermen have just gotten to the point where they say, 'Fuck it all, we're not doing it any more.'"

Ironically, NMFS officials feel misunderstood, too.

*   *   *

One spring day, I visit the Northeast Regional Office of the National Marine Fisheries Service in Gloucester, Massachusetts, to meet with half a dozen people in the Protected Species Division, the group in charge of the Atlantic Large Whale Take Reduction Plan. They have graciously consented to speak to me, even in the throes of their hectic schedules. They seem eager to talk to me about the complex task they face in preventing the extinction of the right whale while allowing fisheries to continue.

I sit at the head of a large conference table on the second floor of the NMFS office building, facing a handful of staffers. Mary Colligan is the assistant regional administrator for protected species, and she must deal with all the special animals under the care of her corner of the agency, everything from Atlantic salmon to harbor porpoises to whales. Dave Gouveia is the marine mammal coordinator, and Diane Borggaard is the large whale coordinator. One person, Dana Hartley, who coordinates the Marine Mammal Stranding Program, joins us from Woods Hole via a speaker phone, an object in the middle of the table that I had initially mistaken for an air filter.

Mary, the senior staff member in the room, fields my first questions. I have observed Mary in meetings and other settings, and she is always calm, even when things become tense. She is also forthright, answering as honestly and directly as she can. Unfortunately, the Take Reduction Plan process rarely provides her and her colleagues with ready, straightforward, and unqualified answers. Perhaps this is one reason that fishermen accuse NMFS officials of being unresponsive to their needs and that conservationists say they are stalling.

In her calm and direct manner, Mary explains the mandate Congress gave to NMFS when they reauthorized the Marine Mammal Protection Act: Work with stakeholders to develop and implement a plan that will reduce serious injury and mortality to below the potential biological removal within six months and to levels approaching zero within five years of implementing the plan.

"So, on the one hand they were saying, 'Work with everyone to do this,'" Mary says, choosing her words carefully, "but on the other hand they were giving us a very short time frame to achieve some very difficult goals when we look at right whales."

"And you are already five years out, right?" I observe. The PBR (potential biological removal) for right whales is zero, but at least two right whales have died from entanglement alone in the past two years. So the Fisheries Service is still a long way from achieving the goal.

"Yeah," Mary nods solemnly. "Right whales are the ultimate test of that law. When zero is your number, it almost doesn't matter whether you're at the six-month goal or the five-year goal. So in the case of right whales, five-year goals become irrelevant because you're held to that standard every day."

Mary stops short of saying the goals of the MMPA are unrealistic. She implies but never says that by failing to reduce take the agency is breaking the law. In her even tone, Mary says it took the agency a great deal of time and effort to decide how to form a team comprised of the various stakeholders and how the team should work.

"It was the agency's intent to bring issues in front of the team, provide enough background so that the team could discuss those issues and make consensus recommendations back to the agency, with the intent that the agency would go forward with those consensus recommendations. It hasn't always worked exactly like that," Mary admits, "because there are some issues that the team has not been able reach consensus on. In some cases recommendations were made to the agency by consensus, but they weren't necessarily things that the agency could simply go forward and develop."

Dave Gouveia adds, "Generally, you think you get a consensus recommendation, but the devil is always in the details." As he speaks, Dave leans over the table and gestures with his hands. "When you start to flesh out what they recommend, you run into obstacles, whether they're legal obstacles or conflicts. And you don't have the luxury to go back and set another meeting to address these other issues. You're under the gun, and you've got to come up with a solution. You've got to work closely with your Science Center, you've got to try and work with individuals on the outside, but it's very delicate and it's very tricky."

Though I hadn't brought it up, Dave and Mary are both trying to explain why the current plan includes changes and measures the team did not endorse, such as DAMs and certain gear modifications that fishermen feel are unrealistic. The main point Mary and Dave are trying to convey is that the cumbersome bureaucracy and the vast array of constituents and mandates make their jobs extraordinarily complex. People outside NMFS, they believe, simply do not understand the degree of complexity they are facing.

Diane Borggaard has been quiet until now. She explains in an unassuming manner that they are trying to improve communication with the TRT by inviting people from various NMFS departments to attend the meetings and give feedback, "to steer the TRT with regards to certain measures that might be unenforceable or unfeasible."

"Sometimes it's not that easy," Dave Gouveia adds. "Sometimes when you're giving that sort of input, you are an obstacle. They say, 'NMFS is in the way again. They don't want us to do this. They have their own agenda. They're trying to tell us what to do.' But you're trying to give them good positive feedback, explaining that it just won't work because of this or it would be easier if you tried to do it this way. But that's not how some members of the industry see it. Then if you get into a situation where you make a rule, you get into the other end: 'Why didn't you tell us this in the beginning? Why weren't you there? We could have used this information at the meeting.' So you really can't win, you really can't."

Now Chris Mantzaris, the protected resources division chief, drops by to join the conversation. Mary introduces us, and he shakes my hand and takes a seat at the table. I'm impressed that he has made an appearance for this interview; apparently the team really is keen to communicate.

In their last TRT meeting in June 2001—the same meeting in which

Gary Ostrom called for Sharon Young's resignation—lawsuits were on everyone's mind. Many outside NMFS believe the plan they rushed to put into effect was the result of the litigation.

"How did the lawsuits influence the time frame for the plan?" I ask the group.

"Going into the last TRT meeting, I don't think we were driven by the lawsuits," Mary says. "I feel we were driven by the fact that we were still having entanglements and serious injuries and mortality. It was really the Biological Opinions that were driving us. So the agency was driven by the need to meet our goals under the MMPA and the ESA. And that really set the timeline. We did of course have the litigation pushing us along as well."

"The court didn't set our time frame," Chris Mantzaris insists. "We really set the time frame ourselves because we were trying to meet the whale's next migration. We were trying to get everything in place so by the time the next migration came along we would have rules out there that would protect the animals. So the court was sort of tracking us more than anything."

In a way, this is a peculiar statement because only a portion of the right whale population actually migrates to the calving grounds in the south for the winter. Right whales are present and could potentially encounter fishing gear in New England waters year-round.

Though it is a sensitive subject, I want to know how these earnest folks perceive the mistrust that pervades their relationships with the various stakeholders.

"I have been speaking with many of the members of the TRT," I tell them, "and I do find that mistrust of NMFS is a central theme that comes up again and again. It also seems that same mistrust is feeding into mistrust between the fishermen and the conservationists. Neither side trusts NMFS. But they mistrust NMFS for different reasons. So that becomes another barrier to everyone sitting down and working things out. I'm hearing from some fishermen on the TRT that they have no intention of participating any longer."

"You could see it, too, in the TRT," Chris Mantzaris leans forward to speak. "That was sort of obvious in a lot of the reactions. The fishermen felt . . . at least it appeared that they were concerned about putting their heart and soul into it because they were mistrustful of people around the table. So they're being protective; sometimes you can't blame them. And I think some of the mistrust came from, was even reinforced when the conservationists filed a lawsuit, because they didn't feel like they were getting what they needed apparently from the Take Reduction Team process."

Chris goes on to say that NMFS is a regulatory agency, so anyone subject to NMFS regulations will be mistrustful at times, in spite of their best efforts to be transparent or inclusive.

"I think it's frustrating," Mary says, her brow furrowed, though her voice is steady. "I think it's incredibly challenging. What I find frustrating is seeing how hard everybody is working and then hearing criticism that we're not talking to folks. We've tried to be very transparent and very up front. So it's hard for me personally to hear, 'You're not telling us what's going on. You don't care and you don't understand or appreciate or even want to know how it affects me as a fisherman.' I don't think that's really fair in my mind. I guess that's just my personal reaction to it. I understand it's a really challenging issue for all of us, and trying to tackle it is hard on everyone. But we're certainly going to be more successful if we're working together."

As I leave the NMFS office building, I realize again that the accusations from people outside the agency contain both truth and untruth. During this visit I have come to understand that the folks at NMFS are far more well-meaning than anyone gives them credit for, but they are defending a system that no one else believes in.

I once asked a NMFS official whether she thought the DAM rule was an effective management strategy. The party line at the time was that DAM was an effective but unwieldy management tool, which was implemented because the agency needed to take decisive action. NMFS planned to streamline the DAM rule as much as possible in the coming years.

So I wasn't surprised when this NMFS official nodded and replied, "Yes, I think it's effective."

"Why do you think it's effective?" I had never gotten an answer to this question that directly addressed the many problems with the DAM rule. I hoped this person, who had not been working on the whale problem for long, still retained an outsider's perspective and could explain.

"Well," she said thoughtfully, "I don't think the agency would have gone through with it if it weren't." I had no way of knowing whether her answer came of naïve optimism or an attempt at toeing the party line, but I could barely contain my surprise at this expression of faith in the agency.

"Are you sure about that?" I asked. "This is an agency which is currently defending itself against a hundred lawsuits." This was an unfair question, but it was out of my mouth before I'd had time to think better of it.

She shrugged.

Whether through faith in the system or resignation to its strictures, NMFS officials adhere to the Byzantine policies and procedures required by law and regulation. People outside the agency are simply baffled when NMFS officials allow policy and procedure to mire the process. The fishermen interpret NMFS's adherence to procedure as bowing to the wishes of the conservationists, and conservationists interpret it as stalling.

At the 2003 TRT meeting, I saw firsthand the consequences of this misunderstanding, as policy and procedure hindered a surprising breakthrough in relations between conservationists and fishermen.

12   A Commonsense Plan

The Devil Is in the Details

The rift between fishermen and NMFS scientists over how to look at the ocean and think about fish fostered a level of discord, doubt, and mistrust that made it almost impossible to convince fishermen and regulators to curb overfishing. It also impoverished our understanding of the ocean, by hindering the exchange of information and perspective.
David Dobbs, *The Great Gulf*

The National Marine Fisheries Service did not convene the Atlantic Large Whale Take Reduction Team in 2002. A few folks complained that the process couldn't go forward unless the team met again. However, given the bitter feelings that came to the surface at the last meeting and the outcry following the implementation of the interim rule, including DAMs, SAMs, and new gear modifications, most were relieved not to face another three days of head butting. Several members of the team had even declared the process beyond repair and either vowed never to attend another meeting or advised NMFS to disband the team entirely. So everyone was surprised when New England fishermen and state fisheries officials came to the 2003 meeting ready to make some important concessions. For their part, conservationists were ready to talk; it was clear by now that current measures were not working, and they hoped to gain something at this meeting that might stem the steady stream of entanglements.

Ironically, it seemed that the unpopular and apparently ineffective DAM rule was the factor that might lead the team to agree on some real solutions. With the exception of one member, David Laist of the U.S. Marine Mammal Commission, every member of the team was ready to give up DAMs, especially if it could be replaced by more palatable measures. The fishermen were willing to give a great deal of ground to get rid of the DAM threat, and the conservationists were eager to use DAMs as a bargaining chip to gain measures that were more effective in preventing entanglements.

*   *   *

In a carpeted conference room in a Warwick, Rhode Island, hotel, some forty members of the TRT are taking their seats at tables arranged in a large square. Around the team, another thirty people are observing the meeting, some sitting in uncomfortable chairs, others networking near the coffee urns. As they arrive, each member of the team collects an enormous binder containing their placard and a ream of background material and agendas. When the moderator finally calls the meeting to order, I note that several of the large binders remain unclaimed. John Our told me a year ago that he'd had it with the TRT, and sure enough, his binder sits on the table with his placard held to it by a rubber band.

For most of the first day of the meeting, the team sits through several speakers updating them on what has happened with the whales and the plan since they met two years ago. The folks in the room are especially eager to hear about DAMs from Diane Borggaard. Referring to a PowerPoint slide, she told them that the DAM was triggered for the first time by a group of right whales sighted off Cape Ann in the spring of 2002, prompting NMFS to implement a mandatory two-week closure. Another DAM began as a mandatory closure and then became voluntary when the weather deteriorated and fishermen complained that they couldn't safely retrieve their gear. All of the triggers thereafter—nine in

2002 and so far one in 2003—were either not implemented because the whales left the area or were just voluntary closures.

Diane tells the group it took an average of two weeks to implement each DAM closure, voluntary or otherwise. Remember that two weeks is the average length of time these aggregations of right whales would last, so most would be over by the time the closures went into effect, even if the fishermen could or would comply.

She goes on to explain the measures that the agency is currently considering for the following year, including gear modification and restrictions on fishing practices in the Southeast. The feds, still clinging to the DAM concept, want the team to consider the idea of using gear modifications instead of closures to implement the DAM rule. So instead of pulling their gear, fishermen could modify their gear at sea in order to keep fishing in the event of a DAM. The team has discussed a few ideas for DAM gear modifications in past meetings, the most realistic and straightforward of which is temporarily removing one buoy line from strings of traps or nets.

When Diane is finished with her presentation, David Laist, looking stern, raises his hand.

"Why do you feel the need to make a rule for a voluntary action?" he asks, sounding exasperated. He's wondering why the DAMs take so long to implement, especially since they are voluntary, and he's reluctant to concede that lobster fishermen can't comply with DAM closures.

"We need to go through the rule-making action," she answers. "It's basically a requirement."

"We have to do it with any trigger," adds David Gouveia, who is sitting at the table in the front of the room.

"I must say I find this ridiculous," says Laist, pursing his lips and looking like he has just tasted something sour. He will wear that expression for most of the three-day meeting. "I'm thinking of it from the perspective of the whales. In my opinion the DAMs should be mandatory, they should be quicker, and they should be applied in critical habitats." Any SAM or critical habitat restrictions in force override DAM closures.

Later in the day, in another discussion about DAMs, Diane acknowledges that the Fisheries Service has received "a great deal of negative feedback" about the DAM rule. Some have informally asked NMFS to simply remove the rule from the plan, she says. Diane and her colleagues don't exactly say that they feel the Fisheries Service made a mistake in implementing the DAM rule, but they make it clear that they are now taking complaints about the DAMs seriously. Also, all recent DAMs have been voluntary, an unspoken indication that they are having second thoughts about the measure.

Diane explains, however, that the measure cannot be removed unless it is replaced with another measure of equal or greater conservation value. If she recognizes the irony in that statement, she hides it well.

For the lunch hour, the team breaks up into caucuses: conservationists, scientists, northeastern fishermen and their state regulators, southeastern fishermen and their regulators, and NMFS officials. The factions move off to rooms or restaurants. They are charged with discussing the proposal for DAM gear modifications that Diane has described. When we return from lunch, the fishermen and state fisheries officials are still caucusing; the door to the smaller conference room where they are meeting remains resolutely shut.

Several people attending a TRT meeting for the first time sit on the sidelines during protracted discussions about traps and trawls, SAMs and DAMs, and gear modifications. The Fisheries Service has recently identified a few additional fixed-gear fisheries that they determined—via a serpentine regulatory process—to be posing a threat of entangling whales. This process recently brought into the fold the sea bass pot, shark gill-net, and hagfish trap fisheries (hagfish are also affectionately known as slime eels). Some of these newbies appear to have been through this mill before, perhaps even with another marine mammal TRT. Others appear, frankly, overwhelmed by the scope and complexity of the proceedings. Eyes wide, mouths agape, clutching cups of cold coffee, they're climbing a steep learning curve and have a long way to go to learn the alphabet soup of acronyms that the older members of the team bandy about with ease. More than once after a particularly arcane exchange of verbiage, I see one of these guys shake his head as if trying to work it all into place.

Looking at these poor souls, I am reminded of something David Mattila of the Center for Coastal Studies once told me: the fishermen who get pulled into the TRT process by the Fisheries Service go through all the stages normally associated with grief, including shock, denial, anger, and resignation. By the looks of it, some of the newer members of the TRT are still in the shock stage.

By mid-afternoon, the northeastern fishermen and state officials are ready to make a proposal to the team. As the team gathers again and takes their seats, Cape Cod lobsterman Gary Ostrom bustles in, followed by his three stout sons. Gary seems a little agitated in his camouflage shirt and matching hat. When I shake his hand, he whispers that he won't be able to stay long. Instead of sitting at the table, Gary makes his way to the back of the room and stands, arms crossed, behind several fisheries delegates. His sons stand fidgeting nearby.

Terry Stockwell, a fisheries regulator with the state of Maine, speaks from his chair, representing all of the northeastern inshore lobster fisheries. His deep voice fills the room.

This caucus would like to see an entirely new set of rules, says Terry, which would replace the interim rule that added DAMs and SAMs to the management regime. The new plan would involve weak-links in all lobster gear and—most significantly—removing all floating groundlines in "high-risk" areas as soon as possible. For everywhere else, says Terry, if fishermen get financial assistance they could phase in "low-profile gear" by 2008, but with a line buy-back program the fishermen could get rid of all floating groundline by 2006. "Money talks," he says. The Seasonal Area Management concept—with a little tweaking—could stay, perhaps even expand.

In reading the previous paragraph, your eyes may have glazed over with the details of gear modifications and phase-in dates, but this proposal holds everyone on the TRT in rapt attention. The details of the proposal are not that important, except that they show a newfound willingness among fishermen and the states to participate in the process. This list of measures, particularly since it issues from the lips of Terry Stockwell, marks a turning point in the take reduction process that many in the room have long wished for.

Terry is a bearded, bearlike former fisherman who takes his job at the Maine Department of Marine Resources very seriously.

"I'm fiercely protective of fishermen," Terry once told me.

As such, he has presented a formidable opponent to implementing whale protection measures in Maine, the bastion of a large and vocal lobster fishery. Maine's fishermen have denied culpability in whale entanglement and fought regulations since the beginning. They were positively apoplectic over the DAM rule.

"Maine is still in denial about the whale problem," a Massachusetts fisherman told me in 2001, "but we were still in denial in '95."

It now seems like Maine is ready to move forward as Terry and his constituents accept that they will need to play a bigger role in whale protection, especially if fishermen could get key exemptions where they fish on rocky bottom and sinking groundline chafes and parts.

A hand goes up and one of the scientists asks what the industry caucus means by "high-risk."

Terry shrugs, suggesting Stellwagen Bank and Jeffreys Ledge as places to start. Then he puts his papers down and looks up at the group to speak frankly. "We need your help in this," he says. "I'm one of the ones who a few years ago said we couldn't do it."

"SAM areas could be a whole lot bigger and the time could be a whole lot bigger," adds Dan McKiernan, a Massachusetts fisheries official. "The SAM areas as they are now don't always capture feeding aggregations."

Gary Ostrom raises his hand to register his displeasure at the form SAMs have taken: lobster trawls can only have one end line. The fishermen had offered to remove one end line as a simple gear modification they could implement in a DAM, but the feds incorporated the measure into SAMs instead. "We volunteered to take one end line off for a trip, and it turned into a three-month session." Gary jabs a finger as he speaks from the back of the room. "We came here, we were asked to do a little more, and now we're getting another box. SAM took a bad hit."

"But the long-term approach here is to do away with DAMs and SAMs and apply Cape Cod Bay rules everywhere," says Bill Adler, executive director of the Massachusetts Lobstermen's Association, summing up the deal the fishermen and the states seek.

"If money came available," asks Sharon Young, "could you implement the plan faster?"

"Could we do it faster?" says Bill. "Yes, we could do it faster."

This is a veritable love-in compared to the last meeting.

* * *

Dan McKiernan speaks very little while the team gets used to the proposal and begins to discuss details, but the mark of his patient and amicable leadership is unmistakable. Of all the regulators in the room, he has probably been grappling with the problem of whale entanglement longer than most.

When Max Strahan won his case against the state of Massachusetts in 1996, he thrust the state to the forefront of efforts to stop entanglement. Dan McKiernan was the Department of Marine Fisheries (DMF) official charged with fulfilling the court order, convening an Endangered Whale Working Group, and developing a plan to reduce the number of whales injured or killed by fishing gear in state waters. With a tight timeline, a relatively small number of fixed-gear fisheries in the state, and less labyrinthine regulatory procedures, the state moved far more quickly than the feds in implementing a plan. In fact, the feds incorporated some of the principles of the state's plan when they finally reached the rule-making stage.

"We have a whale problem because we have whales," says Dan, referring to the biogeographical twist of fate that has endowed Massachusetts with lots of endangered whales.

Dan has an uncanny ability to patiently coax people with diverse interests to listen and understand one another. Tall and lanky with strawberry blond hair, Dan is very persuasive without posturing or grandstanding. He also can be detached enough from a tense situation to laugh at the ridiculous or ironic—opportunities that crop up often in his line of work.

One of the most remarkable feats Dan has accomplished at the helm of the state's whale plan is communicating openly with all sides, apparently without alienating or losing the trust of anyone. With Dan presiding over or participating in all the rule making since 1996, Massachusetts fishermen have made more concessions to whale protection than any other state. Working closely with fishermen in the state, Dan was able to broker a deal to finally end court oversight in the Strahan case. In the settlement agreement, the fishermen agreed to eliminate the use of all floating groundline in Cape Cod Bay by January 2003—and the fishermen I spoke to still trust him.

"Dan McKiernan is the best guy in the Department of Marine Fisheries," says Gary Ostrom, whose trust is not easily won. "He's the best guy I've met. He speaks his mind. He's taught me a lot and got me thinking outside the box."

People on all sides express the same sentiments.

"He's an advocate for the whales, and he understands the industry," says Amy Knowlton, a right whale scientist and an important figure working on the problem of ship strikes. "He doesn't really have an agenda."

"He does have the trust of the industry," Bob Kenney says of Dan.

"Do you trust him?" I ask.

Bob, characteristically, considers the question seriously before answering, "Yup."

"Now there's a guy from the state point of view who has really been trying to solve this problem," says David Mattila. "Dan has been—and it may be because of Max's lawsuits, but he truly has spent a lot of time looking at it."

"These fishermen in the state of Massachusetts have more to lose," says Sharon Young of the Humane Society. "Dan McKiernan, I think, has been really proactive; he's in the lead in trying to get new things through. I think he hates hypocrisy. He doesn't like seeing rules go in that are a sham."

That's high praise from a lot of corners. As I moved among the people involved with the whale entanglement issue, I heard similar praise for some scientists and whale rescuers, but I had come to regard a fisheries regulator as the person everyone (or at least someone) loves to hate. How does Dan do it? I visited him at his office in Boston one day to talk about whales and ask how he manages to be the Teflon fisheries regulator.

"I started my career working on lobsterboats as a state official, and I think that experience really helped me," Dan said, leaning way back in his rolling office chair. "I've even volunteered to continue to take part in some of the sampling, just to stay on the boats and be able to talk to some of those guys about what's happening. I think we're kind of unique here in that I talk to Moe Brown three times a week about the whale survey that's going on; I have a lot of contact with Scott Kraus on the phone about statistics; and I've hired Gary Ostrom to set the gear for me to do an underwater video; I'm paying a bunch of fishermen to go to the gear workshop. I play a different kind of role than any other state people do. If you're in the federal government you have your role—you're a regulator or you're a gear person. But I come at it from all directions." Dan also keeps in touch with Sharon Young of the Humane Society and his counterparts in other New England states.

In 2002, Dan McKiernan worked with fishermen, divers, and scientists to study the way different types of groundline between lobster traps behaved in situ. What kind of obstacle does floating groundline present to a swimming whale, Dan wondered, and do sinking and neutrally buoyant lines really reduce risk? The team used divers and remotely operated underwater vehicles to film and document buoyant loops of floating rope between traps, averaging sixteen feet off the bottom. Sinking and neutrally buoyant line just rested on the bottom. This project accomplished several goals. It brought together a diverse team for a task that really accomplished something while providing additional evidence to himself, NMFS, the scientists, and most important, the fishermen that sinking groundline will save whales. The following year, intrigued by Dan's work, Terry Stockwell and his colleagues at the Maine Department of Marine Resources undertook a similar gear study.

When the interim rule hit the fan in 2002, with DAMs, SAMs, and gear modifications, Dan McKiernan's diplomatic sensibilities told him the meager trust TRT members had was now squandered on rules that would cost fishermen time, money, and patience without doing much to save whales. Weak-links were a major piece of the new gear modifications and were still not proven. Outside of Cape Cod Bay, the ocean was still going to be crisscrossed with floating groundline. So he began doing what he did best.

The state of Massachusetts developed a proposal, which Dan and DMF Director Paul Diodati brought to Washington and presented to NMFS administrator William Hogarth. The plan was simple: Adopt year-round gear modifications over the next five years from Easport, Maine, to Key West, Florida, including weak-links and sinking groundlines on all fixed gear; drop the DAMs; provide financial relief to help fishermen replace their line; work with fishermen to rebuild trust; and urge the Canadian authorities to adopt a similar plan. Dan and Diodati told the administrator they could deliver consensus on the TRT on a commonsense plan such as this.

Hogarth listened intently to their presentation and watched their video showing buoyant loops of floating groundline, but he remained impassive and noncommittal. So Dan went to work on developing support for these measures back home in New England, confident that it was the best course of action for fishermen and whales everywhere.

Could Dan really deliver consensus on measures such as those he presented to Hogarth? In making my rounds to speak with people on the TRT, I made a point to ask. And the answers were pretty uniform.

"I do."

"He just might be able to pull it off."

"I believe Dan can deliver support for a commonsense plan."

*   *   *

The proposals and rhetoric the fishermen and state regulators bring to the 2003 TRT meeting bear a striking resemblance to the proposal Dan offered to Hogarth. The fishermen's proposal gets a boost when Scott Kraus gets up to summarize discussions among the scientists in the group.

"I think you could eliminate DAMs right away," says Scott, now speaking for himself. "They are not biologically informative and they're not very biologically informed."

The rest of what Scott has to say is simple and familiar. Many of the scientists agreed that eliminating lines in the water column will help to minimize entanglements, Scott reports, "for instance by increasing the number of traps per line and requiring sinking or neutrally buoyant groundlines in all locations and all fisheries on the East Coast."

In more caucuses and coffee breaks, the conservationists develop counterproposals that ask for faster phase-ins and offer specific ideas about what could and could not be exempted from a sinking groundline requirement. Bonnie Spinazzola of the Offshore Lobstermen's Association and Peter Cooke, who runs an offshore crab boat, drop in on the conservationist caucus for some informal negotiation.

During one break, I notice Gary Ostrom's three sons sitting in observers' chairs looking so bored they might just slide onto the floor. I sit down nearby with my coffee. Gary's voice carries to us from the area around the coffee urns where he is fervently engaged in a conversation.

"I thought your dad said he couldn't stay long," I said.

The boys all roll their eyes. One of the boys flops an arm in his dad's direction and says, "He's over there doing what he does best."

I don't think Gary Ostrom would mind if I told you he was opinionated. He is one of the few remaining fishermen in my home, Cape Cod, and as near as I can tell, he has stayed in the business through sheer force of will. Gary is outspoken, driven, and cares very much what the future will look like for him and his three boys, so he is very involved in fisheries management issues. He tells me he had to force his way onto the Take Reduction Team.

At one TRT meeting, Gary happened to strike up a conversation with a woman named Carla Bennet. At the time Carla worked for the International Fund for Animal Welfare (IFAW), an animal rights group with headquarters on Cape Cod, and she was attending the meeting as an observer.

"I was watching this girl take notes faster than I could read," Gary remembers. "I wasn't sure who she was, but I made a couple of comments."

Gary told Carla, "It's a waste of time—they're getting nothing done."

"What could we do now?" she responded.

"Well we could get the ghost gear out of the water," suggested Gary. Ghost gear is traps or nets that are either lost or abandoned. Even lost gear keeps fishing and may also entangle whales.

Carla took the idea to IFAW president Fred O'Regan, and they gave Gary twelve thousand dollars for a program to remove ghost gear from the Cape Cod Bay Critical Habitat Area.

"What we did is use common sense," says Gary. "We broke the bay into sections, and I had a fisherman from each of the areas going and looking for the ghost gear. So they were guys who knew whose gear was out there, which gear was lost. I hired full-time commercial fishermen, not guys that were not doing anything. I paid six hundred dollars a day for the boat and the captain, and three hundred dollars for the stern man. So it was well worth the effort. We're not allowed to handle the gear without law enforcement on board, so we were able to get enforcement to go. We worked a deal with Marine Patrol, so it also made the state look good; the state was doing some work for the right whales. And law enforcement, they were amazed. Well, what a concept, using guys that actually know what's going on! And it was funny, it started out law enforcement stepped on board and said, 'We're law enforcement, my name is officer so and so.' By the end of the day it was a first-name basis. It was fun, and it was good because the guys got to see something different too. And we came in under budget." Gary returned $6,500 to IFAW.

"IFAW took a lot of heat for working with me," says Gary. "They were told they were working with the enemy, and they stood up to the heat. I thought, 'I'm stepping out on a big limb, hoping these people don't take my legs out from underneath me.' But they didn't. We don't agree on everything, but nobody does. They were willing to look past the rhetoric that we're out there to kill whales, we're out there raping the ocean, beyond 'let's get a lawyer and sue them,' and sat down and talked."

In March 2002, a consortium of Cape Cod–based environmental groups presented Gary with the Patricia Lambert Award for Marine Protection, honoring him for his work with IFAW and the fishermen of Cape Cod Bay.

*   *   *

At the 2003 TRT meeting, it seems apparent that a consensus is building, though David Laist continues to cling to the notion that DAMs could be workable if only NMFS and the industry would try harder. Many people from all sides feel an urgent need to move ahead quickly to eliminate DAMs and start phasing in sinking groundline now that the idea has widespread support.

The discussion about enforcement seems to harden everyone's resolve. Greg LaMontagne of NMFS and a couple of representatives from the U.S. Coast Guard stand to update the group on enforcement of the measures in the plan. It seems that compliance with the gear modifications, mostly weak-links and requirements about how to configure gear, has been very good. The Coast Guard and the state Marine Patrol officers have written a few tickets, but overall, they see fishermen complying with the new regulations. The three are a little vague when describing enforcement on DAMs. David Laist would like to know more.

"The DAMs have been monitored by the Coast Guard," LaMontagne nods. "The mandatory DAMs were monitored, and some of the voluntary DAMs. We don't have any numbers on enforcement of the DAMs."

"Can you get us some numbers?" asks Laist.

"We can make the effort, yes."

The discussion continues later, and the team learns that the Coast Guard did meet with a few fishermen during the one mandatory DAM closure to warn them to remove their gear.

"During that first DAM," relates Bill Adler, "one fisherman was met at the dock by the Coast Guard with a warning. He was terrified. The ironic thing is that this guy was moving his gear, and it's an impossibility."

"What about when you can't get to the gear?" asks Bonnie Spinazzola, who represents offshore lobster fishermen.

"Yeah," interjects Pat White, a Maine lobsterman and longtime fisheries activist. "What's the penalty?"

The Coast Guard officers consult briefly and then nod to each other. "A hundred thousand," one states.

"What?!" several people exclaim.

"Each count is one hundred thousand dollars maximum," says the officer. "That could be per day."

I glance at Bonnie Spinazzola, who looks as though she's been slapped. All the fishermen and many others shake their heads in disbelief at the fine a fisherman would have to pay for failing to comply with a mandatory DAM closure, a closure with which few lobstermen could comply.

The Coast Guard officers and Greg LaMontagne reassure the group that if fishermen are up front and contact them to say that they are attempting move their gear, the officers would be understanding.

I'm certain that many in the room are thinking DAMs must go. But like Dave Gouveia says, the devil is in the details.

"We can't get rid of DAMs unless we replace it with something of equal or greater conservation value."

It is now the third and final day of the TRT meeting, and the conservationists and the fishermen have come to general agreement on certain changes to the northeastern lobster and gill-net fisheries regulations. The fishermen can phase in sinking or neutrally buoyant groundlines everywhere but in the lowest-risk areas; and if the government or the conservationists can help shoulder the financial burden, phase-in can be shortened. DAMs can go as soon as the government can make them go away, as long as the industry is committed to widespread gear modifications. Dates and areas can be figured out later in smaller working groups. Now it is time for the Fisheries Service to comment.

Dave Gouveia has the unenviable task of providing feedback to the team on the points they have generally agreed upon. He sits in the hot seat at the front of the room and outlines the points the NMFS folks have discussed. He chooses his words carefully, which makes his speech halting and somewhat serpentine.

The main message from the NMFS camp is that anything the agency proceeds with will not be in place for at least eighteen months to two years. With a phase-in plan, it could take six years to fully implement a measure like widespread sinking groundline. A lot of whales could die in six years. Moreover, NMFS has limited resources to focus on the issue, so choosing one measure as a priority may mean putting off another. Ironically, the paperwork involved in implementing DAM closures, even when they are voluntary, takes their time away from moving ahead with more effective measures.

Scott Kraus catches the eye of the moderator, and she calls on him. "I may be chronologically challenged, but I'm having a problem looking at the long-term stuff before we look at the short-term. I mean eight whales died last year, but I don't see us doing anything that would address the problem *now*."

"Can't you do an emergency rule?" someone asks.

Dave looks at a woman sitting among the observers who is a lawyer with NMFS's general counsel office. She's shaking her head, looking like we all should have known that this was not possible. "It's not something you can do in a week," she says, then rattles off a long list of steps that must be taken to make an emergency rule.

"Is there a way you can give us credit for changing over to 25 percent or 50 percent sinking groundline?" Pat White asks.

"That's hard to answer, to tell you what sort of credit we could give you," says Dave Gouveia.

"There's a whole book on 'getting to yes,'" says Sharon Young. "We're dealing with two different issues here, administrative issues and the crying need to do *something*. None of us wants to end up in litigation; it's just not productive. What we need to hear from the agency is what you can do on a short-term basis. There's got to be some way that you can do something on a short-term basis."

"Well, anything we do has to go through a regulatory process," Dave says, his discomfort plain. He is hunched over; his brow is knit. "We do have to analyze and get comments."

The frustration in the room is palpable. Yet again, by explaining the complexity and rigidity of their task, the feds appear to be stalling and uncommunicative. Their attempt to be transparent and responsive has the opposite effect. It's painful to observe. The breakthrough that seemed to be within reach on the first day feels much more distant now, and the gulf of misunderstanding between the feds and everyone else hasn't narrowed. No one in the room has the authority to put common-sense rules in place.

David Laist is nearing the end of his rope. The conservationists are all ready to give up DAMs, but Laist returns again and again to the same problem: "I have little faith in weak-links," he says, "but I feel confident that whales won't get entangled in gear that's not there."

On a break, I ask Sharon Young how she feels about David Laist stone-walling any attempts to reach consensus on dropping DAMs from the plan.

"Well, he is right," she says. "The whales can't get entangled in gear that isn't there. He is taking the strongest possible stance on behalf of critically endangered whales. I wish I could take a strong stance like that, but right now I can't because it would be political suicide." Given the divisive effect the HSUS lawsuit had on the team two years ago, Sharon needs to tread lightly, so this year Sharon is the good cop and Laist is the bad cop.

David Laist grumbles under his breath as the moderator begins to write the points the team has discussed on a large sheet of paper. Going down the list, the moderator asks the members of the team to indicate where they stand to determine if there is consensus. When she asks if there is consensus on getting rid of the DAM rule, Laist shakes his head in exasperation and asks to be recognized.

"Partly I'm opposed to the whole process," Laist complains tersely and asserts, once again, "they can't get entangled in gear that isn't there."

When he is finished speaking his mind, David Laist mutters, "To hell with it. I don't care anymore." He packs his briefcase and marches out of the room.

Conclusion

*Here within sight of the blue shadow of New England's industrial
seaboard . . . moving at daybreak on back roads, the fishermen go their
traditional way down to the sea. They are tough, resourceful, self-respect-
ing, and also (some say) hidebound and cranky, too independent to
organize for their own survival. Yet even their critics must acknowledge
a gritty spirit that was once more highly valued in this country than it
is today. Because their children can no longer afford to live where their
families have harvested the sea and land for three hundred years, [they]
may soon become rare relicts from the past, like the Atlantic right
whales, a cow and calf, that in the winter of 1984–1985 have been
appearing here and there off the ocean beach.*

Peter Matthiessen, *Men's Lives*

What are the consequences if we fail to resolve the conflict between
whales and fishermen? What if trust and cooperation don't emerge? Consider the meaning of the U.S. Endangered Species Act and the newly
enacted Canadian Species at Risk Act. Beyond their various flaws, these
laws represent the will and commitment of nations to protect and trea-
sure natural resources. Extinction, our society has concluded, is not acceptable. Similarly, both nations have an expressed commitment to their
fisheries. Fishing communities, families, economies, and lives are important enough to Canada and the United States to invest legislation,
funds, attention, and consideration.

So which is more valuable? I may value fisheries over whales, while
whales are your overriding concern. Both are in peril, both are passionately defended by many, and if defended wantonly, each could mean the
demise of the other. Should I prevail? Should you? The only answer is
that both must prevail or both will perish. If I decide that small-scale
fisheries must survive, whales be damned, then those who value whales
above all will not rest until the threat I pose is extinguished. The time and

destruction of such a battle would consume us both. It's either whales *and* fisheries or neither whales *nor* fisheries. This is not a new dilemma. It is the hallmark of many high-stakes environmental debates; you could replace the words "whales" and "fisheries" with "spotted owls" and "logging," for instance. Polarizing the debate is the path to ulcers and failure.

The United States has been pouring money and person-power at the whale problem while Canadian officials hope the issue will somehow evaporate if it is starved of funds, and neither strategy seems to be working to protect whales from entanglement and fishermen from liability.

As we have seen, the U.S. Atlantic Large Whale Take Reduction Plan has done little to counter distrust of NMFS. The well-intentioned people who work for the Fisheries Service's Protected Resources Division suffer from three paralytic contradictions: They are driven by constraining legal imperatives that are, in a practical sense, unattainable, yet in some way many still believe—or at least act as though they believe—that the process can work for both whales and fishermen. NMFS officials claim to have done everything in their power to listen to and communicate with members of the TRT, yet they implemented the Dynamic Area Management (DAM) rule when nearly everyone involved told them it could not work. Now the DAM rule is an albatross that consumes precious resources and serves to remind everyone of the dismal relations between the Fisheries Service and the stakeholders. Finally, the Protected Resources Division exists in an agency that manages whole ecosystems by regulating one species at a time, giving rise to tortuous regulatory pathways.

In its latest budget, Congress has drastically increased the amount of money allocated to the disentanglement program. The folks at the Center for Coastal Studies are happy to have ample resources to do their jobs, but the windfall indicates that Congress and NMFS haven't been listening to their mantra: Disentanglement is an expensive and ineffectual Band-Aid.

In Canada, the whale entanglement problem is on the rise again with the growth of the crab, lobster, and turbot fisheries, but this time the whale problem is on the move and more often out of reach. As small trap fisheries creep seaward, more of the entangled whales are dozens or even hundreds of miles offshore, caught in strong deadly gear. A "disentanglement team" comprised of a couple of people in a Zodiac with a few primitive tools can't track and chase whales that are roaming the remote shores of Atlantic Canada or plying the Grand Banks with rope jammed in their baleen. Beyond disentanglement, the concept of preventing entanglement has barely reentered the debate with the renewed growth in the Canadian fishing industry. However, with a new parliamentary mandate to protect endangered species and growing international pressure, the Canadian government will soon need to invest more than a pittance in proactive solutions to the whale problem.

Everywhere around the North Atlantic, in the United States, Canada, and in Europe, fisheries managers are again reining in fisheries, cutting back on lobster trap limits and crab and groundfish quotas. These moves cause rage and despair among fishermen and their communities, many of whom continue to second-guess the science behind the policy.

The turmoil in North Atlantic fisheries and the imminent threats to endangered whales barely form a blip on the radar screen of the general public. Press outlets everywhere mention developments in these stories in a few brief paragraphs—a group of fishermen protesting here, an entangled whale there. Few in the press or the public seem to realize that these are not isolated events but rather indicators of systemic ills. By the time public scrutiny turns to the problem, I worry, it may be too late for whales, fish, and fishermen.

As I delved into these questions over the past few years, there were times when I despaired. More than once, I sat at my computer and cried as I typed the story. But ultimately, telling this story is an optimistic undertaking, a cautionary fable for modern times. So even when I became disheartened I looked for people who were taking a hopeful path.

During a particularly dark period, I paid a visit to Robin Alden, a person who builds things from the ground up. For more than thirty years, Robin Alden has been a quietly formidable force working on behalf of Maine's fisheries. She founded *Commercial Fisheries News,* a New England monthly newspaper for fishermen; she began the Maine Fishermen's Forum; and she had an eventful tenure as Maine's commissioner of marine resources, in which she implemented a unique zone council system that gives fishermen local responsibility in managing the state's lobster fishery. She also served on the New England Fishery Management Council, which advises the National Marine Fisheries Service on management issues.

I had asked to talk with her about her experience addressing harbor porpoise by-catch during her tenure at DMR, but somehow the subject never came up. Instead we talked about our hopes and frustrations in trying to mend the problems before us. We sipped tea and talked at her kitchen table. Her dog nudged me for a pat while my son played with Legos in the living room.

Responsibility and trust, Robin explained, were central to her views on fisheries management. Unfortunately, fisheries management on the federal level leaves little room for either.

"I don't think the current situation can change, with the government afraid of being sued, not being creative," Robin said. "Fishermen have no incentive to change in the current system. The job of the fisherman is to get as much as he can out of the current regulations or just oppose any change."

When you add conservationists to the mix, you add a major sociological gap. The question is how do you escape the vortex of polarized debate and draining meetings and rulings and public comment periods? Robin's answer was to bring fisheries management back to the local level, so responsibility and accountability happen face-to-face and ideas grow from local knowledge.

In other words, make a grassroots end run around the red tape and solve the problem yourself. While speaking with Robin, it occurred to me that the things that have worked in the whale entanglement issue have come from individuals seeing a need and stepping in to fulfill that need. They are practical, well-placed solutions from practical, well-meaning people.

Remember that both Stormy Mayo and Jon Lien began disentangling whales simply because no one else was doing it. Each new tool in the disentangler's arsenal—hooked knives, satellite buoys, syringes the size of a soda bottle—was born of necessity. Dan McKiernan did the leg work to build consensus for a set of simple and effective solutions and put together the resources to do gear research because these tasks had to be done. Gary Ostrom and Carla Bennett matched funds with expertise and equipment to remove ghost gear from Cape Cod Bay, building bridges in the meantime. Each one is an act of responsibility and trust, offering hope that the problem is not intractable.

"I don't underestimate the challenge of human beings working together," said Robin, "but I also know that there is no other option. The only other option is some sort of arbitrary rule. I think that's inevitably going to mean fewer and fewer people will participate."

Robin and her husband, Ted Ames, along with others in their community, have formed the Stonington Fisheries Alliance, working to apply these principals locally. They are part of a growing movement—uniting fishermen, environmentalists, scientists, and others—trying to change the way we think of fisheries management. Among several central tenets of this new philosophy is a holistic, ecosystem-based approach, with management at the community level. Fisheries management decisions, this new thinking goes, should look at fish, fishermen, fishing communities, and all the other organisms involved as interdependent parts of a whole. Responsibility for management and consequences of mismanagement should happen within communities or small regions with shared fisheries resources and with oversight and guidance from national and international bodies. In addition to effectively managing fish stocks and preventing wasteful by-catch, many believe this model will build trust and instill a sense of responsibility for the fisheries among community members.

I can't say where this movement will go and how effective it will be, but the fact that people are recognizing and talking about the importance of trust, responsibility, and holistic thinking is promising for both fisheries and whales.

And now for my own holistic thinking. I am not usually one to engage in millennial philosophizing, but in studying the nexus between fisheries and whales, I cannot help noticing that here, at the turn of the millennium, we have come to a crossroads. In the millennium past, people saw the sea, indeed all living systems, as vast and inexhaustible stores of matter and energy at our disposal. We built families, communities, cultures, and empires on the riches the sea yielded to our ingenious coaxing. But in my generation, we have finally been forced to suffer the consequences of disregarding the laws of physics and nature.

Those who care about fisheries and whales now have their faces pressed hard against the realities; can we—all of us—open our eyes and accept responsibility? The question is not, *which do we save, fish, fishermen, or whales?* Fish, fishermen, and whales all inhabit the same ocean, and they are all utterly dependent upon the intricate global machine to give them what they need to survive. Upsetting the balance affects us all.

If anything good could come out of the ruins wrought by our profligate exploitation of fish and whales, it is this: Perhaps now the truth and shared culpability will be harder to ignore as we make—or fail to make—choices for the future.

Like it or not, things will change. Physics and nature will not brook another millennium like the last, and ultimately it will be the laws of physics and nature that judge us and determine our fate. We—all of us—may still have a chance to decide whether the next millennium will witness the demise or the return of whales and fisheries in the North Atlantic.

References

Acheson, James M. 1988. *The lobster gangs of Maine.* Lebanon, N.H.: University Press of New England.

Aguirre International. 1996. *An appraisal of the social and cultural aspects of the multispecies groundfish fishery in New England and the Mid-Atlantic regions.* Report submitted to the National Marine Fisheries Service under contract number 50-DGNF-5-00008.

Alden, Robin, and Linda Mercer. 2000. Developing a cooperative research agenda for Maine's commercial fisheries. *Maine Policy Review* 9, no. 2: 64–71.

Allen, Scott. 1996. Activist gets whale of a deal. *Boston Globe,* February 11.

———. 1997. Devil doing the angels' work? Irascible environmentalist winning battles in his war to save the right whale. *Boston Globe,* January 13.

Andersen, Raoul, and Cato Wadel, eds. 1972. *North Atlantic fishermen: Anthropological essays on modern fishing.* Institute of Social and Economic Research, Newfoundland Social and Economic Papers, no. 5. St. John's: Memorial University of Newfoundland.

Beardsley, Robert C., K. F. Wishner, M. C. Macaulay, R. D. Kenney, A. W. Epstein, and C. Chen. 1996. Spatial variability in zooplankton abundance near feeding right whales in the Great South Channel. Pt. 2. *Deep-Sea Research* 43, nos. 7–8: 1601–25.

Berrill, Michael. 1997. *The plundered seas: Can the world's fish be saved?* San Francisco: Sierra Club.

Boreman, John, B. S. Nakashima, J. A. Wilson, and R. L. Kendall. 1997. *Northwest Atlantic groundfish: Perspectives on a fishery collapse.* Bethesda, Md.: American Fisheries Society.

Boston Globe. March 1985–December 2003.

Bowman, Robert, Edward Lyman, David Mattila, and Charles A. Mayo. 1999.

Developing a network of marine professionals for the rescue of entangled whales.
Paper presented to the Thirteenth Biennial Conference on the Biology of
Marine Mammals, Maui, Hawaii, November 27–December 3.

Bowman, Robert, Edward Lyman, David Mattila, Charles A. Mayo, and Moira
Brown. 2001. *Habitat management lessons from a satellite-tracked right whale.*
Paper presented to the Fourteenth Biennial Conference of the Society for
Marine Mammalogy, Vancouver, British Columbia, November 30.

Brown, Moira W., S. Brault, P. K. Hamilton, R. D. Kenney, A. R. Knowlton,
Marilyn K. Marx, C. A. Mayo, C. K. Slay, and S. D. Kraus. 2001. Sighting het-
erogeneity of right whales in the western North Atlantic: 1980–1992. *Right
Whales: Worldwide Status,* special issue of *Journal of Cetacean Research and
Management* 2: 245–50.

Brown, Moira W., Marilyn K. Marx, and Owen Nichols. 2001. *Surveillance, monitoring, and management of North Atlantic right whales in Cape Cod Bay, Massachusetts: January to mid-May 2001.* Final report submitted to Massachusetts
Environmental Trust and Massachusetts Division of Marine Fisheries. Boston. October 31.

Buck, Eugene H. 2000. *The Northern Atlantic right whale.* Report for Congress,
Order Code RS20747. Washington, D.C.: Congressional Research Service.

———. 2001. *The North Atlantic right whale: Federal management issues.* Congressional Research Service Report for Congress, Order Code RL30907. March
29.

Cape Cod Times (Massachusetts). January 1995–December 2003.

Corn, M. Lynne. 1995. *The northern right whale.* Report for Congress, Order Code
95–493 ENR. Washington, D.C.: Congressional Research Service.

Caddy, J. F., J. Csirke, S. M. Garcia, R.J.R. Grainger, D. Pauly, and R.F.V.
Christensen. 1998. How pervasive is "fishing down marine food webs"? *Science* 282 (November 20): 1383.

Caduto, Michael J., and Joseph Bruchac. 1991. *Keepers of the animals.* Golden,
Colo.: Fulcrum Publishing.

Carey, Richard Adams. 1999. *Against the tide: The fate of the North Atlantic fisherman.* New York: Mariner Books.

Caswell, Hal, Masami Fujiwara, and Solange Brault. 1996. Declining survival
probability threatens the North Atlantic right whale. *Proceedings of the National
Academy of Sciences of the United States* 96, no. 6 (March 16): 3308–13.

Churchill, W. 1941. Never give in, never, never, never. Speech delivered at Harrow
School on October 29. Harrow on the Hill, Middlesex, England.

Clapham, Phillip J., and Richard M. Pace. 2001. *Defining triggers for temporary area
closures to protect right whales from entanglements: Issues and options.* Northeast
Fisheries Science Center Reference Document 01–06. Falmouth, Mass.:
Northeast Fisheries Science Center.

Commercial Fisheries News (Stonington, Maine). January 1990–December 2003.

Committee on the Status of Endangered Wildlife in Canada website. 2001 (January 21). <http://www.cosewic.gc.ca/eng/sct5/index_e.cfm> (accessed October 12, 2002).

Corey, Tony. 1998. Untangling the issues to save the whales. *International Year of the Ocean,* special issue of *Nor'easter* 10, nos. 1–2: 18–23.

Corson, Trevor. 2002. Stalking the American lobster. *Atlantic Monthly,* April, 61–81.

Cowan, Steve, and Barry Schienberg. 2002. *Empty oceans, empty nets.* San Rafael, Calif.: Habitat Media. Videorecording.

Cullen, Kevin. 1993. Wailing over the whales: A man worth looking up to. *Boston Globe,* July 30.

Dawson, Stephen M. 1991. Modifying gillnets to reduce entanglement of cetaceans. *Marine Mammal Science* 7, no. 3: 274–82.

Dickerson, Reed. 1983. Symposium: The legislative process: Statutory interpretation: Dipping into legislative history. *Hofstra Law Review* 11: 1125–62.

Diver cuts whale free from craypot lines off Kaikoura. 2001. *Regular National,* June 11. <http://www.whalewatch.co.nz/_disc3/00000266.htm> (accessed February 13, 2004).

Diver lost trying to free trapped whale. 2003. *New Zealand Herald,* June 17. <http://www.nzherald.co.nz/storydisplay.cfm?thesection=news&thesubsection=&storyID=3507852> (accessed February 13, 2004).

Dobbs, David. 2000. *The great gulf: Fishermen, scientists, and the struggle to revive the world's greatest fishery.* Washington, D.C.: Island Press.

Dooley, Emily C. 2001. West Coast group offers whale rescue alternative. *Cape Cod Times.* July 8.

Doremus, Holly. 2001. Adaptive management, the Endangered Species Act, and the institutional challenges of "new age" environmental protection. *Washburn Law Journal* 41: 50–89.

Dye, Lavonne R. 1993. The Marine Mammal Protection Act: Maintaining the commitment to marine mammal conservation. (Case Note). *Case Western Reserve Law Review* 43, no. 4: 1411–48.

Ellis, Richard. 1991. *Men and whales.* New York: Lyons Press.

———. 1993. *Physty: The true story of a young whale's rescue.* Philadelphia: Courage Books.

———. 1996. *Monsters of the sea.* New York: Random House.

———. 2003. *The empty ocean.* Washington, D.C.: Island Press.

Environment Canada Species at Risk Program website. <http://www.species atrisk.gc.ca/index_e.cfm> (accessed October 1, 2002).

Feynman, Richard P. 1987. In Timothy Ferris, "The year the warning lights flashed on." *Life,* January, 67–68.

Finzi, Juliette, Charles Mayo, Edward Lyman, and Moira Brown. 1999. The influence of prey patch structure on the distribution of right whales. Paper presented to the Thirteenth Biennial Conference on the Biology of Marine Mammals, Maui, Hawaii, November 27–December 3.

Fishermen's Voice (Gouldsboro, Maine). January 1999–December 2002.

Greene, Charles H., and Andrew J. Pershing. 2000. The response of *Calanus finmarchicus* populations to climate variability in the Northwest Atlantic: Basin-scale forcing associated with the North Atlantic Oscillation. *ICES Journal of Marine Science* 57, no. 6: 1536–44.

Greene, Charles H., Andrew J. Pershing, Robert D. Kenney, and Jack W. Jossi. 2001. Effects of climate on the recovery of the endangered North Atlantic right whales. Unpublished.

Greene, Charles H., A. J. Pershing, A. Conversi, B. Planque, C. Hannah, D. Sameoto, E. Head, P. C. Smith, P. C. Reid, J. Jossi, D. Mountain, M. C. Benfield, P. H. Wiebe, E. Durbin. 2003. Trans-Atlantic responses of *Calanus finmarchicus* populations to basin-scale forcing associated with the North Atlantic Oscillation. *Progress in Oceanography* 58, nos. 2–4: 301–12.

Hall-Arber, Madeline 1993. "They" are the problem: Assessing fisheries management in New England. *Nor'easter* (fall/winter): 16–21.

Hall-Arber, Madeline, Chris Dyer, John Poggie, James McNally, and Renee Gagne. 2001. *New England's fishing communities.* Massachusetts Institute of Technology Sea Grant College Program MITSG 01–15. Falmouth, Mass.: MIT Sea Grant.

Hamilton, Lawrence, Cynthia M. Duncan, and Nicholas Flanders. 1998. Northern Atlantic fishing communities in an era of ecological change. *International Year of the Ocean,* special issue of *Nor'easter* 10, nos. 1–2: 28–31.

Hanna, Susan, Heather Blough, Richard Allen, Suzanne Iudicello, Gary Matlock, and Bonnie McCay. 2000. *Fishing grounds: Defining a new era for American fisheries management.* Washington, D.C.: Island Press.

Himmelman, John. 1990. *Ibis: A true whale story.* New York: Scholastic.

Houtman, Nick, and Kathleen Lignell. 1996. Who should manage the fisheries? An alternative approach in northern New England. *Nor'easter* 8, no. 2: 28–31.

Harris, Michael. 1998. *Lament for an ocean: The collapse of the Atlantic cod fishery.* Toronto: McLelland and Stewart.

Johnson, Tora. 2003. Entanglements: Understanding conflicts and contradictions among fishers and whale advocates in the eastern United States and Canada. In *Proceedings of the International Conference on People and the Sea II: Conflicts, threats and opportunities,* Centre for Maritime Research, Amsterdam, Netherlands, September 4–6.

Katona, Steven K., Valerie Rough, and David T. Richardson. 1993. *A field guide to whales, porpoises, and seals: From Cape Cod to Newfoundland.* 4th ed. Washington, D.C.: Smithsonian Institution Press.

Kavanagh, Patrick. 1996. *Gaff topsails.* London: Hamish Hamilton.

Kellert, Stephen R. 1999. *American perceptions of marine mammals and their man-*

agement. Washington, D.C., and New Haven, Conn.: Humane Society of the United States and Yale University.

Kenney, Robert D. 1998. *Right whales and global climate: Western North Atlantic calving rate correlates with both the Southern Oscillation and North Atlantic Oscillation.* Report to the International Whaling Commission, SC/M98/RW29.

———. 2000a. Are right whales starving? *Right Whale News* 7, no. 2, 1–6.

———. 2000b. What's wrong with North Atlantic right whales? *Whalewatcher* 32, no. 1: 1–9.

———. 2001. Anomalous 1992 spring and summer right whale (*Eubalaena glacialis*) distributions in the Gulf of Maine. *Right Whales: Worldwide Status,* special issue of *Journal of Cetacean Research and Management* 2: 209–23.

Kenney, Robert. D., Charles A. Mayo, and Howard E. Winn. 2001. Migration and foraging strategies at varying spatial scales in western North Atlantic right whales: A review of hypotheses. *Right Whales: Worldwide Status,* special issue of *Journal of Cetacean Research and Management* 2: 251–60.

Kenney, Robert.D., P. M. Payne, D. W. Heinemann, and H. E. Winn. 1996. Shifts in Northeast Shelf cetacean distributions relative to trends in Gulf of Maine/ Georges Bank finfish abundance. In *The Northeast Shelf ecosystem: Assessment, stability, and management,* edited by K. Sherman, N. A. Jaworski, and T. J. Smayda. Cambridge, Mass.: Blackwell Science.

Kenney, Robert. D. and Karen F. Wishner, eds. 1995. The South Channel Ocean Productivity Experiment: SCOPEX. *Continental Shelf Research* 15, nos. 4–5): 373–84. Oxford: Pergammon.

Kibbe, David. 2001. Activist tries to block sedation of whale. *Cape Cod Times,* June 22. <http://www.capecodonline.com/archives/> (accessed June 25, 2003).

Klinowska, M., and D. A. Goodson. 1990. *Some non-acoustic approaches to the prevention of entanglement.* Paper SC/O90/G19 presented to the International Whaling Commission Symposium on Mortality of Cetaceans in Passive Fishing Nets and Traps, La Jolla, Calif.

Knowlton, Amy R., and Scott D. Kraus. 2001. Mortality and serious injury of northern right whales (*Eubalaena glacialis*) in the western North Atlantic Ocean. *Right Whales: Worldwide Status,* special issue of *Journal of Cetacean Research and Management* 2:193–208.

Knowlton, Amy R., Scott D. Kraus, and Robert D. Kenney. 1994. Reproduction in North Atlantic right whales (*Eubalaena glacialis*). *Canadian Journal of Zoology* 72, no. 6: 1297–1305.

Knowlton, Amy R., Marilyn K. Marx, Heather M. Pettis, Phillip K. Hamilton, and Scott D. Kraus. 2001. *Scarification analysis of North Atlantic right whales (Eubalaena glacialis): Monitoring rates of entanglement interaction.* Report on Year One Activities to National Marine Fisheries Service, Contract #43EANF030107.

Kraus, Scott D., Phillip K. Hamilton, Robert D. Kenney, Amy R. Knowlton, and Christopher K. Slay. 1998. *Status and trends in reproduction of the North Atlantic right whale*. Paper SC/M98/RW1 presented to the International Whaling Commission Special Meeting of Scientific Committee towards a Comprehensive Assessment of Right Whales Worldwide, March 16-25, Cape Town, South Africa.

————. 2001. Reproductive parameters of the North Atlantic right whale. *Right Whales: Worldwide Status,* special issue of *Journal of Cetacean Research and Management* 2: 231-36.

Kraus, Scott D., and J. J. Hatch. 2001. Mating strategies in the North Atlantic right whale (*Eubalaena glacialis*). *Right Whales: Worldwide Status,* special issue of *Journal of Cetacean Research and Management* 2: 237-44.

Kurlansky, Mark. 1997. *Cod: A biography of the fish that changed the world.* New York: Penguin.

LeFevre, Lori. 2003. *Report from the groundfish social impact informational meetings.* In *Final Amendment 13 to the Northeast Multispecies Fishery Management Plan, including a final supplemental environmental impact statement and an initial regulatory flexibility analysis,* vol. 1, *Management alternatives and impacts.* Prepared by the New England Fishery Management Council, National Marine Fisheries Service, December 18. <http://www.nefmc.org/nemulti/planamen/final_amend13_dec03_section_1.pdf> (accessed January 30, 2004).

Lien, Jon. Teaching fishermen about whales. 1986. *Whalewatcher* 20, no. 1.

————. 1993. *Field tests of acoustic devices on groundfish gillenets: Assessment of effectiveness in reducing harbour porpoise by-catch.* A report on a cooperative project by Portsmouth Fishermen's Cooperative, Memorial University of Newfoundland, New Hampshire Sea Grant, Manomet Bird Observatory, Coonamessett Farm, International Wildlife Coalition, National Marine Fisheries Service, Centre for Fisheries Innovations, and Canada Department of Fisheries and Oceans, February 15.

————. 1994. Entrapments of large cetaceans in passive inshore fishing gear in Newfoundland and Labrador (1979-1990). *Gillnets and cetaceans,* special issue 15 of *Reports to the International Whaling Commission:* 149-57.

————. 1996. *The human and biological context of marine mammal by-catch, and a review of information on large whale collisions with fishing gear.* Report for the Workshop to Assess the Effectiveness and Effects of Acoustic Devices for Preventing or Reducing the Adverse Effects of Marine Mammal- Fishery Interactions, Seattle, Wash., March 20-22. U.S. Marine Mammal Commission.

Lien, Jon et al. 1980-96. Annual preliminary reports to the Fisheries Development Branch of the Department of Fisheries and Oceans, and the Newfoundland and Labrador Department of Fisheries on entrapment, entrapment assistance, and entrapment prevention.

Lien, Jon, W. Barney, S. K. Todd, R. Seton, and J. Guzzwell. 1992. The effects of adding sounds to codtraps on the probability of collisions by humpback whales. In *Marine Mammal Sensory Systems,* edited by J. A. Thomas, R. A. Kastelein, and A. Y. Supin, 701-8. New York: Plenum Press.

Lien, Jon, Sue Staniforth, and Leesa Fawcett. 1985. Teaching fishermen about whales: The role of education in a fisheries management and conservation problem. In *Marine Parks and Conservation,* edited by Jon Lien and Robert Graham, 1: 231–240. Toronto: National and Provincial Parks Association of Canada.

Lien, Jon, G. B. Stenson, S. Carver, and J. Chardine. 1994. How many did you catch? The effect of methodology on bycatch reports obtained from fishermen. *Gillnets and cetaceans,* special issue 15 of *Reports to the International Whaling Commission:* 535–40.

Lien, Jon, Sean K. Todd, and Jacques-Y. Guigné. 1991. Inferences about perception in large cetaceans, especially humpback whales, from incidental catches in fixed gear, enhancement of nets by "alarm" devices, and the acoustics of fishing gear. In *Sensory Abilities of Cetaceans,* edited by J. Thomas and R. Kastelein, 347–62. New York: Plenum Press.

Lien, Jon, A. Velhurst, T. Huntsman, J. Jones, and R. Seton. 1990. *Reactions of humpback whales to novel sounds: Curiosity and conditioning.* Paper SC/O90/ G51 presented to the International Whaling Commission Symposium on Mortality of Cetaceans in Passive Fishing Nets and Traps, La Jolla, Calif., October 20–25.

The lobster and the whale: 1997. Right whale protectors propose lobster fishing limitations. *Economist,* May 24: 28.

Luloff, A. E., and Mark Nord. 1993. The forgotten of northern New England. In *The forgotten: Uneven development in rural America,* edited by William W. Falk and Thomas A. Lyson, 125–67. Lawrence: University of Kansas Press.

Lyman Edward, Robert Bowman, David Mattila, and Charles A. Mayo. 1999. *A technique for disentangling large free-swimming whales.* Paper presented to the Thirteenth Biennial Conference on the Biology of Marine Mammals, Maui, Hawaii, November 27–December 3.

MacKay, Paula. 1990. Whaling and dealing: The politics of whale conservation. *Christian Science Monitor,* July 12.

Maine Department of Marine Resources. *Commercial Fisheries Landings.* <http://www.maine.gov/dmr/commercialfishing/commercialfishing.html> (accessed December 8–10, 2002).

Malik, Sobia, Moira W. Brown, Scott D. Kraus, Amy R. Knowlton, Phillip K. Hamilton, and Bradley N. White. 1999. Assessment of mitochondrial DNA structuring and nursery use in the North Atlantic right whale (Eubalaena glacialis). *Canadian Journal of Zoology* 77: 1–6.

Malik, Sobia, Moira W. Brown, Scott D. Kraus, and Bradley N. White. 2000. Analysis of mitochondrial DNA diversity within and between North and South Atlantic right whales. *Marine Mammal Science* 16, no. 3: 545–58.

Mate, Bruce R., Sharon L. Nieukirk, and Scott D. Kraus. 1997. Satellite-monitored movements of the northern right whale. *Journal of Wildlife Management* 61, no. 4: 1393–405.

Matsen, Brad. 1998. *Fishing up north: Stories of luck and loss in Alaskan waters.* Anchorage: Alaska Northwest Books.

Matthiessen, Peter. 1986. *Men's lives: The surfmen and baymen of the South Fork.* New York: Random House.

———. 1987. *Wildlife in America.* Revised and updated. New York: Viking.

Mattila, David K., and Jooke Robbins. 1998. *Monitoring of entanglement scars on the caudal peduncle of humpback whales in Gulf of Maine.* Report to the National Marine Fisheries Service, Order no. 40EMNF700232.

———1999. *A directed, photographic technique for estimating large whale entanglement rates.* Paper presented to the Thirteenth Biennial Conference on the Biology of Marine Mammals, Maui, Hawaii, November 27–December 3.

Mayo, Charles A., B. H. Letcher, and S. Scott. 2001. Zooplankton filtering efficiency of the baleen of a North Atlantic right whale, *Eubalaena glacialis.* *Right Whales: Worldwide Status*, special issue of *Journal of Cetacean Research and Management* 2: 225–29.

Mayo, Charles A., Edward Lyman, and Amy DeLorenzo. 2000. *Comparison of the yearly caloric availability in Cape Cod Bay with North Atlantic right whale calving rates: 1984-2000.* Report to the federal Marine Mammal Commission, St. Petersburg, Fla., October 12.

McGinn, Anne Platt. 1998. *Rocking the boat: Conserving fisheries and protecting jobs.* Worldwatch Paper #142. Washington, D.C.: Worldwatch Institute.

McLeod, Brenna. 2003. *DNA analysis of 58 sixteenth-century whale bones from Basque sites in Labrador.* Paper presented to the Annual Meeting of the North Atlantic Right Whale Consortium, New Bedford Whaling Museum, New Bedford, Mass., November 4–5.

Mederer, N. J. 1996. Surviving the changes: Families respond to fishery management. *Nor'easter* 8, no. 2: 12–15.

Melville, Herman. 1930. *Moby Dick, or The whale.* Illustrated by Rockwell Kent. New York: Random House.

Moore, Michael, Andrew Stamper, Scott Kraus, and Rosalind Rolland. Report of a workshop on large whale medical intervention—Indications and technology development. Falmouth, Mass., February 7, 2000.

Moscrop, J. 1999. In deep water. *Geographical* 71, no. 12: 26.

National Fisherman (Portland, Maine). January 1990–February 2004.

Neis, Barbara, and Lawrence Felt, eds. 2000. *Finding our sea legs: Linking fishery people and their knowledge with science and management.* Saint John's, Newfoundland: ISER Books.

Nelson, Dawn L. 1990. *A review of gear and animal characteristics responsible for incidental catches of marine mammals in fishing gear.* Paper SC/O90/G48 presented to the International Whaling Commission Symposium on Mortality of Cetaceans in Passive Fishing Nets and Traps, La Jolla, Calif., October 20–25.

Nelson, Dawn L., and Jon Lien. 1990. *Responses of naive, captive dolphins to proto-type whale alarms.* Paper SC/O90/G49 presented to the International Whaling Commission Symposium on Mortality of Cetaceans in Passive Fishing Nets and Traps, La Jolla, Calif., October 20–25.

Newell, Dianne, and Rosemary E. Ommer, eds. 1999. *Fishing places, fishing people: Traditions and issues in Canadian small-scale fisheries.* Toronto: University of Toronto Press.

New York Times. January 1999–December 2003.

Pauly, Daniel, and Jay Maclean. 2003. *In a perfect ocean: The state of fisheries and ecosystems in the North Atlantic Ocean.* Washington, D.C.: Island Press.

Payne, Roger. 1995. *Among Whales.* New York: Scribner.

"People." 2003. *Right Whale News* 10, no. 4: 10.

Pershing, Andrew J., and Charles H. Greene. Impact of climate variability on the endangered North Atlantic right whale. *Nature,* in review.

Philbrick, Nathaniel. 2000. In the heart of the Sea. New York: Penguin.

Porter, Gareth, Janet Brown, and Pamela S. Chasek. 2000. *Global environmental politics.* 3rd ed. Boulder, Colo.: Westview Press.

Portland Press Herald (Maine). January 2000–December 2003.

Prado, J., and A. Smith. 1990. *Possibilities of reducing incidental catch and mortality of marine mammals in drift net fisheries.* Paper SC/090/G14 presented to the International Whaling Commission Symposium on Mortality of Cetaceans in Passive Fishing Nets and Traps, La Jolla, Calif.

Reeves, Randall R. 2001. Overview of catch history, historic abundance and distribution of right whales in the western North Atlantic and in Cintra Bay, West Africa. *Right Whales: Worldwide Status,* special issue of *Journal of Cetacean Research and Management* 2: 187–92.

Reeves, Randall R., Jeffrey M. Breiwick, and Edward D. Mitchell. 1999. History of whaling and estimated kill of right whales, *Balaena glacialis,* in the northeastern United States, 1620–1924 (statistical data included). *Marine Fisheries Review* 61 (3): 1–12.

Reeves, Randall R., E. Josephson, and T. D. Smith. A suspected historical offshore right whale ground in the offshore N. Atlantic, "Maury's Smear," shown to be apocryphal. <http://www.cmrh.dk/maurys%20smear%20apocryphal.pdf> (accessed February 10, 2004).

Reeves, Randall R., Rosalind M. Rolland, and Phillip J. Clapham, eds. 2001. *Causes of reproductive failure in North Atlantic right whales: New avenues of research.* Northeast Fisheries Science Center Document 01–16. Report of a workshop held April 26–28, 2000, at Northeast Fisheries Science Center, Falmouth, Mass.

Reeves, Randal R., Tim D. Smith, Robert L. Webb, Jooke Robbins, and Phillip Clapham. 2002. Humpback and fin whaling in the Gulf of Maine from 1800 to 1918. *Marine Fisheries Review* 64, no. 1: 1–12.

Reynolds, John E., and A. Rommel Sentiel, eds. 1999. *Biology of Marine Mammals.* Washington, D.C.: Smithsonian Institution Press.

Right Whale News. The Newsletter of the Southeastern United States Implementation Team for the Recovery of the Northern Right Whale and the Northeast Implementation Team, July 1994–November 2003. <http://www.graysreef. nos.noaa.gov/rightwhalenews.html> (accessed September 2002–February 2004).

Robbins, Jooke, and David Mattila. 1999. *A directed, photographic technique for estimating large whale entanglement rates.* Paper presented to the Thirteenth Biennial Conference on the Biology of Marine Mammals, Maui, Hawaii, November 27–December 3.

Safina, Carl. 1997. *Song for the blue ocean.* New York: Henry Holt.

Schaeff, Cathy M., Scott D. Kraus, Moira W. Brown, and Bradley N. White. 1993. Assessment of the population structure of western North Atlantic right whales (Eubalaena glacialis) based on sighting data and mt dna data. *Canadian Journal of Zoology* 71: 339–45.

Smolowitz, Ronald J., and Cliff Goudey. 1990. *Mitigating cetacean mortality in fisheries: Appropriate alternative.* Paper SC/O90/G40 presented to the International Whaling Commission Symposium on Mortality of Cetaceans in Passive Fishing Nets and Traps, La Jolla, Calif.

Smolowitz, Ronald J., and David N. Wiley. 1992. A model for conflict resolution in marine mammal/fisheries interaction: The Harbor Porpoise Working Group. In *Proceedings, MTS'92; Global Oceans Partnership Conference* 1: 354–60.

Taking of marine mammals incidental to commercial fishing operations; Atlantic Large Whale Take Reduction Plan regulations. 1997. (Interim Final Rule) *Federal Register* 62, no. 140 (July 22): 39157–88.

Taking of marine mammals incidental to commercial fishing operations; Atlantic Large Whale Take Reduction Plan regulations. 1999. (Final Rule) *Federal Register* 64, no. 30 (February 16): 7529–56.

Taking of marine mammals incidental to commercial fishing operations; Atlantic Large Whale Take Reduction Plan regulations. 2000. (Interim Final Rule) *Federal Register* 65, no. 246 (December 21): 80368–80.

Taking of marine mammals incidental to commercial fishing operations; Atlantic Large Whale Take Reduction Plan regulations. 2002a. (Final Rule) *Federal Register* 67, no. 6 (January 9): 1133–42.

Taking of marine mammals incidental to commercial fishing operations; Atlantic Large Whale Take Reduction Plan regulations. 2002b. (Interim Final Rule) *Federal Register* 67, no. 6 (January 9): 1142–60.

Taking of marine mammals incidental to commercial fishing operations; Atlantic Large Whale Take Reduction Plan regulations. 2002c. (Final Rule) *Federal Register* 67, no. 7 (January 10): 1300–1314.

Taking of marine mammals incidental to commercial fishing operations; Atlantic Large Whale Take Reduction Plan regulations. 2002d. (Final Rule; correction) *Federal Register* 67, no. 63 (April 2) 15493–94.

Taking of marine mammals incidental to commercial fishing operations; Atlantic Large Whale Take Reduction Plan regulations. 2002e. (Final Rule; technical amendment) *Federal Register* 67, no. 208 (October 28): 15493–94.

Taking of marine mammals incidental to commercial fishing operations; Atlantic Large Whale Take Reduction Plan regulations (ALWTRP). 2003a. (Temporary Rule) *Federal Register* 68, no. 72 (April 15): 18143–45.

Taking of marine mammals incidental to commercial fishing operations; Atlantic Large Whale Take Reduction Plan regulations. 2003b. (Final Rule; technical amendment) *Federal Register* 68, no. 76 (April 21): 19464–65.

Taking of marine mammals incidental to commercial fishing operations; Atlantic Large Whale Take Reduction Plan regulations. 2003c. (Final Rule) *Federal Register* 68, no. 165 (August 26): 51195–201.

Tande, Kurt S., and Charles B. Miller, co-conveners. 1999. Symposium on population dynamics of Calanus in the North Atlantic. Results from the trans-Atlantic study of *Calanus finmanrchicus,* Tromsø, Norway, August 24–27.

Todd, Sean K., Jon Lien, and Jacques-Y Guigné. 1991. *The acoustics of fishing gear; implications for humpback whale net entrapments in Newfoundland and Labrador.* Paper presented to the Ninth Biennial Conference on the Biology of Marine Mammals, Chicago, December.

Todd, Sean K., J. Lien, and A. Verhulst. 1992. Orientation of humpback (*Megaptera novaeangliae*) and minke (*Balaenoptera acutorostrata*) whales to acoustic alarm devices designed to reduce entrapment in fishing gear. In *Marine Mammal Sensory Systems,* edited by J. A. Thomas, R. A. Kastelein, and A. Y. Supin, 727–39. New York: Plenum Press.

Todd, Sean K., and Dawn L. Nelson. 1994. A review of modifications to the webbing and setting strategies of passive fishing gear to reduce incidental by-catch of cetaceans. *Gillnets and cetaceans,* special issue 15 of Annex F of *Reports to the International Whaling Commission:* 67–69.

United Nations Food and Agriculture Organization, Fisheries Department. Statistical databases and software, 2001. <http://www.fao.org/fi/statist/statist.asp> (accessed December 14, 2002).

United States Department of Commerce, National Marine Fisheries Service. Fisheries Statistics website, 2002 Fisheries of the United States. 2001 (August 14). <http://www.st.nmfs.gov/st1/fus/fus00/index.html> (accessed December 10, 2002).

United States Department of Commerce, National Marine Fisheries Service. Northeast Fisheries Science Center website. <http://www.nefsc.noaa.gov/> (accessed January 2001–January 2004).

United States Department of Commerce, National Marine Fisheries Service.

Northeast Fisheries Science Center website. Fisheries Historical Information page. <http://www.nefsc.noaa.gov/history/> (accessed November 14, 2002).

United States Department of Commerce, National Marine Fisheries Service, Protected Resources Division. Protected Resources Division Office of Protected Resources website. <http://www.nmfs.noaa.gov/prot_res/prot_res.html> (accessed January 2001–January 2004).

———. Atlantic Large Whale Take Reduction Plan. <http://www.nero.nmfs.gov/whaletrp/> (accessed January 2001–January 2004).

———. Stock assessment reports for marine mammals. <http://www.nmfs.noaa.gov/prot_res/PR2/Stock_Assessment_Program/sars.html> (accessed January 2001–January 2004).

———. Recovery plans required under Section 4 of the Endangered Species Act. <http://www.nmfs.noaa.gov/prot_res/PR3/recovery.html> (accessed January 2001–January 2004).

———. 2001. Environmental assessment of the final rule amending the Atlantic Large Whale Take Reduction Plan Dynamic Area Management. Gloucester, Mass.: NMFS Northeast Regional Office.

———. 2002a. Harbor Porpoise Take Reduction Plan. <http://www.nero.nmfs.gov/porptrp/> (accessed August–November 2002).

———. 2002b. Guide to the Atlantic Large Whale Take Reduction Plan: An evolving plan to reduce the risk to North Atlantic right whales and to humpback, fin, and minke whales posed by lobster pot/lobster trap gear and gillnet gear in the U.S. Atlantic Ocean. Gloucester, Mass.: NMFS Northeast Regional Office.

———. 2003. Final environmental assessment of the Final Rule amending the Atlantic Large Whale Take Reduction Plan Dynamic Area Management Gear Modifications. Gloucester, Mass.: NMFS Northeast Regional Office.

U.S. Congress. Senate. Committee on Commerce, Science, and Transportation. Subcommittee on Oceans and Fisheries. 1997. Hearing, *Whale protection and the impact on North Atlantic Fisheries.* April 26. Washington, D.C.: Government Printing Office.

Vail, David, Mark Lapping, Wilfred Richard, and Michael Cote. 1998. *Tourism and Maine's future: Toward environmental, economic and community sustainability.* Augusta: Maine Center for Economic Policy.

Van Zile, Dexter. 2000. Prince of whales: If fixed-gear fishing is outlawed off New England, it won't hurt Max Strahan's feelings. *National Fisherman* 28, no. 3, May.

Volgenau, Lisa, Scott D. Kraus, and Jon Lien. 1995. The impact of entanglements on two substocks of the western North Atlantic humpback whale, *Megaptera novaeangliae. Canadian Journal of Zoology* 73 (9): 1689–98.

Warner, William W. 1984. *Distant water: The fate of the North Atlantic fisherman.* New York: Penguin.

Weinrich, Mason. 1999. Behavior of a humpback whale (*Megaptera novaeangliae*) upon entanglement in a gill net. *Marine Mammal Science* 15, no. 2: 559–63.

Whitehead, Hal, and James E. Carscadden. 1985. Predicting inshore whale abundance—whales and capelin off the Newfoundland coast. *Canadian Journal of Fisheries and Aquatic Science* 42, no. 5: 976–81.

Winn, Howard E., C. A. Price, and P. W. Sorensen. 1986. The distributional biology of the right whale (*Eubalaena glacialis*) in the western North Atlantic. *Right Whales: Past and Present Status*, special issue 10 of *Reports to the International Whaling Commission*: 129–38.

Weber, Michael L. 2002. *From abundance to scarcity: A history of U.S. Marine Fisheries policy*. Washington, D.C.: Island Press.

Whale rescuer's death case of good intentions gone wrong. 2003. *New Zealand Herald*, June 17. <http://www.nzherald.co.nz/latestnewsstory.cfm?storyID=3507860&thesection=news&thesubsection=general&thesecondsubsection=latest> (accessed February 13, 2004).

Williams, C., and M. George. Whaling in Dildo, Trinity Bay, Newfoundland. <http://www.nfld.com/nfld/other/whales/trinitybay/story0001.html> (accessed December 17, 2002).

Young, Nina M. 2001. The conservation of marine mammals using a multi-party approach: An evaluation of the take reduction team process. *Ocean and Coastal Law Journal* 6, no. 2: 293–346.

Young, Nina M., and Suzanne Iucidello. 1997. Blueprint for whale conservation: Implementing the Marine Mammal Protection Act. *Ocean and Coastal Law* 3, nos. 1–2: 149–216.

Index

Pages with illustrations are in italics.

Conservation Law Foundation (CLF), 230–34

consolidation of fisheries, 80, 200–202

Conway, Jerry, 105

Cooke, Peter, 254

cooperation, 150–53, 209–10, 213–17, 255–56, 263

copepods *(Calanus finmarchicus)*, 46–48, 55–58

crab fisheries, 71, *141*, 209–10, 217–18, 254

critical habitat areas, 155–57, *165*, 166

currents, 55–57

cyamids. *See* whale lice

DeLorenzo, Amy, 52–53

Department of Fisheries and Oceans (Canada), 26, 31, 172–73, 186, 261–62

deterrent, whale, 125, 144–46

"Devil Doing the Angels' Work" (Allen), 96–97

diatoms, 46–47

Dildo, Newfoundland, 29–30, *170*

disentanglement: costs, 108–110; dangers, 86–87, 119–23, 187–92, 219, 222–23, 226; illegal, 127, 313, 149–50, 225–27; Newfoundland, 30–31, 36, 37, 169–91; success rates, 86, 135–36, 138, 147; tools and technology, 84–90, 99–103, 174, 181–84, 222–23; training fishermen, 220–28; whale reaction to, aggressive, 86–87, 117, 119–23, 128, 187–92; whale reaction to, other, 119–20, 125–26, 215–16, 222, 26. *See also* entanglement
—of individual whales: Churchill, right whale #1102, 84, 88, 98–101, 102–103, 107; Ibis, humpback whale #0125, 7–8, 13–15, 19–22; right whale #2030, 86–88; Saucy Whale, 169–91

diving with whales, 119, 122–23

Dobbs, David, 245

Downeast Lobstermen's Association, 160

Dowser (humpback whale calf), 22, 23

draggers, 78

Dynamic Area Management, 148, 159–68, 243–44; compliance, 160, 163–64, 230, 256–57; enforcement, 161–64, 256–57;

delays in implementation, 161–64, 246–47; and risk of entanglement, 160, 164–66; scientific justification, 159–60; in Take Reduction Team Meeting 2003, 246–48, 254, 256–59; trigger, 160

economics of fishing communities, 78–80, 208; and gear loss, 11, 27, 30, 35; post-moratorium, 70–72, 196, 200–13, 217–19. *See also* fishing industry

economics of litigation, 233–36

educating fishermen, 38

Ellis, Richard, 29, 113–15, 119; *Men and Whales*, 113–14; *Monsters of the Sea*, 114

endangered species. *See* finback whale; humpback whale; right whale, North Atlantic
—attitudes about, 4, 37–38, 168, 260–61

Endangered Species Act of 1973 (ESA), 72, 74, 93, 155–57; attitudes about, 168, 260

enforcement: Dynamic Area Management, 161–64; illegal disentanglement, 225–26; Marine Mammal Protection Act, 75–78, 226

entanglement: anchored whale, 7, 20, 71, 169–91, 213–16; cod trap, 36–37; free-swimming whale, 19–22, 20, 81–111; gill net, 6–22, 25–27, 30–31, 169–91, 213–16; historical, 7, 68, 216; lobster gear, 7; offshore, 71–72; press about, 90–92, 102, 108, 122–23, 262; preventing, 144–46, 147; scars from, 45, 64–65, 125, 138, 149. *See also* disentanglement; fishermen, disentangling whales; fishermen, reporting entanglement; fishing gear, modifications to reduce entanglement; frequency of entanglement; illegal disentanglement; injury, from entanglement; physiological effects of entanglement; preventing entanglement. *See also individual whales*

Entrapment Assistance Program (Newfoundland), 31–32, 35–36, 35–38, 170–72, 179 entrapment of whales. *See* entanglement; cod trap; gill net

environmental groups: Conservation Law Foundation, 230–34; Greenpeace, 37–38; Humane Society of the United States, 148, 232–36, 250, 252, 258–59; International Fund for Animal Welfare, 255–56; GreenWorld, 92, 93, 95, 96–97, 110

environmentalists: attitudes about whales, 219, 234; priorities, 132–33

ESA. *See* Endangered Species Act of 1973

Essex (whale ship), 117

Eubalaena glacialis. See right whale, North Atlantic

euthanasia of whales, 106

Exclusive Economic Zone, 39

Federal Register, 160, 161

Feynman, Richard, 154

finback whale *(Balaenoptera physalis)*, 29–30

fishermen: code of silence, 226–28, 230; disentangling whales, 127, 131, 149–50, 213–16, 220–28; environmental values, 131–33; income, 234–37; lying, 237; priorities, 132–33; reporting entanglement, 127, 149–50, 223–28, 230; values about whales, 131–33. *See also individuals by name*

fishery closures: critical habitat areas, right whale, 155–56; Dynamic Area Management, 159–68, 230; threats of, 74, 93, 150–51, 159–68, 225–30

fishery regulations: due to litigation, 93; gear modification, 139–44; socioeconomic impacts, 78–80; for whale protection *(see* Take Reduction Plan, Atlantic Large Whale; Dynamic Area Management)

fishing communities, 67, 78–80, 132–33, 199–209; pre-moratorium, 67, 199–200, 203, 206–207; post-moratorium, 200–201, 203, 205, 207–210, 217–18

fishing dangers, 67

fishing down the food chain, 40, 207–208

fishing effort: increase in, 39–40; latent, 80, 177, 200–201, 209

fishing gear: changes over time, 66–72, 176–77; consequences of loss, 11, 27, 30, 35, 38; modifications to reduce entanglement, 139–46, 148, 151, 156–59, 163; proliferation, 39–40, 70–71; research, 77, 139–44, 149, 252; "whale safe/friendly," 149. *See also individual gear types*

fishing industry: landings, 70–72; pre-moratorium, 66–70, 78–79, 199–200; post-moratorium, 70–72, 78–80, 200–203, 209–213, 217–18

fish net. *See* fishing gear; gill net

food web, North Atlantic, 46–48, 52–53, 55–57, 60–61

frequency of whale entanglement: humpback, 2, 38, 125; right, 1, 45, 63–66, 136, 138

Gaff Topsails (Kavanagh), 193

gear, fishing. *See* fishing gear

gear modification: definitions, 77, 148; lines, 139–44; weak links, 142–44

George, Miriam, 29–30

Georges Bank, 44, 46, 107

ghost gear, 255–56

"Gift of the Whale" (Caduto and Bruchac), 81

gill net: described, 10, *11*; fishery, 78–80, 184–86, 199, 210–17, 248; on entangled whale, 6–22, 25–27, 30–31, 169–91, 213–16; hauling, 185–86, 210–13; modifications required, 140–46; pingers, 144–45; setting, 9–10, 199

global warming, 59

Gouveia, David, 161, 239–41, 247, 257–58

Grand Banks, 71

Grand Manan, New Brunswick, 131

grappling hooks, 20, 84

Great Gulf, The (Dobbs), 245

Great South Channel: Churchill rescue effort, 98–100, 102–103, 107; maps, *44, 109, 165*; productivity, 46, 48, 56; right whale habitat, 46, 48, 56, 156, 166

Tora Johnson teaches human ecology and geographic information science at the College of the Atlantic in Bar Harbor, Maine. Also a freelance writer, she served as the marine reporter for the *Martha's Vineyard Times* from 1998 to 2000 and has published, with Arlene De Strulle, *A Guide to Freshwater Animals without Backbones* (1997), as well as numerous articles in magazines and newspapers.